Jacka VC

ROBERT MACKLIN is one of Australia's most exciting and wide-ranging authors, with novels (*Fire in the Blood*, *The Queenslander*, *Juryman*, *The Paper Castle*) and non-fiction works (*100 Great Australians*, *The Secret Life of Jesus* and the memoir, *War Babies*) to his credit. With co-author Peter Thompson he wrote *The Battle of Brisbane*, *Kill the Tiger*, *Keep Off the Skyline* and *The Man Who Died Twice*, the life and adventures of Morrison of Peking, recently translated for publication in China. He lives in Canberra, where he divides his time between books, plays and screenwriting.

Jacka VC

AUSTRALIAN HERO

Robert Macklin

2 Aug, 2007.

Dear Uncle Allan —

I hope this is of some interest to your VC
research —

Love, Inga xx.

ALLEN&UNWIN

To Rob and Ben,

my personal heroes

First published in Australia and New Zealand in 2006

Allen & Unwin
83 Alexander Street
Crows Nest NSW 2065
Australia
Phone: (61 2) 8425 0100
Fax: (61 2) 9906 2218
Email: info@allenandunwin.com
Web: www.allenandunwin.com

National Library of Australia
Cataloguing-in-Publication entry:

Macklin, Robert, 1941- .
      Jacka VC : Australian hero.

          Bibliography.
          Includes index.
          ISBN 978 1 74114 830 5.

      ISBN 1 74114 830 8.

      1. Jacka, Albert, 1893-1932. 2. Soldiers - Australia -
      Biography. 3. World War, 1914-1918 - Australia - Biography.
      I. Title.

      940.41294

Maps by Ian Faulkner
Index by Russell Brooks
Set in 12/18 pt Requiem by Midland Typesetters, Australia
Printed by Griffin Press, South Australia

10 9 8 7 6 5 4 3 2 1

CONTENTS

Author's Note

The research for this work exposed me to a great deal of military literature. These works varied in quality, but, almost without exception, they incorporated an attitude towards death in war that I found deeply troubling.

The premature, violent death of a single human being is a shocking tragedy. Often, it involves terrible agony. Always, it represents the denial of great human potential. Without exception, it causes the most devastating anguish and pain among those who loved the young man—for they are overwhelmingly young men—who is suddenly no more. One life is gone forever; other lives are scarred in ways that can never be repaired.

Yet, when we write of the deaths of soldiers, we employ words like gallantry, honour and sacrifice to somehow justify the horror. And we speak, not of single deaths, but of armies—millions—in a murderous obscenity. And we do so with a kind of fatalist calm that is in itself horrific.

I do not excuse myself from the charge, though I have tried, wherever possible, to expose the enormity of the crime against humanity. If I have glorified a hero, it is because within the context of war, he not only gave himself to the struggle against the enemy, he fought just as hard against the appalling arrogance and incompetence of the leaders on his own side who were sending his mates to a needless death.

And then he fought another war, almost as terrible.

I am deeply grateful to Elizabeth Moss, the adopted daughter of Albert Jacka and his wife, Vera, for breaking a lifetime of silence to speak of her parents. As she said, 'As time passes, you can become quite detached from your past—as if it belonged to someone else. I prefer to keep it that way.' Nevertheless, she was prepared to make the journey back in time and to provide vital clues to an element of Albert Jacka's story that has previously passed unnoticed and helped to reveal a much fuller picture of the man than previously portrayed.

Other members of the Jacka family—most notably his niece, Josephine Eastoe—have been equally generous with their time and have provided hitherto unsuspected insights.

I am deeply in debt to Anthony Staunton, the internationally recognised authority on the Victoria Cross—and indeed the military minutiae of World War I—for his willingness to read the manuscript at an early stage to eliminate errors of fact. If any remain, they may be put down to my obduracy in the face of superior knowledge.

Greg Gilmore was of great assistance in researching Jacka's early sporting activities.

My thanks to Nigel Beusst for permission to quote from his excellent film, *Jacka VC,* and to Fred Brenchley and Peter Thompson for their help and support, and to Claire Cayzer for permission to use her Anzac photographs.

The poem 'On Scratchbury Camp' by Siegfried Sassoon is reproduced by kind permission of the Estate of Mr George Sassoon.

The Port Phillip City Council was generous in providing documentary and pictorial material on Jacka's time as lord mayor of St Kilda. I thank the Australian War Memorial for permission to reproduce photographs from their files. And my warmest thanks to the staff of the AWM for their patience and helpfulness in the research effort that underpins the work.

Similarly, I stand in awe of the ever-obliging staff of the newspaper repository of the National Library of Australia who never seem to tire of instructing the technologically challenged to manipulate the viewing and copying instruments of their busy bailiwick.

Finally, it is my pleasure to thank Ian Bowring, my publisher at Allen & Unwin, for his support and encouragement, and my editor Angela Handley for her unique gifts of charm and diplomacy in demanding the highest standards from her irascible charge.

R.M.

robert@robertmacklin.com

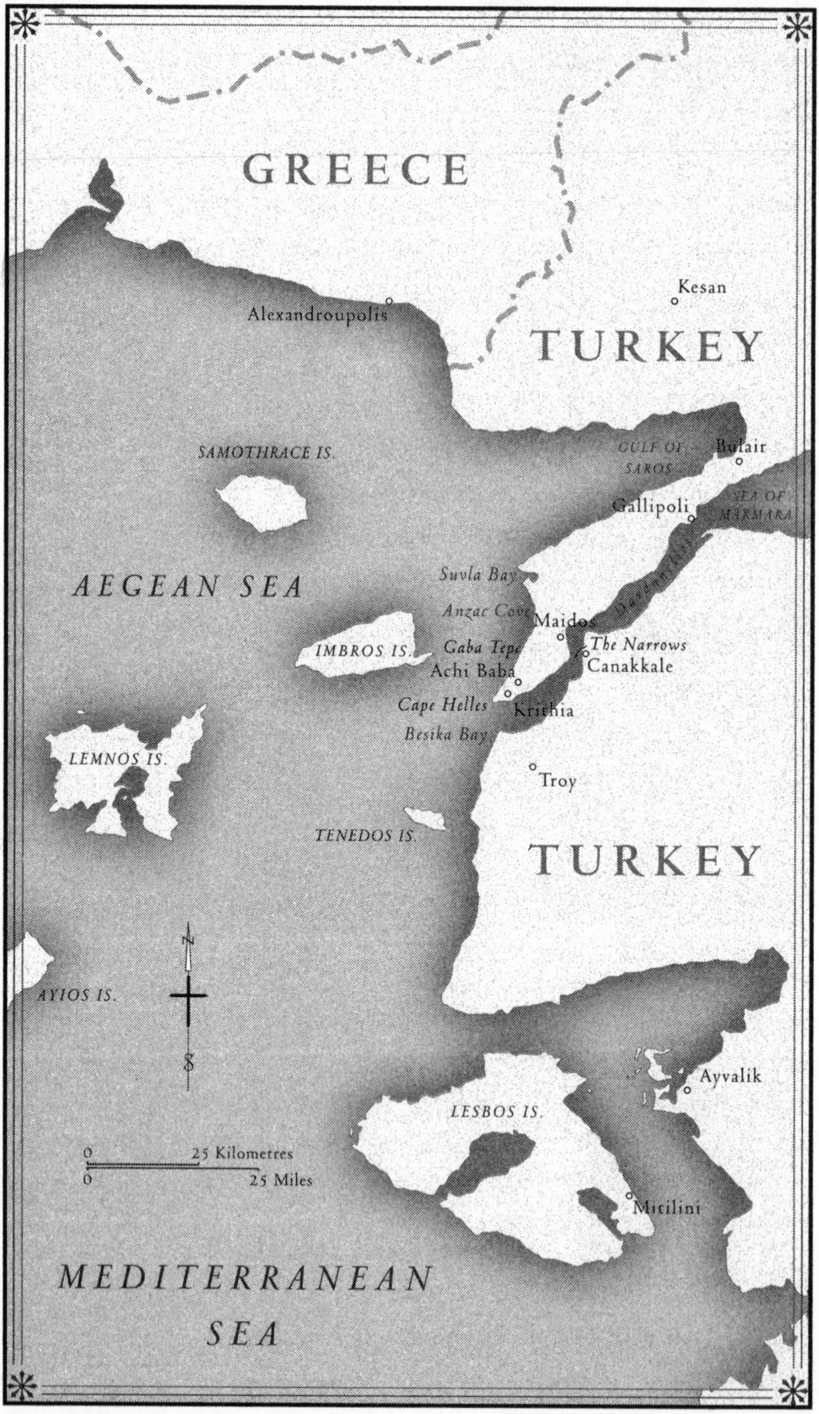
GREECE
Kesan
Alexandroupolis
TURKEY
SAMOTHRACE IS.
GULF OF
SAROS
Bulair
Gallipoli
SEA OF
MARMARA
AEGEAN SEA
Suvla Bay
Anzac Cove
Maidos
IMBROS IS.
Gaba Tepe
The Narrows
Canakkale
Achi Baba
Cape Helles
Krithia
Besika Bay
LEMNOS IS.
Troy
TENEDOS IS.
TURKEY
N
AYIOS IS.
S
Ayvalik
LESBOS IS.
0
25 Kilometres
0
25 Miles
Mitilini
MEDITERRANEAN
SEA

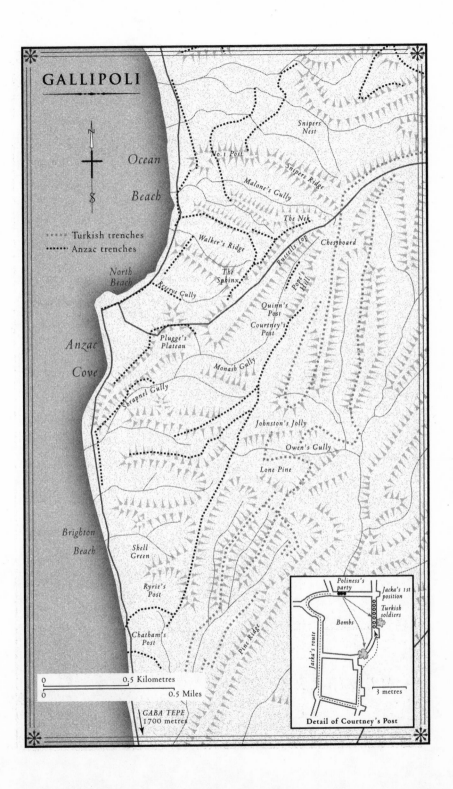

GALLIPOLI

Turkish trenches
Anzac trenches

Ocean

Beach

*North
Beach*

*Anzac
Cove*

*Brighton
Beach*

Snipers
Nest

No. 1 Post

Snipers Ridge

Malone's Gully

The Nek

Walker's Ridge

Chessboard

Russells Top

Pope's Hill

*The
Sphinx*

Reserve Gully

Quinn's
Post

Courtney's
Post

Plugge's
Plateau

Monash Gully

Shrapnel Gully

Johnston's Jolly

Owen's Gully

Lone Pine

Shell
Green

Ryrie's
Post

Chatham's
Post

Pine Ridge

0   0.5 Kilometres

0   0.5 Miles

*GABA TEPE
1700 metres*

Poliness's
party

Jacka's 1st
position

Turkish
soldiers

Bombs

Jacka's route

3 metres

Detail of Courtney's Post

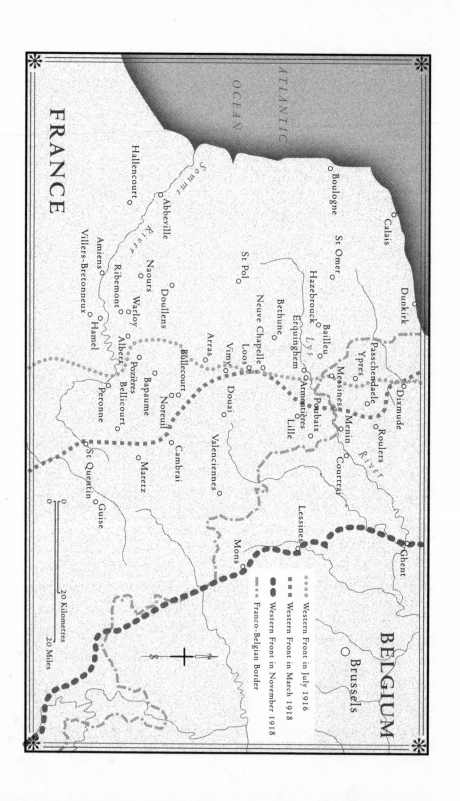

1

PROLOGUE

A single wreath adorned the handsome memorial to Albert Jacka in St Kilda Cemetery. My companion, Pearl Donald, a tiny grey-haired woman with a lively smile, lifted it reverentially from the marble gravestone. Pearl was a trustee of the cemetery and she held Jacka's grave in special regard. Each year she attended the service his family, friends and admirers held there to honour his memory. The ceremony had been conducted every year since his death on 17 January 1932.

She passed me the wreath, a ring of faded red plastic flowers on a black background. It had lain there for several months. The cardboard centre was weathered but the inscription on the attached card was quite clear. I read it aloud: 'In grateful memory of ALBERT JACKA VC, A Great Soldier, and all Australians who fought for the old country in the Great War 1914–18, in whose valiant footsteps we have trod on the Battlefields of France.' It was signed, 'The London Metropolitan Police Service 1977–2004'.

Nearby a raven screeched, the sound rising on the wintry wind above the urgent murmur of afternoon traffic on Dandenong Road. I read it again, silently this time. It seemed extraordinary that a civil police force should be honouring a man who died from wounds suffered almost a century ago in that terrible conflict. Jacka had won his Victoria Cross at Gallipoli, the first Australian so honoured in the war to end all wars. And he had been decorated again and again as he fought the Prussian militarists in France and Belgium. Indeed, the best judges believed he had earned two more VCs in those horrific killing fields. But what could this possibly mean to a team of British bobbies in the 21st century?

A week later, on 7 July 2005, five terrorist bombs exploded in the Underground and on a red double-decker bus in the heart of the British capital. Suddenly London was a war zone. The Metropolitan Police Service was in the front line. In 90 years the battleground had shifted; the form of the conflict had changed; but the struggle against men of ill will went on. There was still a need for heroes. Suddenly the wreath made sense.

1

Getting the buggers

I n August 2005, I was on the five-hour drive between Istanbul and Gallipoli, the road Jacka and his mates would have taken to the Turkish capital if only they had been able to break through the defences on the Gallipoli peninsula. We travelled beside the Sea of Marmara and, as we approached the narrow strait that opened into the Aegean at the Dardanelles, the undulating farmland was an ocean of sunflowers. In sharp irony, their bright green and gold proclaimed the Australian colours triumphant.

Across the entrance at the tip of the peninsula was the ancient settlement of Troy, which had itself been the object of foreign conquest, destruction and rebuilding a dozen times in a long, bellicose history. When we visited it, one wit told the pedantic guide to the ruins that Australia had a proverb that covered the situation perfectly: 'If at first you don't succeed,' he said, 'troy, troy, troy again.' For a moment, the irreverent larrikinism that so characterised the Anzacs flashed a spark across the Dardanelles. The guide was not amused.

There was nothing amusing, however, about the glowering heights of scrubland that rose up from Anzac Cove as we reached the place where the Australians had landed on 25 April 1915. Landing here was the first of many blunders visited upon Jacka and his mates by their British masters. Later, the then Field Marshal Sir William Birdwood would admit, 'This landing farther north than was intended naturally caused some temporary difficulties; for these I must take the blame, for they were caused by my insistence on landing before daylight.'[1] The 'temporary difficulties' would be measured in 8000 young Australian lives in eight months of hellfire from an impossible position. At the time, however, rather than admit to a blunder, he pretended it was all part of a clever plan since the Turk would never anticipate an invasion in an area so perfectly designed to favour the defending force.

A tiny strip of beach, a prospect of precipitous cliffs, low scrub, blind gulches, waterless gullies and stony ground, all in a bowl the lips of which were securely in enemy hands—little wonder the Turks left it only lightly defended. They could hardly improve on Nature.

This was the place of Jacka's baptism of fire and his first experience of incompetence from 'the heads'.[2] He would take each to heart and together they would help to define the man who would come to be 'Australia's greatest frontline soldier'.[3]

Late that afternoon, the door of the small bus that had taken me to Gallipoli opened, and I made my way through the scrub towards the area known as Courtney's Post. It was a fine, clear day and, to the west, down below the cliffs of Shrapnel Valley, lay Anzac Cove and beyond that Homer's wine-dark sea, with the islands of Imbros and Lemnos bulking formidably on the horizon. Above the scrub-line, the Aegean was innocent of watercraft, whereas during the Gallipoli campaign a huge British taskforce of battleships, cruisers, destroyers and other vessels down to small steam pinnaces and whaleboats crowded the area, and German U-boats made deadly forays into their midst.

Suddenly the scrub parted and I found myself standing in the same place where Jacka had stood 90 years before—the front line of the Anzacs. The trenches were mostly filled in now, but as the darkness gathered I could hear the Turks begin their wild charge that terrible night of 19 May 1915, screaming the name of their God— 'Allah, Allah, Allah'—as they hurled themselves at the Australians and New Zealanders to prise them from their trenches and drive them into the sea.

It was at Courtney's Post that the Anzac line wavered and threatened to break. Directly behind it was a steep fall about 20 metres to a dugout that served as front-line headquarters for the 4th Brigade's Australian commander, 49-year-old Colonel John Monash. A rope ran from the furthest trench down to the dugout. From time to time, Monash would send one of his junior officers to climb it to survey the scene and brief the field commanders.

On that night, Monash and Colonel Harry Chauvel, commander of the Australian Light Horse Brigade, had only revolvers to defend themselves. If Jacka's platoon in D Company of the 14th Battalion could not hold the enemy back, the Turks would skid down the cliff on top of the flimsy dugout. Two glittering military careers would be ended almost before they began. And once they poured through the gap, a rout would surely follow. The Australians would be split, their supply lifeline cut to pieces.

The officers could hear the wild cacophony of battle above: the Turkish band in the background raising the aggressors to patriotic frenzy, the machine guns and rifles, the screams of wounded men, the fierce appeals to the God of Islam. The Very lights and the exploding hand-bombs tossed from both sides lit the sky and made treacherous shadows among the flashes.

In the trenches at Courtney's Post, Acting Lance Corporal Jacka and his comrades bore the assault. It was not the first time he had confronted the enemy from this post, or from Quinn's, 100 metres to the left. On 1 May at Quinn's Post he confided to his diary, 'Turks making great attacks on our trenches. They are brave but are going to certain death. Mowing them down in the hundreds.'

This night was different. All along the line, the Turks were charging into a fusillade of machine-gun fire, but as they fell, their compatriots ran over the bodies and hurled themselves at the Australian trenches. Now it was hand-to-hand combat, both sides firing at point-blank range, and a dozen metres to Jacka's right, in the trenchline ahead of his, the Turks broke through, tossing bombs and killing two Australians, wounding two more and driving six others out. The Turks ran to Jacka's right and into the intersecting communication trench.

Jacka had been protected from the bomb blasts by his firestep dug into the front of the trench, and from there he fired into the milling Turks who took cover and held on. Then, as other enemy soldiers rushed to join the attackers, Jacka shouted, 'Turks in the trench!' and loaded another magazine into his Lee Enfield 303. In front of him lay the open mouth of the communication trench to the front and rear. An Australian officer, Lieutenant Bill Hamilton, a young Duntroon graduate, suddenly appeared there, firing his revolver at the Turks, but was cut down before he'd emptied the chambers.

Jacka needed to break the stalemate before his ammunition ran out. 'Officer wanted,' he called. Below in Monash's HQ, Major 'Bobby' Rankine ordered Lieutenant Keith Wallace Crabbe up into the communication trench.[4] Jacka heard him coming and stopped him with a shout. 'Look out. Turks in there!'

Wallace Crabbe: 'What's the situation?'

Jacka told him.

Wallace Crabbe: 'If I get men to back you up, can you charge them?'

Jacka: 'Yes. I want two or three.'

Wallace Crabbe disappeared. Jacka moved about the trench firing at an angle, using other men's rifles and reloading in a single motion as he went. Whenever a Turkish rifle appeared around the corner he fired. Again and again he ducked bullets and retreated to his firestep.

Wallace Crabbe gathered three volunteers from A Company, all Bendigo boys—Privates Frank Poliness, Stephen De Arango and Bill Howard. It had been Poliness who responded to the officer's entreaty, 'Will you back Jacka up? It's a tough job.'

He nodded. 'It's sink or swim,' he said.

As the bullets flew overhead, and the screams of men *in extremis* rose above the roar of battle, they reached the communication trench near Jacka's line. Wallace Crabbe reported his return. Jacka slung his rifle over the top of the trench towards them and followed it, landing in the communication trench with them. The officer took charge. They would fight their way forward up the communication trench to the new front line and meet the Turks head-on.

Jacka turned to the privates. 'Fix bayonets,' he said. It was his first order. His second typified the man. 'I'll go first. Follow me.'

Jacka dashed across the exposed area of the communication trench, back to his firestep in the line. Howard followed but the Turks were too quick and he was hit by three bullets. Jacka dragged him out of the firing line and warned the others to stay where they were. Howard was badly hurt but he would survive.

Wallace Crabbe's tactic wouldn't work. Now Jacka took charge. He called to the lieutenant to open fire up the communication trench while he circled to the rear of the Turks. The officer instantly accepted the authority of the lance corporal.

Bending low and carrying his rifle with the bayonet fixed, Jacka hurried left up the slight rise through the darkened trenches, past dead comrades and the severely wounded Lieutenant Harold Boyle. He passed one communication trench, then took the other leading to the forward line where the Turks were gathering themselves for the final push through the Australian defenders to the battalion HQ.

The trench line was slightly angled, and this gave Jacka a little cover when he moved into it. Then, out of sight of the Turks, he climbed over the parapet into no-man's-land. Wallace Crabbe and his men kept firing up the communication trench to hold the enemy back. The Turks responded with rifle and revolver. Suddenly Jacka loomed above them.

There were ten bullets in his magazine as he leapt into the trench and began firing. Five men fell to gunshot before his ammunition ran out and he used the bayonet to dispatch two more. As the others attempted to flee, Poliness shot two of them dead. Three others surrendered. Turks from further down the line saw the panic and joined in a wild retreat. The action was over. The line was restored.

Lieutenant Wallace Crabbe cautiously rounded the corner of the trench where he had glimpsed Jacka jumping down, and heard the gunfire and the cries of men. Dawn was breaking. In the soft light, the trench was literally filled with the dead—the seven Turks were lying on top of the Australians who had been killed by the Turkish bombs. Only Jacka, his face flushed, his rifle loosely at hand, remained alive.

In his detailed account, the officer said, 'All right, Corporal?'

Jacka nodded. 'Well, I managed to get the buggers, sir.'[5]

Word of Jacka's extraordinary action sped through the ranks on Anzac. Wallace Crabbe reported the event to the battalion commander, Lieutenant Colonel Richard Courtney after whom the post was named. But Courtney was in no condition to process the recommendation and was evacuated. He would die in Melbourne of illness, attributed to Gallipoli, in 1919.

Jacka's own diary entry that day was laconic to a degree. 'Great battle at 3am,' he wrote. 'Turks captured large portion of our trench. D Coy called into the front line. Lieut. Hamilton shot dead. I lead a section of men and recaptured the trench. I bayoneted two Turks, shot five, took three prisoners and cleared the whole trench. I held the trench alone for 15 minutes. Lieut. Crabbe informed me that I would be recommended.'

In fact, the recommendation would have been lost in the confusion of war had not the men of the line spread the word that reached the ears of Monash, and then of the division commander, Major General Sir Alexander Godley. When Monash dined a week later with General Sir Ian Hamilton, the officer commanding the expedition to Gallipoli, on his seaborne HQ the *Arcadian*, Hamilton knew the story already from Godley. He and Monash agreed over dinner that Jacka had earned the Victoria Cross, the first to be awarded to an Australian in the Great War.

Monash, the ambitious Victorian engineer struggling to overcome his German-Jewish background in the rarefied milieu of the British High Command, shared Hamilton's admiration for the Australians' fighting qualities. He would base an extraordinarily successful military career on his command of the Anzac Corps. He wanted the story out immediately the award was approved.

However, Monash could not rely on normal channels for his propaganda offensive, at least in the Gallipoli engagement. Charles Bean, the official Australian war correspondent, had taken an immediate dislike to the 'pushy Jew'[6] and concentrated his reporting on the 1st Division, commanded by British-born General William Throsby Bridges. Bridges, the creator of Duntroon Military College, was much more to the liking of the British-educated journalist.

The 1st Division were all Australians, whereas Godley's division, which included Monash's 4th Brigade, was a mix of Australian and New Zealand battalions, together with Chauvel's Light Horse, albeit without their mounts which were back in Egypt. Bean attached himself to Bridges' command and he was unaware of Jacka's award until it was gazetted. Monash complained, 'Charley Bean seldom comes our way.'[7]

However, once final approval came through from London, Monash had a story to tell. Bean then approached Wallace Crabbe, who provided him with a full written report. Less than a month later Wallace Crabbe was killed in action.

Bean's failure to interview the VC himself was of not the slightest concern to Jacka, who went straight back into the line. He would actively resist personal publicity and the trappings of fame for the whole of his life. Nor did it prevent his remarkable feat, and the honour it secured, being disseminated to a wide Australian readership. Monash saw to that.

The newspapers trumpeted the story of the nation's first hero of the Gallipoli encounter. The politicians leapt upon it as proof of their wisdom in committing Australia to the glorious defence of the British Empire and all she stood for. Jacka and the Anzacs were covering the nation in glory. And when the recruiting posters went up in the capital cities showing Jacka in action, young men flocked to enlist.

That single action at Courtney's Post was enough to secure a place for 22-year-old Bert Jacka among his country's favourite sons. But what neither the papers, the generals, nor the politicians knew was that the shy lad from Wedderburn in country Victoria had only just begun his astonishing journey. In the months and years that followed, his deeds on the battlefields of France and Belgium would make his name a legend and inspire an entire battalion of 1000 men to designate themselves 'Jacka's Mob'.[8] In peacetime, his reputation for decency and good fellowship would take him to the pinnacle of success and happiness before the life was crushed from him on an alien battlefield with no rules of engagement.

But, as with Gallipoli itself, there seemed to be something at the heart of Jacka that we could not know completely. He was a hero to the common man. He was beloved by his comrades at arms with an intensity unmatched in our military history. But so determined was he to ignore the code of unquestioning obedience to those who outranked him when they put his men in jeopardy, that some in the military establishment retaliated.

They had feted him. They had decorated him. They had promoted him. But in a system and a conflict that regarded human beings as expendable—not just in their hundreds, but in their hundreds of thousands—Jacka would not fit himself to their mould. So they put an end to his promotions, downgraded his recommendations for valour, and began to call him 'crude', and imply he was 'unsound', 'out of control', and somehow undeserving of his nation's whole-hearted respect. By omission and commission they called his character into question.

For 90 years the truth of the matter has proven elusive. But it is there to be found.

2

JACKA COUNTRY

Albert Jacka was not born to soldiery. On the contrary, his family were hard-working country folk from Wedderburn, 60 kilometres north of Bendigo, Victoria. His father was a Labor man who would fiercely oppose conscription in 1916 and again in 1917, even when success meant that fewer reinforcements might be sent to his sons in their struggle. When young Bert Jacka heard the call to arms at 21, he was working in solitude in the backblocks of Victoria, repairing the native forests that had been all but denuded by the goldminers in their frantic need for timber supports.

Solitude suited him. He was shy in company. Like most Australians he was mad for sport, but because his job took him from town to town on the fringe of the great Murray River he rarely played in local team competitions. Instead, he tested himself in events that celebrated the individual—cycling races and boxing. He excelled at both. The local newspapers of the region recorded his triumphs.[1]

He was not a tall man—standing only 5 feet 6½ inches (169 centimetres) in his stockinged feet when measured by the recruiting officer. But his chest expanded a full 2 inches when he breathed deeply; the cycling had given his legs a hard muscularity; the boxing had developed his upper body; and both had contributed to an athlete's perfect balance.

In the boxing ring, as on the battlefield, he was not roused to anger quickly. But once his blood was up he became a fierce and uncompromising fighter. He fitted perfectly into that unique brand of Australian soldiery: the volunteer for king and country, impatient with military formalism, contemptuous of slackers, loyal to his unit and proud of his mates; but most of all, eager to get the job done, the enemy defeated, the aggressor punished and the world put to rights.

Like many others in the Australian Imperial Force, he would earn an early reputation as a rebel, reluctant to salute the officers, particularly the British variety who paraded themselves about the streets of Cairo on the lookout for antipodean insolence. But unlike many of his comrades, he quickly learned the value of the chain of command and joined it so he might take a greater part in the struggle. As his seniors fell around him, Bert Jacka would pick up the gauntlet of authority. But he never lost the sense of urgency, the need to get the job done as soon as possible so he could return to the land he loved and get on with life.

The Wedderburn Express burst into life in the lively former gold-mining town on Saturday 16 June 1889. There had been a robbery of a large quantity of pickled beef from Mr Wilson's butchery in High Street; and at the Salvation Army Barracks on Sunday last 'Captain Peter Wong Woy, a Chinaman, testified to the congregation and read from the Bible in English and Chinese'.

Captain Wong Woy's bilingual testimony notwithstanding, the inhabitants of Wedderburn valued their peace and quiet. The *Express* hosted a heated argument in its Letters column for an entire year over the right of the Salvos to play their drums in the streets of the town. In the end, two Salvation Army captains were fined and had to pay costs.

Not that Wedderburnians didn't appreciate their music. The year 1889 saw the formation of the town's brass band, followed soon after by a local minstrel troupe. But henceforth the Salvos played only trumpets and triangles.

By then the Jackas had been in the district for at least two decades. Wedderburn, which was named after the South African-born police constable who patrolled the area in the pioneering days, had its gold rush in the 1850s when the town population swelled to 40,000; but, as the fever lured the prospectors north, Wedderburn returned to agricultural pursuits. Periodically, new finds would bring mini-rushes well into the 20th century, but there is no record of the Jackas' involvement in the quest for easy riches. It's also unlikely that the Jackas were founding members of either the band or the blackface melody-makers.

Albert's grandfather, Josiah, had arrived in Victoria on the *Fortune* with three brothers and a sister in 1854. His parents, Nathaniel and Elizabeth (nee Kettle), had married in the Wedderburn Church of England in 1884 but went farming near Winchelsea in the Geelong district soon after. Elizabeth had been born in England in 1864 and had come to the Geelong area with her family as a girl. They later moved to Clifton Hill, then on the outskirts of Melbourne.

Winchelsea, one of Victoria's earliest settlements, became a centre for shearers and other tradesmen needed to service the big properties of the district. There Elizabeth gave birth to their first child, David Samuel (known as 'Sam') in 1886, Fanny the next year, Elsie in 1891 and Albert on 10 January 1893, the year Winchelsea installed its first fifteen gaslights in the main street.

But the 1893 Depression crippled the farming community and forced Nathaniel off the land. To put bread on the table, he joined the Victorian police force and served in the area. Another son, Sidney, came along in 1894, but soon Nat Jacka had had enough of the constabulary and in 1897 the family returned to Wedderburn. Until Nat built his own house, they moved in with his parents at the southern end of town where the railway spur line from Bendigo terminated. He also leased a few acres and was soon describing himself as a farmer and carter, hauling goods in his big dray back and forth between the settlements and the railhead.

Two more children—the last—were born to the couple: Bill in 1897 and Bessie in 1899. Nathaniel built his own house in Ridge Street 500 metres away from his parents' home. By then Albert was six and just starting school at the solid-brick building that still stands on the corner of Reef and Ridge Streets.

Most of Albert's schoolmates lived in the town, and they walked to school, but those from nearby farms would arrive in gigs, buggies or riding their own horses. Every Monday morning, Albert and the 90 or so other pupils would salute the flag and sing 'God Save the King'. On Tuesdays they had half an hour of religious instruction. Every Friday afternoon the girls were taught sewing while the boys played football or cricket.

In class they would scratch out their letters on slates, ruled on one side and plain on the other, under the strict supervision of the teachers. The hours were long, the learning largely by rote, but school did have its lighter moments. On one occasion a boy was late and the headmaster demanded an explanation. 'Me mum's making jam', said the wide-eyed truant, 'and she sent me down to the cemetery to get some jars.'[2]

Albert was a good student with a clear, flowing hand. He scored well in every examination. But his great love was for sports of all kinds, from cricket and football to rifle shooting and especially cycling. As he rose through the classes, slates were replaced by books, and slate pencils by pen and ink.

He was mild mannered as a rule, but according to his younger brother Bill, if anyone threatened a family member he was soon on the scene with fists raised. 'We always felt safe when Albert was around,' he said.[3] This need to protect others—particularly those whom he regarded as 'family'—would almost assume the form of a compulsion in later life.

The Wedderburn Miners' Literary Institute and Free Library had opened in 1859 and was expanded in 1899. The Jackas patronised it like most of the townsfolk, but once Albert received his Merit Certificate at the end of primary school it would be the only source of further learning available. There was no high school in the town and no money in the big family for Albert or his brothers to board in Bendigo. So at thirteen he joined his father on the dray.

It was a varied life. They cut sleepers and fence posts for the railway, repaired roads on contract to the government, brought goods from Bendigo to the Wedderburn stores, and serviced the bigger properties. With their small farm providing milk and vegetables, they made a decent living. With the few shillings his father paid him, Albert graduated from hard-wheeled bicycles to the new pneumatic tyres.

Nathaniel had become a non-conformist who believed in hard yakka and the rights of the working man. He was a very active president of the local Political Labour Council, the forerunner of the Australian Labor Party. Like his son, he was prideful and, when challenged, sure of his ground. He rarely took a backward step.

The Wedderburn Express is silent on the fate of the minstrel troupe (though the brass band brought great distinction to the town) so we cannot know whether young Albert ever joined the chorus. We do know, however, that he would develop a fine tenor voice. According to brother Bill, Albert joined the Presbyterian choir as a teenager, not so much out of religious conviction (since he was raised a Wesleyan), but because he was 'sweet' on the organist, Elsie Raff, the parson's daughter. But his pursuit of Elsie was conducted within the strictures of a puritanical framework. Indeed, about this time Albert joined the local chapter of the Independent Order of Rechabites, a Friendly Society dedicated to the abstinence of 'all liquors of an intoxicating quality, whether ale, porter, wine or ardent spirit, except as medicine'.

The name of the order was taken from the Old Testament. When tempted by Jeremiah to partake of a loving cup, the Rechabites nobly replied that, 'We will drink no wine for Jonahab, the son of Rechab, our father, commanded us saying, "Ye shall drink no wine neither ye nor your sons forever".' The modern order was formed in England in the 1830s and by 1847 had reached Australia, with the Victorian chapters easily the most active in the country. For Jacka, the teenage pledge would become a lifelong commitment.

It is apparent that Albert absorbed many of his father's attitudes and opinions during the long hours and years they spent together. The bond became so close that at a crucial time in his life the VC winner would refuse orders from his commanding general out of concern that the result would cause an unbridgeable rift between father and son.

But it cannot have been easy for the strong-willed teenager to remain a follower and, at seventeen, Albert stepped out of the paternal shadow. For several months he worked as an engine cleaner for the railways in Bendigo. Then he applied for entry to the Victorian Forestry Department and was accepted in their training program. After courses in reforestation, fencing and the tending of native forests, at eighteen he was given charge of his own bailiwick.

Over the next three years he would board with various families in all the towns within his area of responsibility, from Wedderburn itself to Cohuna (where today they proudly display a fence post cut by Albert during this time), to Koondrook, Lake Charm and Heathcote.

Motorised transport was becoming available, but Albert had ambitions to become a professional cyclist and wherever possible he rode his bicycle while on the job. The country just south of the Murray was flat and the roads uncluttered. Jacka relished the challenge and pushed himself to the limits of endurance. In the solitude and the silence, broken only by the chortling magpie and the wild scream of the white cockatoo, he would find the self-knowledge and strength of purpose common to all athletes who test themselves to breaking point. And on Friday nights, when the amateur boxing contests were held in the local halls, or in the open air, he would test himself against his fellows with satisfying results.

He was a young man in his prime.

3

Gathering for the fray

When war broke out in Europe in August 1914, Albert was boarding with the MacArthur family in Heathcote where he had stayed long enough to be picked in the local Aussie Rules football team. His three years with Forestry had been a good, active, outdoor time, but because of his lack of education there were few prospects for advancement. His vague ambition to become a professional cyclist was unfulfilled and the peripatetic demands of his job weighed against it. The recruiting ads in the local papers were offering six shillings a day—a big jump from his modest wage—and the prospect of adventure in the great, wide world.

The papers also told of the peril facing the Empire from the mad ambitions of the German kaiser, and of Australia's fearful isolation among the yellow hordes should the solid bulwark of imperial protection be toppled by the Prussian militarists. But most of all, it was a call to arms for a young nation that until so recently had been no more than a collection of colonies whose roots lay in the shameful past of penal settlement and fierce division between privilege and poverty.

Now there was a new spirit abroad, a prideful restlessness, a growing sense of Australian identity as expressed in the ballads of Henry Lawson and Banjo Paterson, the international recognition of figures like Nellie Melba, herself a Melbourne girl, and George Ernest 'Chinese' Morrison, born not more than 20 kilometres from Jacka in Geelong and whose amazing travels and journalistic exploits at home and in the Dragon Court of Peking had made him world famous.[1] Boxer Les Darcy, who like Albert, had left school early to become a carter, was beating all comers. Victor Trumper, the best batsman in the world, had thrashed the English bowlers in the 1912 Test series and though Australia lost the Ashes 1–nil with two matches drawn it was a near-run thing. The days of English *noblesse oblige* on the cricket field were long gone. The Australians were a force to be reckoned with.

Throughout the country, as with Jacka himself, there was a powerful sense of frustration at unrealised potential. Australia was young and strong. Opportunities were limited by distance and a scarcity of educational resources. But the country was growing to manhood and bursting with the need to prove itself to its seniors. This European war in defence of the motherland was made to order. There was no time to lose.

In late August 1914, Albert sought an indefinite leave of absence from Forestry. It was approved immediately and, having left his fencing tools with a mate, he presented himself to the recruiting officer at the Heathcote Town Hall on 8 September to sign up for the duration. Like so many of his compatriots, his biggest fear was that the fighting would be over before he arrived.

Almost immediately, he ran up against official incompetence from the higher-ups. When he arrived in Melbourne a week later to begin training, his papers had been lost and he had to sign up again. He was declared fit except for some teeth which he had neglected. A visit to the army dentist would soon put that right. He pocketed his pass and headed out to the training camp at Broadmeadows, 16 kilometres north of the city centre.

There he was assigned to the unit that would become his wartime family for the next four years, the foundation of his loyalty and his support, his comrades in horror and hellfire, tribulation and triumph: 14th Battalion AIF. Soon it would be combined with the 13th, 15th and 16th to become the 4th Brigade, which under John Monash proved to be one of the most potent fighting forces of the conflict.

Also in training at the time in the 16th was George Mitchell, who Jacka would come to know at Anzac and in France and who epitomised the larrikin digger of swift-growing legend. After the war Mitchell would write one of the most powerful and least appreciated books of the Great War. 'Our only home was our unit,' he wrote. 'Pride in ourselves, in face of a world of friends and enemies, was our sustaining force.'[2]

The 14th had a fighting force of 1000 men, most from Bendigo and the towns around Wedderburn. Some of them, like Bill Earle and George Bolam, Jacka knew already; others he would get to know in the long months of training. But he formed no special friendships with individuals. That was not his way. He was content with his own company and mixed easily, if unobtrusively, in the rough and tumble of a man's world. Others could be the life of the party. In those early days Jacka preferred the quiet, telling word or phrase that cut to the core.

Their commander was Lieutenant Colonel Courtney, a Melbourne solicitor who at 45 was well suited to the training regime. He instilled as much parade ground discipline as was possible for a group of volunteers who felt their role was to fight and saw no value in the inanities of military rank and privilege. Jacka was typical. At first he resented the orders and the appalling lack of organisation that could barely outfit the new recruits, let alone arm them with the weapons of war.

But, as the army whipped itself into shape, Jacka came to appreciate the orderly framework of the military system. He relished the route marches, the rifle drill, bayonet practice and skirmishing skills passed on by the NCOs from Australia's small professional army. Indeed, he soon sought to join their ranks by attending classes for junior NCOs conducted at Broadmeadows in the evenings. By the end of November he was an acting lance corporal.

When he returned to Wedderburn on embarkation leave he was the pride of the family. Younger brothers Sid, now 20, and Bill, 17, also declared themselves ready to join up. However, Nathaniel and Elizabeth put their parental foot down and the brothers would not enlist until they turned 21 and 18 the following year.

At a ceremony in the Mechanics' Hall, John Pettard, the bank manager and head of the local Rechabite chapter, presented Albert and two other young soldiers with medallions to remind them of their pledge. Townspeople crowded on to the platform as the train made steam for the run to Bendigo and Melbourne. The girl he had admired from the choir stalls, pretty Elsie Raff, threw her arms around him and kissed him on the lips. According to young Bill, Albert blushed ruby red and hastened inside the carriage. The scene at Wedderburn was repeated in the small country towns and the burgeoning cities across the land. The flower of Australian youth was heading off to fight the Hun and to cover the nation in glory.

On 17 December, the 14th Battalion lined up with their compatriots for the celebrated march of the 4th Brigade through cheering crowds lining the streets of Melbourne. As Newton Wanliss, the 14th Battalion's historian, wrote later, 'Few who saw that march will ever forget it—thousands of picked Australians of magnificent physique and highly trained, marching with the confidence and bearing of veterans.'[3]

The men's only experience of war was from history books, with their tales of triumph at Waterloo, and the newspaper stories of Boer War skirmishing and sharpshooting on horseback. The Germans, they knew, were made of sterner stuff than the Boers. But the Prussian militarists had pitted themselves against the greatest empire the world had ever seen. Britannia not only ruled the seas, she had millions of eager recruits responding to the call to arms, from the British Isles to the vast plains of Canada, to the teeming cities of India, and to the strong young farmers of New Zealand. But best of all, she had the Australians. Their British-born prime minister, Andrew Fisher, whose schoolteacher wife had taught her groom to read and write, now spoke for them all when he promised to defend the Empire 'to the last man and the last shilling'.

Such were the castles in the air of December 1914.

THE OLD WORLD BECKONS

'Bert' Jacka, as he was now known by his mates in the 14th, opened his new diary three days before Christmas. 'Embarked on H.M.A.T. *Ulysses* at 4.30p.m.,' he wrote. 'Put out to sea at 8p.m. Anchored for the night at 10p.m.' As a diarist, Jacka was no Samuel Pepys. Terse and laconic, he seems to have used the diary reluctantly, as though responding to a plea from his mother, to keep track of his great adventure. His entries quickly became intermittent and would end with the withdrawal from Anzac. However, they do provide glimpses of character, not least by their simplicity and directness.

The *Ulysses* was waiting for the other troop transports to assemble before heading across the Great Australian Bight to Albany where, with ships already gathered, they would become the Second Fleet heading to war in Europe. It was 124 years since the notorious Second Fleet bringing convicts from Britain to Australia had arrived two years after the penal settlement was founded in 1788. Also known as the Death Fleet, it recorded a casualty rate of almost a third of its human cargo. The sobriquet would prove—in the long term—just as applicable to Jacka's convoy.

As commander of the 4th Brigade, Monash was in charge of the nineteen-ship convoy and, with his almost obsessive organisational skills, he would see to it that the officers and men were fully occupied during the five-week voyage. In the mornings, there were weapons classes, physical training and drill on deck. In the afternoons, cricket matches were organised and in the evenings singsongs were popular with the men. Jacka quickly made a name for himself in the boxing ring.

But, as the volunteers for king and country tried in vain to celebrate Yuletide in the heaving seas of the Bight, they had little or no idea of the great forces at play in the Old World. By the end of 1914 vast armies had swept across Europe in blind obedience to ancient hatreds and prejudice, new-found hubris and vaulting imperial ambition. The vicious royal intrigues of yesteryear were colliding with the huge technological advances of the industrial revolution to produce an unprecedented human slaughter. And the prerogatives of class would ensure that millions of young men would be turned into cannon fodder by their rulers with absolute impunity.

These were foreign concepts to the Australians of 1914. They knew little and cared less about the regal absurdity that had triggered the conflict—the assassination of the 51-year-old, extravagantly moustached Archduke Franz Ferdinand, heir to the imperial throne of Austria and Hungary, on 28 June 1914.

Though there was absolutely no evidence connecting the assassin with the Serbian government, Ferdinand's uncle, the Emperor Franz Josef, demanded of the Serbs an act of abject contrition. Belgrade's response went only part way to meeting Vienna's demands, so, in an excess of self-righteousness, and armed with a 'blank cheque' from Germany's Kaiser Wilhelm, Austria–Hungary declared war on Serbia.

That was a clear threat to Russia, for if the Austro–Hungarians took control of the Ottoman states of the Balkans, that would give them political ascendancy over Constantinople, the gateway to Russian trade through the Black Sea to the Mediterranean. So Tsar Nicholas II mobilised the armed forces in support of the Slavs of Serbia.

However, the real enemy was not the tottering Austro–Hungarian Empire but the Prussian militarism behind it, personified by the vain, garrulous, strutting figure of Nicholas's cousin, Wilhelm II. He regarded the tsar, with some justice, as 'only fit to live in a country house and grow turnips'. He and his officer corps believed implicitly in Germany's 'manifest destiny', its 'historic mission', and indeed the 'biological necessity' to make war as the natural law of humankind to establish the leadership of the strong. So, seizing his chance, on 31 July Wilhelm sent an ultimatum to cousin Nicky: 'Demobilisation must begin within twelve hours.'

The Russians refused. The following day Germany declared war on Russia. The Old World trembled on the brink.

Nowhere had the course of events been followed more closely— and with such a mix of trepidation and delight—than in France. For more than four decades successive French governments had sworn that one day they would reclaim the border territories of Alsace and Lorraine that had been the price of their defeat by Germany in the war of 1870. They had swallowed their traditional Anglophobia and developed common cause with Britain, culminating in 1904 in the Anglo–French Entente. This was expanded to incorporate Russia in the Triple Entente of 1907.

In the years since, French military leaders had developed strategies with the British generals to combat German aggression. And the French generals had planned a counter-punch, an attack aimed to penetrate friendly Alsace and strike at the heart of Germany in the south.

The Germans had made their own detailed preparations. By 1914 they had a plan, designed and refined to the last detail by Count Alfred von Schlieffen, the former head of the German general staff, that would sweep their armies around the north of Europe towards France like a right hook, the fist of which would land on the figurative jaw of Paris and knock France out within a few months. Wilhelm himself had examined the plan and pronounced it a work of German genius. So, two days after he declared war on Russia he did the same to France, which immediately returned the compliment.

Germany then demanded free passage of its troops through Belgium. King Albert of the Belgians refused. And when the German armies invaded on 3 August he pleaded for assistance. Britain delivered an ultimatum to Germany and, when the kaiser failed to step back from the brink, Britain entered the war. That evening the mordant foreign secretary, Sir Edward Grey, standing with a friend in his Whitehall office, found immortality in the melancholy observation, 'The lamps are going out all over Europe; we shall not see them lit again in our lifetime.'

Despite a spirited resistance, the Belgians were overwhelmed by the German advance before Britain could deploy. Their one decisive stroke was to destroy their railway lines to cut the flow of German supplies and reinforcements before retreating to Antwerp. This gave the Allies time to organise their defence in northern France. The government of Herbert Asquith, nicknamed 'Squiffy' because of his fondness for the bottle, dispatched the bulk of the regular army in the British Expeditionary Force (BEF) under General Sir John French, whose brave words in high council would stand in stark contrast to his erratic behaviour in the face of the enemy.

After one notable conflict at Mons, when two British divisions found themselves suddenly confronting the massive advance of two German army corps, General French began to retreat at ever increasing speed and by the end of August was proposing to depart altogether. Only the personal intervention of Lord Kitchener, the secretary of state for war, kept him on the Continent at all.

But as the Germans swung round into the 'hook' in northern France a sudden flaw appeared in the Schlieffen plan—a growing gap between their two great columns of advance that opened up their flanks to a potentially fatal counterattack. General Joseph Gallieni, the military governor of Paris, spotted the flaw and charged in to exploit it. But his commander in chief, Marshal Joffre, had other ideas, and the decisive blow never fell. Instead, the German advance trundled slowly to a stop. Then on 8 September, as Albert Jacka on the other side of the world was signing up in the Heathcote Town Hall, the German commander Helmuth von Moltke ordered a brief retreat. An enraged Kaiser Wilhelm immediately sacked him.

By now the Belgians were only just holding on in Antwerp and the British first lord of the Admiralty, Winston Churchill, dispatched 3000 marines in support, with himself as prospective commander. It was the first of Churchill's flamboyant—not to say quixotic— interventions. It was too little too late. But that seems only to have whetted Churchill's appetite for more. Nevertheless the Belgian resistance, combined with the determined French resistance to the German war machine, sapped the resources of the invader. By mid-October, the armies were ranged against each other on a Western Front drawn from Switzerland to the sea. The kaiser's expectations of a short, decisive war evaporated.

At Ypres, they dug trenches; the line thickened on both sides and the daily slaughter began. Sir John French became erratic and contradictory. Soon the BEF would be all but wiped out and Lord Kitchener would tell the Cabinet that only armies of 'millions', raised from the civilian ranks, would provide any hope of victory.

In the south, the Gallic strike at the German heart through Alsace and Lorraine immediately ran into trouble. The machine gun, with its power to cut down an advancing force from the flanks, ensured that aggression became synonymous with death and disaster. Paradoxically, in this new battlefield, the best method of attack was defence.

That lesson would not be learned by the Allied generals for months, and in some cases, years. Even when they knew their tactics were sending untold thousands to their certain death, still they attacked and sacrificed in heedless futility. Now the two opposing armies settled into a stalemate of attrition.

In the east, the expected 'Russian steamroller' simply broke down. Hopelessly equipped and led, one Russian army was utterly destroyed by the Germans, with 90,000 prisoners taken. Another fell back in disorder. Further south the Russians confronted the Austro–Hungarians, who were almost their equal in incompetence. Confusion reigned until a German army arrived and restored a semblance of order to the battlefield. The Russians retreated and dug in. Once more the engines of war were immobilised.

By New Year's Day 1915, as the Australian Second Fleet steamed across the Indian Ocean, the war in Europe had assumed the pattern it would maintain for the next four years—armies entrenched in confrontation; commanders in their relatively luxurious staff head-quarters behind the lines making plans that would send their soldiers on futile sorties to death and terrible injury; war ministries at home rousing their populations to greater and greater sacrifice.

The politicians quickly realised that they were no longer in charge. They had passed the mantle of authority to the men whose business was the battlefield and, as ever, those at the top were bound root and branch to their glory days fighting the last war. With the rarest excep-tions, the generals were unable to accommodate the new imperatives wrought by the industrial revolution. Sir John French declared in 1914 that 'Nothing will ever truly replace the cavalry charge.'

Occasionally a politician would break ranks with a daring and seductive plan to end the stalemate and the war. Winston Churchill was a serial offender. His defence of Antwerp with the Royal Naval Division had been a costly gambit. His subsequent decision to with-draw the British North Sea Fleet to the west of Scotland, then the west of Ireland, for fear of U-boat destruction, had removed a powerful aggressor from the chessboard of battle. But now he had a brilliant scheme that had leapt fully formed into that fertile brain: the conquest of Constantinople by his Mediterranean Fleet. In a single stroke he would take Turkey out of the war; then the Allied armies would drive up through the Balkans to certain victory over the hated Hun.

When Franz Ferdinand fell to the Serbian assassin, Turkey was divided and anxious. Her Ottoman Empire had been 'the sick man of Europe' for a century and in 1908 the Young Turk revolution usurped the power of the sultan. Under their 'little Napoleon', Enver Bey, they sought to rejuvenate the country. Kaiser Wilhelm saw a chance to engage the new government through their common hatred and fear of Russia. And for once his diplomatic overtures were welcomed.

In July 1914, the Turks began negotiations in earnest with Germany, seeking immediate protection from a Serbian advance down through the Balkans. But then a split began to form in the ranks of the Young Turks, a substantial number preferring an alliance with Britain. With impeccable timing, Churchill chose that moment to 'requisition' two Turkish battleships, the *Sultan Osman* and the *Reshadieh*, that had just been built in British yards. The split healed instantly. The same day, 3 August, Turkey signed a treaty of alliance with Germany.

However, much to the kaiser's chagrin, their new ally did not immediately declare war on Russia. Having secured German protection, the Young Turks wanted to see which way the bigger battle might go before declaring themselves.

In the previous two days a hide-and-seek drama had begun in the Mediterranean as British warships sought to prevent two German battleships commanded by Admiral Souchon from reaching the Dardanelles prior to the declaration of war. The British cruisers *Indomitable* and *Indefatigable* happened upon their quarry six hours before the expiry of Britain's ultimatum to Germany to respect Belgium's neutrality. 'Very good,' cabled Churchill. 'War imminent.' But by the time the clock ticked to midnight the Germans were beginning to out-distance their pursuers.

By the following evening the two German ships were well clear as they approached the plains of Troy on the southern arm of the Dardanelles. At 9 p.m. they entered the narrows. As soon as they were through, the German military attaché in Constantinople, Colonel von Kress, demanded that Enver Bey give the order to fire on any British pursuers. Enver hesitated. He needed to consult his Cabinet. But Kress was insistent. 'Are the English to be fired on or not?'

Finally Enver answered, 'Yes.'

The Germans pressed their advantage by offering to 'sell' Turkey the two warships as a replacement for those Churchill had 'requisitioned'. The Young Turks accepted with pleasure and the populace applauded.

For nearly three months the Allies blustered and badgered, seeking to break the alliance of convenience between Germany and Turkey. At times French *politesse* and urbanity seemed about to carry the day, but on 28 October Admiral Souchon finessed his rivals when he took his ships into the Black Sea and shelled the Russian cities of Odessa, Sevastopol and Feodosia.

The Turkish government was stunned but they were also under threat. Souchon could just as easily turn his guns on Constantinople itself. The game was up. Russia declared war on Turkey on 4 November, followed by France and Britain 24 hours later.

On 25 November, as Bert Jacka and his mates were learning the basics of hand-to-hand combat at Broadmeadows, Prime Minister Asquith called to order the first meeting of the War Council, comprising himself, Kitchener and Churchill. The First Lord immediately presented his plan to rescue the situation in Turkey—a naval action to blast through the defences at the Dardanelles, blow the German cruisers out of the water, and confront Constantinople from the Bosphorus. The Young Turks, he believed, would quickly bow to the superior British force of arms.

Churchill played his cards carefully. No ground troops would be lost from the Western Front since only a naval action was contemplated. Nor would his plan reduce the strength of the navy in the North Sea, since only older battleships of the Mediterranean Fleet would be used. Every objection was met and trumped by the former war correspondent turned military zealot. Finally he carried the day. The War Council approved the proposal on 15 January 1915.

On that day Jacka wrote in his diary: 'Sailed from Colombo at 8am. A number of troops missing.' This was not surprising. More than 2000 virile young men had been penned together for nearly a month. When they had docked at the Ceylonese capital two days earlier, Jacka noted, 'Beautifully fine morning. Palms making a pretty background to the white houses. During the day a lot of fun was caused by Major Steel chasing the troops who had broken ship. Sergeant Major Blainey was threatened with being thrown overboard for drawing and firing a revolver at a nigger plying a boat for hire.'

In fact, the clash was more serious than Jacka's laconic tone implies. Leave was tightly rationed and the volunteers resented it. They were starved of fresh fruit and vegetables, to say nothing of female company. Hundreds broke out and, once having sampled the tropical delights, some were reluctant to return to the regimen of shipboard life. Others got so drunk they did not recover until the Ulysses had left. And those on board showed their displeasure at the substandard fare provided them in dramatic fashion. Jacka wrote, 'Four corporals reduced to the ranks for breaking ship . . . soldiers dumped 13 bags of potatoes overboard.'

Monash took the outbreak personally. He had been deeply concerned about the epidemic of measles that had struck the ship, followed by two outbreaks of typhoid. He had asked for a contingent of nurses on board but the headquarters staff were afraid of 'incidents' between the sexes. Next time, he decided, he would brook no refusal. Only Monash's multifarious 'activities roster' kept morale steady until the accoutrements of war appeared off the ships' bows to seize the young soldiers' imaginations.

On 28 January they reached Port Suez at 3 a.m. and Jacka wrote, 'Rumour has it that we are held up on account of the Turks attacking the Canal last night. Ship just passed with her bridge sand-bagged up.' The next day a huge British cruiser saluted the Australian and New Zealand flagship with rousing cheers from the 'blue-jackets' lining the rails. Monash took the salute. Then, on both sides of the canal, British troops, as well as Sikhs, Bengal Lancers and even Ghurkhas, welcomed the Australasians to the fray.

'Both banks are fully entrenched and held by infantry,' Monash wrote. 'Every half-mile or so is a huge redoubt or field fortification, bristling with rifles, guns and machine guns . . . A considerable Turkish and Arab Army is within a few miles of us, led by German officers.'

Finally, three days later they docked at Alexandria, the second-largest city and the main port of Egypt. In 1915 it was linked to Cairo by a highway and railway line and, with beaches stretching 140 kilo-metres along the Mediterranean from Abu Qir to Al-Alamein, it was a summer resort for the wealthy. But Jacka and his 14th Battalion saw only its back-street slums as they marched through the city. They entrained for Heliopolis at 8 p.m. on 2 February and arrived at dawn next day.

In ancient times Heliopolis was, as its name suggests, the principal seat of sun worship, and in time the men of Monash's 4th Brigade would come to understand why. Now it was a southern suburb of Cairo, an 18-kilometre ride by electric tram from the centre of the city. The troops' Australian money was changed for Egyptian coinage. In the camp itself two marquees were erected, one for soft drinks and the other for beer, but most found the Egyptian brew undrinkable and Jacka was not tempted to break his Rechabite pledge.

Now the 4th Brigade was combined with the New Zealanders and the Australian Light Horsemen to become the New Zealand and Australian Division under Major General Sir Alexander Godley, the first formal recognition of the Anzac force. Godley, the son of a British Army captain, had been sent to New Zealand in 1910 to command that dominion's armed forces. But neither the Australians nor the Kiwis were impressed with their new commander, as they footslogged through the sand under a blazing sun. And they wouldn't have a bar of his ever-present wife who, rumour had it, whispered to her husband, 'Make them run again, Alec.'[1]

Nor were they much enamoured of their Egyptian hosts. But there was little else to do with their free time so, with or without leave, they crowded into Cairo, first for a feed at one of the better restaurants, then to the red-light district of the Haret el Wasser which they immediately nicknamed 'the Wozzer'. After a few drinks they hired donkeys from the persistent local hangers-on and raced them down the narrow lanes with little care for the vendors' displays on each side. They gambled and fought, laughed and sang their raucous ballads. They went out of their way to refuse to salute the British officers, who regularly reported this outrage to the Australian command. The Anzacs quickly came to despise the entire country which, they reckoned, was full of shit, sand, sin and syphilis. And when they were ready to return to camp, they would leap aboard a tram, throw the driver off and drive the thing themselves at break-neck speed.

Godley responded with long desert marches and pickets on the road to Cairo. Jacka was not interested in the boozing and whoring in the Wozzer, but it was at Heliopolis that he had his first brush with authority. On 24 February, he wrote, 'Had two charges put in against me by Sergeant Cowie. Awarded one day's defaulter on each charge.' His transgressions were not recorded, but it was the beginning of a nettlesome relationship with his superiors. Time and again, his sins would be those of the angry warrior, impatient with formality, careless of insubordination and outraged by the incompetence that was endangering his own life and sending too many of his mates to a needless death.

PARRY AND THRUST

On 19 February 1915, Churchill's grand plan found voice in the roar of naval gunfire. Admiral Sir Sackville Carden, who had been a reluctant recruit to the Churchillian cause, fired salvos on Turkish positions in the Dardanelles from the massive 15-inch guns of the battleship *Queen Elizabeth* and his fleet of older vessels. The initial attacks went well. British marines landed and met little or no resistance. However, once Carden's ships ventured inside the straits they ran into minefields; and heavy gunfire from the forts along the banks made mine-sweeping hazardous. The attack ground to a halt. Carden withdrew then collapsed in nervous prostration. He was replaced by his deputy, Rear Admiral Sir John de Robeck.

It was only now that any consideration was given to the army's involvement in the plan. While there are conflicting versions about who raised the issue first, it is clear that Kitchener sought the views of his former military secretary, General William Riddell Birdwood.

Born in India, where his father worked in the Civil Service of the Raj, 'Birdy' saw action in South Africa as a cavalry officer and on Kitchener's Boer War staff. In November 1914 as Secretary for War Kitchener selected him to command the Anzacs in Egypt. Now he ordered him to report on the naval attack and make recommendations for the way ahead.

Birdwood saw his chance. In a series of telegrams he declared that the operation could not be successfully completed by the navy alone. A military landing was essential. The entire expedition, he hinted, should be placed under his command.

Back in Cairo, he dined with Monash, who was not impressed. 'A small, thin man,' he wrote. 'Nothing striking or soldierly about him.' Birdwood's limitations, it seems, were also apparent to his mentor, for on 12 March Kitchener turned to another protégé, the well-connected General Sir Ian Hamilton, who numbered not only Winston Churchill but the king himself among his admirers. The supremo's orders to Hamilton were as seductive as they were succinct: 'Capture Constantinople. If you do, you will have won not only a campaign, but the war.'[1]

A slim, prissy character with a neatly clipped moustache, Hamilton had been born in Corfu in 1853 and, after graduating from Sandhurst, was posted to India, spending the next 25 years overseas and seeing action in the Afghan War and the Boer War. He established a minor reputation as a poet and columnist. His military reports were marked by an unusually striking turn of phrase. In the traditional cavalry charge of the day, he was a gallant soldier and was twice recommended (unsuccessfully) for the Victoria Cross.

In 1887, he married Jean Muir, the daughter of a Glasgow businessman, and the couple were popular members of the social establishment. It would seem that by 1915 Hamilton was as much concerned with military punctilio as he was with the hard business of war and preferred to remain aloof from the death and gore of the battlefield. He would command Gallipoli almost entirely from the comfort of his seaborne stateroom. Moreover, with only 75,000 soldiers to accomplish his mission, Hamilton faced a very different challenge from that which confronted the nervous Carden.

The February bombardment had given the Turks fair warning that a major attack was planned. Turkish forces were being recalled from operations in the Balkans and on the Suez Canal. For the first time in modern history, the Turkish homeland was threatened.

Meantime, Jacka and his mates in Heliopolis were still slogging through the sand and making short work of the hessian-covered dummies used for bayonet practice. The desert marches became longer and more arduous. The 14th's historian, Newton Wanliss, wrote, 'The heavy tramping, together with the additional weight of the equipment, tried the men's pluck and stamina to the utmost. But the fear of ridicule of their comrades stimulated the weary to the required effort and it became a point of honour not to fall out.'[2]

In the evenings, Acting Lance Corporal Jacka studied for promotion. The young man from Wedderburn had grown comfortable in the company of his comrades of the 14th. They were from his part of the world. They talked the same language. They shared a mutual respect. And it looked as though they would soon have a job to do.

In February, the Turks had attacked British positions across the Suez Canal. They were soundly trounced and when they retreated two companies of Ghurkhas played havoc with them. The Turks lost 2000 men and a further 700 captured. Now the rumour mill reckoned the Australians and New Zealanders would not be going to Europe at all, but would be used to knock Turkey out of the war.

To some, particularly in the lower ranks, this was a blow. They had volunteered to fight the Hun in defence of the Empire. They wanted to go in against the A Grade team, not the bloody Reserves. However, when Monash got the hint from Birdwood that Gallipoli might be the theatre where his troops were blooded he was not displeased. Early victories were good for morale and casualties could be minimised. The problem was that no one seemed to know how, where or when the attack might be made. And it seemed little effort was being made to understand the topography of the place or the likely strength of the enemy.

When he heard that Hamilton would be in charge, Monash recalled their meeting at Lilydale outside Melbourne in 1913. At the time the illustrious visitor was inspector-general of British overseas forces and Monash put his 2500-strong brigade through a battle exercise on the dusty Lilydale plains. It had been a triumph of organisation and Hamilton had been suitably impressed. That was a good start. Monash found the man charming and surprisingly cosmopolitan, though perhaps lacking the necessary ruthless streak for high command.

Hamilton arrived in Cairo on 18 March with a hastily assembled staff. His entire background intelligence had been supplied by Kitchener—two small travel guidebooks on Turkey and a textbook on the Turkish army. And this was the day Admiral de Robeck had chosen to mount his concerted attack on the passage to Constantinople. With a modicum of good fortune and a fair wind, he believed, he would smash his way through the Turkish defences to the accompaniment of wild hosannas from his impatient First Lord of the Admiralty. This would allow Hamilton's soldiers to advance the 230 kilometres along the northern side of the Sea of Marmara in a mopping-up operation with all the panoply of a triumphal march.

Luck, however, was not on de Robeck's side. In an action that is still celebrated annually throughout Turkey, the massive Allied fleet of sixteen capital ships faced 200 defending guns, fixed torpedo tubes set into the banks on both sides of the narrows, submarine nets and scores of mines. With *Queen Elizabeth* in the lead, the great grey ships powered into the azure waters of the strait with the dun-coloured hills of Gallipoli glowering on their portside.

The battle raged from 9 a.m. to 5 p.m., the great guns pounding the shore batteries and forts with the Turks responding in kind. In the afternoon, mine-sweeping trawlers crewed by civilians were sent forward to clear the way for the battleships. But they soon wilted under fire and fled. Just then the French battleship *Bouvet* struck a mine, capsized and sank. Then HMS *Inflexible* was holed by a mine and limped back out to sea, listing heavily. HMS *Irresistible* was abandoned after hitting another mine and HMS *Ocean* was crippled. De Robeck signalled his fleet to withdraw.

Not a single mine had been cleared, nor a single Turkish gun destroyed. Seven hundred Allied lives had been lost and three capital ships sunk. But what de Robeck did not know was that the Turkish forts were almost out of ammunition. One final thrust and the fleet might well have made its way through. Even if he had returned the next day, he would have found a battered Turkish force on the verge of collapse. However, de Robeck lacked the stomach for it.

As the sun dipped below the Aegean on the evening of 18 March, the British had lost two-thirds of their battle fleet in the Dardanelles and de Robeck had little idea of what to do next. Someone suggested using destroyers to clear the minefields, but that needed time to organise. Then Hamilton, urged by Birdwood, proposed that the army take over and the navy play a supporting role. De Robeck hesitated for several days, then on 22 March he and Hamilton made a joint decision: the naval fleet would sail to Alexandria to reorganise itself while Hamilton prepared his force for a land battle.

Much later, the instigator of the Gallipoli campaign, Winston Churchill, would claim this decision was taken without the knowledge of himself or his government. 'No formal decision to make a land attack was even noted in the records of the Cabinet or the War Council,' he wrote. 'This silent plunge into this vast military venture must be regarded as extraordinary.'3

Extraordinary indeed. So too was the fact that the War Council did not meet for another two months. Even the general officer commanding Egypt, Sir John Maxwell, wrote, 'Who is co-ordinating and directing this great combine?'4 Maxwell's comment was apt. Hamilton commanded the army on the ground, de Robeck the navy, while Maxwell was General Officer Commanding Egypt, where the troops were based. No one was given overall charge. Hamilton simply assumed it and decided on a landing at Gallipoli.

This meant that in the absence of firm guidance and support from Allied High Command—by now struggling to hold the Germans on the Western Front—Hamilton and his senior commanders were dangerously out of their depth. But to a man they believed that their opposition was simply not up to the standards of the British, French and Anzac troops. Imperial hubris reigned.

CLOSING IN

On 23 March, the whole of the New Zealand and Australian Division formed up in the desert for inspection by General Maxwell. By now, Monash had chosen navy blue as the 4th Brigade's colour and the 14th Battalion combined it with their gold to produce a unique patch on each man's uniform. Jacka and his compatriots stood-to for inspection, then marched past the commanders.

Henry Nevinson, special correspondent for *The Times*, watched the exercise in wonder. 'A finer set of men than the Anzacs after their three months training on the desert sands could hardly be found in any country,' he wrote. 'They walked the earth with careless and daredevil self confidence.'[1]

Monash rode alongside Hamilton in the march-past. The British general recalled their meeting at Lilydale. 'Well, Monash,' he said, 'when we sat under the gum tree 12 months ago we didn't think, either of us, we should meet again so soon.'[2]

Jacka had been neglecting his diary. On this occasion he merely recorded that the 'Battalion turned out with full Division under

Major General Godley.' The waiting was beginning to play on everyone's nerves.

On Good Friday, the Anzacs let off steam with a visit to 'the Wozzer' that ended in a full-scale riot as they torched the brothels and terrorised the spivs and pickpockets. The authorities responded, but the Australians chased off the military police and returned to camp only when the British commandant ordered his Lancashire Territorials to fix bayonets and prepare to advance.

Finally, on 10 April, the order came to break camp. On the following day, the 14th Battalion struck their tents and lined up for the march from Heliopolis to Helmia railway station. The bands played as the men of the 14th loaded into the train for Alexandria, the Light Horsemen cheering them enviously on their way.

At the port, Monash addressed his troops: 'You may be faced with privation and hardships, sometimes hunger, often tired and miserable. But this is what soldiering amounts to. I call on you with confidence to do your level best for the sake of your manhood, for the sake of Australia and for the sake of the British Empire.'[3] The brigade responded with a rousing cheer.

Then Monash and his headquarters staff shared the decks of the rat-infested Rangoon trader *Seang Choon* with the 14th on the wind-tossed journey to Lemnos Island. Jacka suffered the swells. 'Nearly died of sea sickness,' he wrote. By the time they arrived at the island's commodious harbour, Mudros, at about noon on 15 April, the entire battalion was in similar shape. But they were quickly distracted by the deep blue of the calm harbour waters and the astonishing collection of seacraft already assembled—British, French and Russian battleships, torpedo boats, mine-layers, balloon and hydroplane ships, mine-sweepers of various shapes and sizes, and transports crowded with noisy troops.

Newton Wanliss wrote, 'Even at night there was much to excite interest, including the twinkling lights from every class of vessel, signals flashing in Morse code and rows of green lights indicating hospital ships.'[4] The transports were lashed together in twos and threes. The *Seang Choon* lay alongside the *Ionus* containing the New Zealanders, who were not pleased when they discovered the men of the 14th were sharing the fresh meat and vegetables and newly baked bread served to Monash and his staff while they had to make do with bully beef and biscuits.

However, according to Wanliss, there was no time for grousing. 'The few days spent at Mudros were occupied getting everyone in trim, practising ascending and descending rope ladders in full marching order and rowing about the harbour in the ship's boats.'[5] Jacka and a few mates 'rowed over to the *Queen Elizabeth* and went on board'. A true leviathan of the seas, the flagship of the fleet was the fastest battleship in the world. Costing more than £3 million, she had been completed only in January and was fitted with an anti-torpedo bulkhead from forward to rear magazine. Her fittings and facilities ensured her officers and guests would want for little.

Back on the *Seang Choon,* the battalion had a visitor: the flamboyant British war correspondent Ellis Ashmead-Bartlett, who would soon contribute more to the making of the Anzac legend than any but the men themselves. The eldest son of a distinguished politician, at 33 he had already made a reputation for bravery under fire and for bright, engaging despatches. In 1897, as a teenager he accompanied his father to Turkey as the guest of the sultan and followed the Turkish army in its campaign against the Greeks.

In 1898, he left his legal studies to serve in the Boer War and in 1904 abandoned both the law and the military to cover the siege of Port Arthur by the Japanese in the Russo–Japanese conflict—otherwise known as 'Morrison's War'—entering the city with the Japanese victors. There he met his first Australian—Morrison of Peking himself, the special correspondent for *The Times* in the Chinese capital. Later, as Reuters' special correspondent, Ashmead-Bartlett covered wars in Morocco and Italy. And in 1913 he chronicled the crushing of the Ottoman Turks in the Balkans for *The Telegraph*.

Between wars, he made several unsuccessful attempts to follow his father into Parliament and became good friends with fellow conservative, Winston Churchill. At the outbreak of war he tried to rejoin his regiment but was declined on health grounds. However, the scent of war would not be denied and he applied to the National Press Association to be their representative on the Dardanelles Campaign. They were delighted to have him and he reached Mudros optimistic that his political friend's most recent adventurism would soon score a great success.

The appearance of the Anzacs that day, 21 April, was a revelation. 'This is the first time I have been brought into contact with the Australian troops, and they certainly create an excellent impression with their fine physique and general bearing,' he wrote. 'A truly magnificent body of men; but their ideas of discipline are very different from those of our old regular army. The men seem to discipline themselves, and the officers have very little authority over them through the holding of military rank—personality plays a much more important role.'[6] They were, in short, his brand of soldier.

Initially, he was also on convivial terms with Hamilton. The next day, 22 April, he met the general on the quay of Mudros Harbour. 'He seemed to be extremely confident, in excellent spirits,' he wrote. 'He even told me a funny story about some Australians.' However, even at this stage, Ashmead-Bartlett had begun to fear that the adventure 'was almost certainly doomed to failure', not least because Hamilton felt the most critical period was the landing itself.

Ashmead-Bartlett's experience told him otherwise. 'Knowing the Turks from the Balkan Wars,' he wrote,

> and judging from the fact that they were now under German command, I did not believe they would concentrate the mass of their men to oppose the landing as they would come under the fire of such a number of warships and would be crushed or demoralised . . . I felt we would encounter the same high level of skill in defence on land as the fleet had met when it attempted to force the Straits by sea, only with this difference: the Turks had received ample warning of our intentions, and have had plenty of time to make their preparations.[7]

He was also concerned about the woeful intelligence effort. 'The general is about to launch his troops on a mere blind attack, leaving the answers to so many all important considerations on which accurate information is essential, to be discovered, not by the researches of the intelligence staff, but by the infantry at the bayonet's point.'[8]

However, Jacka and his mates on the *Seang Choon* were blissfully ignorant of the failings of their commanders. Whatever they may have felt about the British officers' insistence on the protocols of class, they had an abiding faith in the men who ran the imperial forces. They represented the Empire and all it stood for—decency, fair play and responsibility for each and every subject of the king.

Monash, who was closer to 'the heads', was less sanguine. He was prepared to write his first orders of the landing 'without a tremor', but already he admitted to becoming 'disillusioned' with his divisional commander, Alexander Godley, who was showing signs of nerves. He became 'irritable and cross' when discussing the minutiae of the landing plans.[9]

Godley's nervousness was probably understandable. When Ashmead-Bartlett heard the plans on the eve of battle, he was aghast. Hamilton had decided that the British 29th Division under General Hunter-Weston would land on five small beaches at Cape Helles, at the southern end of the peninsula; the 7000-strong Anzac Corps—made up of the 1st Division under General Bridges and the New Zealand and Australian Division under Godley—would land further north, just south of a jutting promontory called Gaba Tepe; elements of the French Corps expeditionnaire d'Orient, including four Senegalese battalions, would launch a feint—a 'landing' at Besika Bay south of the strait on the plains of Troy—but the main French contribution would be at Kum Kale to protect the 29th Division. Thus, the relatively small Allied force would be distributed over a very wide front with no particular objective other than to confront and, if possible, rout an unknown defence. They would be supported by the massive gunfire of the fleet which would be helpful initially but of little use once they had scaled the first ridge.

Ashmead-Bartlett was not the only one astounded by the strategy. The clear alternative was to concentrate the force on the narrowest part of the peninsula—Bulair, in the north—thus cutting off the Turkish supplies. Indeed, this is where the German commander of the Turkish forces, General Liman von Sanders, expected the assault. To oppose it he had a force of only 62,000 fighting men with second-rate supplies and equipment with which to cover the entire peninsula.

Von Sanders believed there was no point in attempting to meet a landing on the beaches with so few resources. Far better to establish defensive positions in the hills above. Having surveyed the entire area it was clear that Bulair was his weakest point. But he could not afford to put all his forces in the north. They had to be spread from one end to the other with reserves held back in case his defences threatened to buckle. The one place he didn't need to worry about was the area north of Gaba Tepe. Only a fool would order a landing there.

On the *Seang Choon* the orders arrived. Jacka wrote, 'Hear we will be heading for Gallipoli any minute.' However, when the orders were read out, the men of the 14th were fiercely disappointed. Instead of leading the charge, they were told that Bridges' 1st Division would land at dawn. Monash's 4th Brigade of the New Zealand and Australian Division would be first in reserve and the 14th Battalion the reserve of the brigade. In the officers' mess and among the infantry they feared they might miss out on the fun. Newton Wanliss wrote, 'Bets at short odds were freely made that they would be in Constantinople within three days of the landing, whilst the more cautious who were only prepared to bet on being there within a week could obtain almost any odds they wished to lay.'[10]

ANZAC DAY

Jacka crossed over to the New Zealand troopship *Ionus* during the night of 24 April. At midnight the interminable wait was punctuated by a sudden dive into the harbour by a fellow lance corporal, Ted Lewis. He was rescued by a boat that put out after him. Jacka was as bemused as the rest. 'He was a strong swimmer and returned up the gangway a few minutes later.' To the jeers of his mates—'Why didn't you wait for tomorrow and earn a VC for it'—Lewis reached the deck claiming he knew nothing about it till he hit the water.[1]

Finally, the *Seang Choon* put out from Lemnos at 10 a.m. on Sunday, 25 April. As they left the harbour, the battalion chaplain, the Reverend Andrew Gillison, held the final church parade before they went into combat. By midday, Jacka wrote, 'Can hear the terrible gunfire' as they approached the distant peninsula.

At Anzac Cove, 1500 men from three battalions had landed on a front of almost 800 metres on the wrong side—the northern side—of Gaba Tepe. Instead of the gentle slopes of their briefing, they were confronted by a surreal landscape of scrub-matted cliffs and jagged gullies. Undeterred, they swarmed up the ridges under withering machine-gun fire.

Above on the hilltop, the senior Turkish commander, Colonel Mustapha Kemal, found soldiers falling back from the Anzac advance.

'Why are you running away?' he shouted.

'They come, they come,' was the reply. 'Our ammunition is finished.'

'You cannot run away. You have bayonets.' He confronted the leaders. He ordered them to fix bayonets and lie down. As the Anzacs reached a crest they followed suit. In the brief pause he told his men, 'I don't order you to attack. I order you to die. In the time it takes for us to die, other troops and commanders can come and take our place.'[2]

The Turks fired their last shots then ran towards the Anzacs, engaging them in hand-to-hand fighting. It worked. Within half an hour the 57th Turkish Regiment of more than 2000 men arrived from their reserve position behind the sheltering peaks and poured down a blistering fire on the Australians and New Zealanders. Kemal held the line. While many of his 'runaways' perished, the action was the beginning of a brilliant military-political career. Kemal would lead his nation after the war and be raised to glory as Atatürk, father of the modern secular Turkish state.

George Mitchell of the 10th Battalion had landed at about 10 a.m. and was now pinned down on the jagged slopes, unable to dig into the hard ridge beneath him, while all around his mates were dying in agony. Then he heard an order: 'Fix bayonets and prepare to charge.' Later he wrote, 'We rejoiced as we gripped our rifles. The long waiting should be terminated in one last glorious dash, for our last we knew it would be, for no man could live erect in that tornado.'[3] The order was never given. The officer was shot dead as he rose. When there was a let-up in the fusillade, the men scrambled for cover.

Mitchell's diary, scribbled in pencil whenever the opportunity presented, is the most graphic account of the Gallipoli engagement penned by a participant. 'We had come from the New World for the conquest of the Old,' he wrote. 'Fierce we expected it to be, but fierce as it was we never dreamed.'[4]

All the time snipers were at me. Not knowing where they were it was impossible to use cover as one did not know on which side of it to get. Then came another shock to the system. There was a weird shrieking note somewhere in the air which increased in volume every fraction of a second. It culminated in a deafening report and a cloud of smoke some 30 yards on my right and 30 feet high. Simultaneously there was a swishing sound as the bullets beat down bushes and swept the earth and a devilish scream as large pieces of the case spun through the air.

Still he went forward.

Continually in my progress I came across groups of men all going ahead but as our opinions differed as to the easiest route we were constantly split up. After climbing a precipice I came upon the real meaning of war. A sturdy Australian lay on his face, congealing blood flowed from a ghastly wound in the head, streaking his face and forming a crimson pool. His flesh was the waxy colour I was to grow so familiar with. Lt Col Hallcombe stood by studying the situation ahead. He gave no heed to the dying soldier. All round our unprotected bodies the bullets thrashed through the barely concealing bushes.

Horror piled on horror.

'We settled down to a musketry duel. The men began to get hit. A terrible cry was wrenched from the bravest as the nickel demon ripped through flesh, bone and sinew . . . Alec Gilpin had been fatally wounded in the stomach,' he wrote. 'All day he begged to be shot.'

Later, 'No stretcher bearers could approach our position without being shot down. The wounded and dying had to lie in their own blood and ask for things they could not have. Some begged to be shot. Others asked their mates to load and pass the rifles so they could end themselves . . .'

Reinforcements arrived. One man dropped beside me laughing, 'You've got yourself into the hottest corner you'll ever strike'. He fired a few shots and again I heard the sickening thud of a bullet. I looked at him in horror. The bullet had fearfully smashed his face and gone down his throat rendering him dumb. But his eyes were dreadful to behold. And how he squirmed in his agony.

There was nothing I could do for him but pray he might die swiftly. It took him about 20 minutes and by then he had tangled his legs in mine and stiffened. I saw the waxy colour creep over his cheek and breathed freer.

I felt thirsty after that but not caring to deplete my water bottle so early in proceedings I unhitched the dead man's, had a long drink and passed it on. All the time the hot sun was beating down on us. Between the incidents that occupied my attention I actually dozed.

A British aircraft flew over to reconnoitre the Turkish positions. Immediately all enemy guns were redirected. The Anzacs appreciated the respite, but the massive fusillade revealed the strength of the force ranged against them.

'Every now and again above the fiendish din of battle came the WOOM-PAH, at which ground, sea and sky seemed to get up and sit down again,' Mitchell wrote. 'It was Big Lissie arguing with her 15-inch toys. And when her shells landed—suffering sinner, they shifted a hill—arms, legs and other curios flying in all directions . . .'

At 4 p.m. Jacka was in a whaleboat heading for the thick of it and noted, 'In amongst the warships ready to go ashore. Some sight this. Shells from warships bursting all over the island [*sic*]. Troops landing on the beach; heavy rifle and machine gun fire. All the hills covered in smoke, reminds me of a bushfire.' He had been chosen as part of the advance party from the 14th—100 men ordered to provide support to the wounded on the beach and to reconnoitre the area for the main force.

Streams of casualties were leaving the shore. Jacka recorded, 'Eight boat loads of wounded arrived at our boat.' Then at 7 p.m. he was in the first contingent of the New Zealand and Australian Division to reach Anzac Cove. 'Going ashore with 30 D Coy men to help with the wounded.'

By the time he reached Birdwood's self-confessed blunder, a kilometre north of Gaba Tepe, the 'temporary difficulties' visited upon the Dominion forces were all too apparent. Dead and wounded men were lying all over the beach and masses of equipment were tossed everywhere. Sailors from the landing parties were trying to clear those wounded who could be saved. Lance Corporal Jacka and his platoon bucked in.

Jacka's first taste of war could hardly have been more horrific. The beach was virtually unprotected. The shrapnel tore down from the Turkish guns. Men's bodies were ripped to pieces. Others lost limbs and senses. Nothing in his training had prepared him for this. It was hell on earth. Only the darkness brought surcease.

It also brought a chance for the staff officers to review the actions of the past sixteen hours and to decide what to do next. The landings of the 29th Division at Cape Helles under Aylmer Hunter-Weston ('Hunter-Bunter' to his many enemies) had been a disaster. On some beaches the Turks were waiting for them, well dug in and with machine-guns set to cut down the invaders in crossfire as they made for the foothills. The result was a slaughter.

In other areas they simply 'captured the beach' as ordered, then waited for further orders that never came. Confusion reigned. Hunter-Weston was establishing a reputation for bumbling incompetence rarely matched by other generals in the Great War.

Across the strait, the French feint had scored the most notable success, meeting relatively little resistance. However, Hamilton had no 'Plan B' to take advantage of this and withdrew them.

By day's end there was no chance that the Anzac advance could make any further progress without a terrible loss of life. Already the 7000 troops had sustained 2000 casualties. The survivors were scattered through the scrub and in sheltered pockets. If they were

to remain on the peninsula at all, a new strategy was desperately
needed.

Hamilton and his staff on the *Queen Elizabeth* were betwixt and
between. Ashmead-Bartlett had been ashore at 9.30 p.m. and spied
a group of officers. When he joined them, Godley was writing a
dispatch to Hamilton as Birdwood dictated in the semi-darkness.
Though dressed in the language of bureaucratic blame-shifting, it
was a plea to cut and run. It ended, 'I know my representation is
most serious but if we are to re-embark it must be done at once.'[5]

The reporter accompanied the messenger back to the flagship
and later secured a copy of Hamilton's response. It was not sent until
hours of dithering had passed and an infelicitous piece of news had
reached the general from another remarkable Australian adventure,
the voyage of the country's only operative submarine, *AE2*, under
Captain Henry Hugh Stoker. Setting out that morning Stoker had
dodged the mines and the nets of the narrows, fired a torpedo and
hit a Turkish destroyer, then signalled his success to the flagship. The
AE2 was later captured without further harm to the Turks, but at the
time the one bright spot in a day of disaster clearly influenced
Hamilton.

'Your news is indeed serious,' Hamilton told Birdwood,

but there is nothing for it but to dig yourselves right in and stick it
out. It would take at least two days to re-embark you, as Admiral
Thursby will explain to you. Meanwhile the Australian submarine
has got up through the Narrows and has torpedoed a gunboat at
Chanak. P S You have got through the difficult business. Now you
have only to dig, dig, dig, until you are safe.[6]

As dawn broke on the 26th, Jacka was still on shore. Like the rest, he had worked through the night to help bring order to the chaos. He welcomed the arrival of the rest of the 14th Battalion when they reached the cove at 10.30 a.m. In the lead boat was Sergeant William Patrick Murphy of Warracknabeal, an old imperial soldier who had only recently arrived in Australia before war broke out. Now as he stood to leap into the gentle surf a bullet struck him in the heart. He toppled into the water.

Jacka recorded the death in his military family. 'First man killed,' he wrote.[7]

Monash arrived on the beach with the 14th and immediately began gathering his scattered brigade. Taking a 'bodyguard' from the 14th—most likely including Jacka who was among those who knew the lay of the land—he made his way into the triangle held by the Anzacs. At its apex was a series of knolls facing the Turkish position and into which the Anzacs had begun to dig defensive positions. Soon they would be named for the commanders within the 4th Brigade who held them—Pope's Hill, Quinn's Post, Courtney's Post and Steele's Post.

The most crucial position at this stage was at the very point of the apex—Quinn's Post—and this was the one chosen for Jacka and his mates to hold 'at all cost'. Lieutenant John Gordon Hanby, from Brighton, who had won Monash's shield at Broadmeadows, led the platoon up Shrapnel Gully to what had immediately become Monash Valley. The summit was a crescent with Quinn's at one end and Pope's Hill at the other. As they climbed, they passed fallen comrades in the rictus of death who had fought their way up the slope the day before. When they reached the post, a lance corporal was the most senior soldier left; the situation was critical. The Turks were almost on them.

The newcomers took up the challenge and a volley of shots stopped the enemy advance in its tracks. Other soldiers scattered in the vicinity then joined the men of the 14th to consolidate the position. Major Robert Rankine of A Company took charge. As the men dug in, machine-gun and rifle fire arrived from unexpected angles. Captain Bill Hoggart, a Victorian schoolteacher, rose on his knees, field glasses in hand, to try to make some sense of it. He was shot through the head.

Then from the right a Turkish machine-gun opened up and, within seconds, twenty men were dead, including Lieutenant Hanby. Others writhed in agony. At first the defenders thought the firing had come from their own 15th Battalion and this added to the confusion. Some of the men put their caps on their rifles and held them up to show they were Australians. Jacka was not among them. He was more concerned to take the gun out of action. He and a small party circled and knocked it out. By mid-afternoon the situation had settled down.

That night it rained, but this did nothing to discourage the Turks. On the contrary, Monash, now established in a rough headquarters below Courtney's, was kept awake by the explosions, bullets and shrapnel bursting above. There was never more than ten seconds' silence between them. In his laconic way, Jacka wrote of that night, 'Having a hard time in the trenches. Terribly cold at nights. Without overcoats or blankets of any description.'[8]

Wednesday morning, 28 April, began with Turkish snipers just ahead of Pope's Hill taking a toll of the defenders. As the day progressed, the Turks found their range and the implications of Birdwood's 'temporary difficulties' became ever more apparent. Major Rankine sent a message to Monash seeking the right to withdraw if the position worsened. Monash replied, 'I cannot allow you to withdraw, nor can I send men to relieve you . . . all you have to do is hold your ridge.'[9] By nightfall Chaplain Gillison was required to read a burial service over 39 men in a common grave. Newton Wanliss wrote, 'While the grave was being dug an attack threatened the post. Fortunately, our artillery obtained the range up Shrapnel Gully and the attack did not materialise.'[10]

That night it rained again. Lieutenant Wallace Crabbe and his men worked to build a covered trench or sap to provide some protection and by morning, according to Wanliss, 'it was now fairly safe to move about Quinn's'. However, he wrote, 'By now, all ranks were showing signs of exhaustion.'[11]

Finally came permission to withdraw. That morning they were, in Jacka's words, 'relieved by Marine Light Infantry at 8am. Rested behind the trenches.' In the area in front of Quinn's they left behind so many Turkish dead that, according to Major Charles Dare, 'it looked as though a battalion was sleeping in the open'.[12]

The British marines, whom Churchill had sent briefly to Antwerp, immediately got the Australians off-side when they sat smoking on the graves of the casualties from the 15th Battalion. Only the arrival of Captain Hugh Quinn of the 15th reassured the 14th that all their hard work and sacrifice had not been in vain. Even then, according to Jacka's diary, they were ordered back to the front line that night, this time to relieve the 13th Battalion. 'Turks counter-attacked,' he wrote, 'but were repulsed.'

By now the 14th battalion had lost one officer with 43 other ranks killed, three officers and 102 other ranks wounded, and 39 other ranks missing, mostly at Quinn's Post. All talk of the Reserve Grade or the Second XI was silenced. Wanliss wrote, 'The Australians had met in the Turk an enemy as brave as themselves and, at this early stage of the war, more cunning at sniping and ruses.'[13] And the major counterattack was yet to come.

THE FIRST VC

From 1 May, the 14th Battalion was given charge of Courtney's Post, named after the battalion commander who was already showing signs of strain. By comparison with the sister battalions of the 4th Brigade, the 14th's casualties had been relatively light. There was even talk that Monash had been favouring them, a suggestion that did not sit well with Jacka and his mates. However, from the moment they took over Courtney's Post from the British marines they were in the thick of it.

They had barely settled themselves into the forward trenches when at 3 p.m. the expected massive counterattack began. By now the Turks were well supplied with the forerunner of the hand grenade—hand-held bombs about the size of cricket balls which they hurled against the defenders. While at first they could be countered by throwing a greatcoat over them when they landed in the trench, soon more powerful devices cut the Australians to pieces. Their own supplies of hand-bombs were on the way.

Meantime, the Australians had mounted their machine-guns to

enfilade the charging Turks and cut them down from both sides; the infantrymen's rifles were running hot. Jacka wrote, 'In the trenches, hardest fighting we have had yet. Turks making great attack on our trenches. They are brave, but are going to certain death. Mowing them down in hundreds.'[1]

Then in a break in the fighting he scribbled, '4.30. Turks still attacking. Now storming our trenches. Lieutenant Rutland [the machine-gun officer] killed. One Turkish officer led a bayonet charge right up to our trenches and was shot dead right on our parapet.'

Later he wrote, '9pm. Battle has been won by us. Can hear Turks out in front collecting their wounded.'

By now Ashmead-Bartlett had been caught up in the action and had cabled his reports to London and thence to Australia. 'No finer feat of arms was ever performed than this sudden landing in the dark, this storming of the heights, and above all, the holding of the positions just won,' he wrote. 'These raw Dominion troops in these desperate days proved themselves worthy to fight side by side with the heroes of Mons, the Aisne, and Ypres.'[2] In fact, the Anzacs knew little of these battlegrounds and the British soldiers who fought there. The job at hand was all-embracing.

In response to the first Turkish counterattack, the New Zealand and Australian Division made a concerted effort to clear the Turks off the high ground that dominated Monash Valley. Jacka and his platoon remained in the trenches. 'Our [D] company relieved by A Company at sunset,' he wrote. 'We are resting just behind the front line. Troops on our left made a bit of a charge and captured a bit of Turkish trench.' Then the Turks began digging towards Quinn's Post and a platoon from the 14th was assigned to fight them off.

By dawn, Jacka was asleep in a dugout just behind the lines when a shell burst over his position. Next to him was Lieutenant Quinton Smith, a former clerk from Essendon. The nose cone of the shell slashed into the officer's legs, amputating one and badly tearing the other. Smith very soon died of his wounds; Jacka, right beside him, could barely credit that he had escaped. 'I was unscathed,' he wrote.[3]

By now the 14th Battalion had been in the firing line for more than a week, and on 6 May reinforcements arrived from the Light Horse Brigade, who had left their mounts in Egypt. Some 62 newcomers took their places beside Jacka, who spent the night on the front line then 'pulled in the German officer who was shot in the battle of 1st May'. The wounded man, it seems, had lain undetected for five days and nights. Stretcher bearers took him back behind the lines for interrogation.

Jacka and his mates then rested at the foot of the hill. But every night they returned to the front line where every moment held the possibility of sudden death. On 9 May, he wrote, 'got letters from home, the first since we landed on Gallipoli'. It was a welcome break in the routine.

On his luxurious floating HQ, Hamilton was counting the cost of his latest foray on Cape Helles where the day before he had sought unsuccessfully to advance the 29th to take the town of Krithia. Ashmead-Bartlett caught the moment with typical vigour. 'With the complete repulse of the final attack on Krithia and Achi Baba on the evening of May 8th 1915, the first stage of the Dardanelles Expedition came to an end,' he wrote. 'From that hour it developed on entirely different lines from what was originally intended by its unhappy sponsors. At this critical hour in the fortunes of the Empire, it suddenly grew to premature manhood, throwing an immense strain on our limited resources by its incessant demands for men, ammunition, guns, material and ships.'[4]

There was also a significant change in the nature of the conflict. Until then, the army's task was to overcome resistance on land and clear the way for the navy to drive up the Sea of Marmara. Now the naval incursion up the Dardanelles was abandoned. Gallipoli became a military conflict, as Ashmead-Bartlett wrote, 'of limitless magnitude, confronted by an enemy whose strength was being augmented day by day, whilst we had failed to gain a single position of any real or strategical importance'.

However, because of Hamilton's strict censorship and overly optimistic reports to Kitchener, Ashmead-Bartlett could not get the real story out. 'It is heart-rending work having to write what I know to be untrue and in the end having to confine myself to giving a descriptive account of the useless slaughter of thousands of my fellow countrymen when what I wish to do is tell the world the blunders that are being daily committed on this bloodstained Peninsula.'[5]

Hamilton relocated to the *Arcadian* amid rumours that German submarines were on the way to the eastern Mediterranean. In fact, the *Queen Elizabeth* decamped entirely the next day. 'What a moral loss to the Army,' Ashmead-Bartlett wrote. 'No more will the weary infantry ashore listen to the sound of those huge shells rushing through space like express trains passing overhead, or watch the gigantic explosions as they strike the enemy's line.'[6]

For the Turks, the withdrawal of the capital ship came at a most opportune time. Von Sanders and the newly promoted Colonel

Mustapha Kemal were planning a massive counterattack. Whatever the cost, this time they would drive the Anzacs into the sea.

The attack was scheduled for the pre-dawn hours of 19/20 May and the plan was simplicity itself. Four divisions of Turks—about 35,000 men—would charge down the hills and gullies, prise the 12,500 Anzacs from their trenches and send them scuttling down to the shore in a massive wave of death and destruction. Not a man would be left alive.

The point of the attack where the greatest force would be concentrated was that arc where the opposing trenches were closest—Pope's, Quinn's and Courtney's. According to Birdwood, if the total Turkish force had been employed there the line would have broken. And this was the preference of the Turkish commanders. But von Sanders insisted that the attack be made all along the trench line.

The defenders knew something big was on. That afternoon reconnaissance aircraft had spotted the enemy massing behind the ridgeline. And in the early part of the bright, clear night there was an ominous silence from above.

At Courtney's, Major Rankine was in command. The Light Horsemen under Harry Chauvel were waiting in reserve together with two companies from the 14th. The other two—B and Jacka's D Company—were in the line.

Out in the Aegean, the Allied battleships set up a firing line above the defenders. The Turks absorbed the bombardment and when it faded at midnight the Turks opened with a tremendous onslaught of heavy machine-gun and rifle fire together with a new version of their hand-delivered 'football bombs'. It lasted for about half an hour and according to Wanliss, 'Many men were partially deaf for days afterward.'[7]

Then there was a long pause as the defenders' nerves strung ever tauter until finally at 3 a.m., with the raucous band music and the screams of 'Allah' splitting the air, the Turks charged the Anzac lines. George Mitchell wrote, 'Every bush seemed to hide a Turk. Instantly across the whole line there was a leaping, flickering sheet of flame. The roar of musketry was like nothing else I ever heard.'[8]

Wanliss: 'Our men would spring on to the fire steps, fire rapidly into the semi-darkness in front and then disappear and reload.' The Turks were slaughtered in their hundreds but still they came, climbing over their own dead to reach the Australians. Everywhere the Australian line held. 'The firing was so furious', Wanliss wrote, 'that the woodwork of some rifles became almost too hot to hold.'[9]

But then came the breakthrough, as a dozen Turks made it into the forward trench at Courtney's Post. The weight of numbers pressed down. The line wavered. Suddenly the Turks were in the Australian trenches. They wrestled and fought man to man. Then the hour produced the man.

Wanliss: 'Hearing that the Turks were in our trenches, Jacka, on his own initiative, set out to investigate. An attempted approach along the direct communication trench proving impracticable, so with true tactical intuition, he made a flank movement and secured a position behind the traverse in a fire trench which blocked any attempted Turkish advance.'

Wanliss's description of the action that won Jacka the VC differs slightly from the official citation, to say nothing of Jacka's own laconic summary. According to Wanliss, Jacka held off the Turks until the arrival of Lieutenant Wallace Crabbe. 'Jacka then volunteered to lead a bayonet charge to clear out the Turks if ten others would follow him. Four agreed to do so (three of them Bendigo men). Jacka then rushed the trench, but finding himself alone among a number of Turks, and apparently unsupported, had to beat a retreat.'

Privates Bill Howard and Bickley (a former grocer's boy from Hastings, Victoria) following him had been wounded and put out of action. 'This direct frontal attack having failed', Wanliss wrote, 'it was decided to endeavour to shift the Turks with bombs. Only two bombs were available, however, and both were thrown by Private McNally [a former labourer from West Leederville, W.A.], the first being a failure.

'The second bomb, bursting on the parapet, raised a cloud of smoke and dust.' This was Jacka's chance.

Under [this] cover Jacka ran the whole length of the trench and, springing into it from the rear, cleared it single-handed, bayoneting the first two Turks he met (one an officer) and shooting five more.

A number of other Turks in the trench bolted, startled by the whirlwind attack, and Jacka shot two (in addition to the seven officially credited to him) as they were disappearing over the parapet.

Jacka himself never claimed the two additional enemy casualties. By the time Wanliss wrote his account, the war was over and the aura surrounding both Jacka and the action had been enriched by other extraordinary deeds.

The action may well have occurred as Wanliss described it. He was a meticulous researcher. But at the time the focus was on an individual feat of arms that had changed the course of battle. The official citation, having passed through many hands, can be read to incorporate both Wanliss and Wallace Crabb's versions of the action:

> For most conspicuous bravery on the night of the 19–20th May, 1915 at Courtney's Post, Gallipoli. Lance Corporal Jacka, while holding a portion of the trench with four men was heavily attacked. When all except himself were killed or wounded, the trench was rushed and occupied by seven Turks. Lance Corporal Jacka at once attacked them single-handedly and killed the whole party, five by rifle fire and two with the bayonet.

At the time the men of the 14th, Jacka included, were preoccupied with the task of simply staying alive. Again and again, the Turks returned to the fray. The area between the Australian and Turkish trenches resembled a slaughterhouse.

Wanliss: 'The morning of 20 May disclosed a revolting scene. The bodies of Turks were lying in heaps and the sufferings of the wounded must have been appalling.' In the manner of traditional military historians, he found a greater good within the slaughter. 'Doubtless, in the main, our opponents were rough and illiterate men, but they had fought like heroes and given their lives freely in defence of their country.'[10]

Jacka withheld his admiration. He wrote in his diary, 'Resting at the foot of the hill. Some of the enemy advanced under the White Flag and arranged an armistice for them to bury their dead from yesterday's battle. One Captain and two men, all Turks, deserted to us.'

Then on the next day after another long night in the front line: 'Our company went into the firing line at 7pm. Early this morning two more Turks gave themselves up.'

Despite the brief burial armistice of 20 May, the killing fields were still crowded with bodies. The smell was almost unbearable and great clouds of flies thickened the air. On 24 May at 7.30 a.m. a nine-hour armistice was declared. Burial parties from both sides exchanged words and cigarettes. Monash was not pleased. He wanted nothing to interfere with the determination of his men to kill or be killed.

But the message coming back from the Turks was gratifying. George Mitchell wrote, 'They regard the Australians as fiends incarnate, mad devils when it came to the bayonet. They would sooner meet the devil and all his legions.'[11]

Ashmead-Bartlett toured the Anzac area with Birdwood and some other officers. 'I found the Australians and New Zealanders very pleased with themselves,' he wrote. 'As Birdwood passed, one of them caught a glimpse of his row of ribbons and remarked, "The bloody army isn't going to know me long enough to get a row like that." In fact they greeted the general in a familiar manner which would have caused many deaths from sudden apoplexy at Aldershot in the old days.'[12]

The Anzacs' sense of triumphant satisfaction was short-lived. On the following day the German submarines finally arrived and at 12.15 p.m., according to Jacka up the hill at Courtney's Post, 'The cruiser *Triumph* was sunk. We saw her go down.' He did not dwell on it. His next (and final) sentence of the day's entry reads, 'Very wet afternoon.'

Ashmead-Bartlett was lunching on the nearby *Swiftsure* when a young signalman came to the wardroom with news of the strike. 'We rushed on deck where every officer assembled,' he wrote. 'And there, sure enough off Gaba Tepe, lay the unfortunate battleship with a heavy list and stricken to death. Fortunately there was a trawler close to the *Triumph* at the time, which was able to take off a number of her crew.'

He continued:

The battleship hung at an angle of forty-five degrees for about eight minutes then turned bottom upwards, floating in this position for twenty minutes, looking like a whale at rest. The admiral, the officers and the crew of the *Swiftsure* stood to attention, bareheaded, when she made her final plunge beneath the waves in a cloud of smoke and steam.

We returned to finish our lunch, somewhat chastened in spirits, and fortified ourselves with a few extra glasses of port.

That evening the British war correspondent allowed himself a moment of sad reflection.

Just a month before, our mighty armada had sailed from Mudros full of high hopes and expectations, with the admiral and his staff in proud possession of the finest battleship in the British Navy, or in the world. Of the whole armada, only the old *Majestic* remained. Gone are the mighty *Queen Elizabeth*, the *Agamemnon*, the *Lord Nelson* and that great fleet of pre-dreadnought battleships which had sailed so proudly out of Mudros Bay, chased into protected ports by one or two miserable little submarines.[13]

For Hamilton on the *Arcadian* there was 'wailing and gnashing of teeth' as de Robeck announced he could no longer be responsible for safeguarding the ship against submarine attack. Therefore, the staff must move their quarters to shore, on Imbros Island, just off the coast.

In the front line, Bert Jacka had a couple of quiet days. But that only gave the men time to contemplate the shocking conditions they had to endure. By now the summer heat was becoming unbearable. The stench of rotting corpses was overpowering. The snipers never let up. Sleep came between fearful dreams and deadly gunfire.

Then on 28 May two of his mates from Wedderburn were shot. 'Sam Wilson', a German immigrant whose real name was Holtum, and Walter Earle, who was carrying water to the post, received terrible head wounds within minutes of each other. Jacka kept his feelings to himself. In his diary he simply wrote, 'Both died.'

That night the *Majestic* herself—with Ashmead-Bartlett on board—was also torpedoed and sunk. Most escaped unharmed, the journalist among them, but it meant that the Gallipoli expedition had lost the final vestiges of Churchill's grand naval plan. Now it was Hamilton's show entirely—a military campaign with nowhere to go but up the impossible slopes of Anzac or the heavily defended hills of Cape Helles with a force that had suffered terrible losses. Moreover, the flies and bad food were taking an even greater toll on the troops than the enemy as enteric dysentery spread through the ranks. It was a challenge that would have tested Wellington himself.

9

The heights of folly

Prissy, poetic Ian Hamilton was no Wellington but he did have a substantial figure of history in support of his quest. In Cabinet, Winston Churchill pressed for massive reinforcements to the Gallipoli expedition. And he was largely successful. No fewer than four new divisions were assigned to the campaign; and from Australia and New Zealand—where the newspapers had been full of the Anzacs' daring exploits—came shiploads of reinforcements.

The enthusiasm for Gallipoli was easy to appreciate. On the Western Front the Allies had lost 300,000 men in recapturing a mere 12 kilometres of territory from the Germans; and there was no prospect of a major advance. To the War Office, beguiled by Hamilton's misleading reports, Gallipoli provided an opportunity for a dramatic breakthrough. To the public of Australia, whose knowledge was confined to the lively reportage of Ashmead-Bartlett and the fulsome dispatches of Charles Bean, the nation was engaged in a heroic coming-of-age that needed only one more effort to secure a great victory.

Then on 31 July came official news that swept the nation—the first Australian soldier of the Great War, Albert Jacka from Wedderburn, had won the Victoria Cross, the highest accolade his sovereign could bestow. Nathaniel and Elizabeth Jacka received telegrams from Prime Minister Fisher and the minister for defence, George Pearce. The town's Patriotic Committee gathered in the Shire Hall and composed a rousing message to the hero of the day, and to the wounded of the 14th Battalion. The children from his old school had a special parade and saluted the flag. Then, to their astonishment and delight, the principal declared a school holiday. The Reverend Raff, whose daughter Elsie had caught the hero's eye, rang the Presbyterian Church bells at 2 p.m. on 1 August. The Wedderburn Rechabites gloried in the exploits of their favourite son.

In Melbourne *The Age* and *The Argus* made the announcement headline news, and the major dailies in the other capitals followed suit. At a time when recruiting figures were starting to fall, the news of Jacka's VC was just the tonic needed to replenish the lines at town halls across the nation.

The Army was quick to capitalise and within days had commissioned posters of an idealised Jacka in glorious combat with the enemy. His sporting prowess was remembered and embroidered. His 'straight arrow' character, his humble country background and his teetotal commitment all served to create the ideal image of heroic manhood of the day. Indeed, the principal poster suggested that Jacka himself was calling upon his sporting comrades at home to 'Join together, train together, embark together, and fight together'. They should 'Enlist in the Sportsman's Thousand' and 'Show the enemy what Australian sporting men can do'.

To this was added the mystique of the Victoria Cross, which had been created by Queen Victoria and was struck from captured Russian artillery pieces of the Crimean War. There was something about it that appealed directly to the Australian psyche, for as the warrant stated, 'neither rank nor long service nor wounds nor any other circumstance save the merit of conspicuous bravery shall establish a sufficient claim for the honour'.

There was even something about the name 'Jacka', with its faint Aboriginal overtones, its simple directness and its ease of recall, that contributed to the strength of the national response. A 'Clarence Throsby-Morton' would never have grabbed the Australian imagination like an Albert or a 'Bert' Jacka. In fact, the Christian name quickly faded from general usage and in the public mind he became 'Jacka VC', the decoration assuming the role of the patronymic.

The prominent Melbourne businessman, bookmaker and Catholic layman, John Wren, donated £500 and a gold watch, honouring his promise to reward the first Australian VC winner. He made his intention known in a letter to Nathaniel and Elizabeth. And while Jacka himself did not hear of it for some weeks, the gesture would have the most far-reaching consequences for his later life.

Among his mates in the 14th there arose a special bond. On 15 July his promotion to lance corporal had been confirmed and, even before the events of 19 May, they had come to regard him as a fearless and formidable fighter. Now, almost effortlessly, he seemed to grow into the role of VC winner as if he'd been measured for it. He was not one to put on 'side' or 'airs'. He had always been prepared to state his view and to act upon it. Now when he did so his comrades listened the harder and followed the faster.

At the time of the announcement he was on a brief four-day leave at Imbros Island, where he contracted a dose of the flu complicated by severe diarrhoea, and had to be hospitalised on nearby Lemnos. The celebration planned by Monash had to wait. 'We are all very jubilant about it,' Monash wrote to his wife. 'Unfortunately we can't have a ceremony until he returns to duty.'

When it came, it represented the first occasion when the two most celebrated Australians of the war met in mutual regard. It marked the beginning of a relationship that would endure and grow throughout their lives.

By then it was 5 August and Monash's 4th Brigade was to take a leading role in the 'breakthrough' Hamilton had promised his sponsors in the War Cabinet. When Ashmead-Bartlett heard the plan that day he despaired. Once again, instead of homing in on the vulnerable neck of the peninsula at Bulair, Hamilton had opted for an advance along a wide front, from Cape Helles to the Anzac bottleneck and beyond to Suvla Bay in the north.

The Helles incursion would be an elaborate feint designed to tie up the Turkish defenders in the south. The major attack would come from the Anzacs, who would be called upon to cut through the Turkish siege on the heights. The 9th British corps, to be landed at Suvla Bay, would then join up with the Anzacs in a 'left hook' that would take them all the way to the highest point of the peninsula, Chunuk Bair. Once they commanded the heights, the Allies would forge ahead to . . . well, that was yet to be decided.

The British contingent at Suvla Bay was commanded by a new arrival, General Sir Frederick Stopford, who had been retired since 1909 and was so enfeebled that he could not lift his Gladstone bag into the train when he left London for the Dardanelles.[1] Born in 1854, he had joined the Grenadier Guards as a twenty-year-old and had spent his military career in administrative posts. By 1914 he had been shuffled off to the sinecure of Lieutenant of the Tower of London. However, because of his position in the list of seniority, he had the required rank for the appointment. And Hamilton lacked the authority to demand a more appropriate man.

The Anzacs themselves were in no condition to attack. Jacka was among the 80 per cent of the corps struck down by the fly-borne dysentery that left them weak and nauseous. George Mitchell suffered a severe case of 'combat fatigue' and like many others was hospitalised in Egypt, then sent to England for further treatment. Monash had four medical officers check each man in the brigade and they reported that most of the veterans were unfit for a major advance. However, some 30,000 reinforcements had arrived, so he could hardly claim a lack of manpower. Thus, when Birdwood and Godley outlined the task they had chosen for the 4th Brigade, he reluctantly shouldered the responsibility on behalf of his men. The one saving grace was that the action offered the prospect of escape from the stinking latrines and vile putrefaction of the slopes and gullies above Anzac Cove.

Godley, the stiff-necked Britisher who Monash knew to be a 'ditherer' under pressure, would command the charge towards the high ridgelines. Once again, the 14th Battalion would be in the thick of the action. They would make for the distant heights over ridge and gully towards the packed defences above.

As Monash addressed his men on the morning of 6 August, trying to bring every man into the picture and firing them with a spark of patriotic fervour, the Turks began shelling the position. No one moved until he had finished, though shrapnel hit some men in their cliff-side 'pigeonholes'. Then, in Jacka's words, they 'Started to move out for attack on the left in conjunction with the landing of British troops at Suvla Bay.'[2]

To his right, the Australian 1st Brigade made a feint at the central position of Lone Pine. It too was designed to tie down Turkish forces to permit a freer advance for the main force. But it quickly developed into a mutual massacre in which 2000 Australian troops were killed and three times that number of Turks. It was a terrible, futile sacrifice. Though the Australians fought bravely and well, the award of no fewer than seven VCs provided an aura of sanctity that served to stifle any public outcry. The Anzacs finally held the position but at a cost beyond all proportion to the territorial gain.

At Helles to the south, the other elaborate feint had resulted in yet another killing field, with more than 4000 British casualties. Moreover, when the 4th Brigade marched along the beach then hurled themselves at the slopes, they found that the Turks under Mustapha Kemal had anticipated the manoeuvre. They were waiting with massed artillery that ripped the brigade to pieces. 'We had not gone half a mile', Monash wrote, 'when the black tangle of hills between the beach road and the main mountain range became alive with flashes of musketry and the bursting of shrapnel and star shell.'[3]

Soon the battalions became separated and disoriented, and as dawn broke, Turkish sniping became so intense that any movement brought a storm of fire. The few maps drawn up from seaborne observation prior to the operation were all but useless, and the field officers relied on local guides, who made matters worse. Wanliss wrote, 'Some of the guides were Levantines of doubtful character, whilst the terrain was so intricate that whole columns lost their way and our men sometimes came under a murderous fire from their own artillery.'[4]

After the first night, the brigade had advanced to the heart of enemy territory, but most of the troops were now exhausted. On 7 August Jacka wrote, 'Lost count of everything but heavy fighting.' Monash urged them to greater effort and by mid-morning they were in a position to look down at the landing to their left at Suvla Bay.

What they saw was a disaster. The confused and indecisive Stopford gave inadequate and contradictory orders to his field commanders, with the result that within hours the landing had degenerated into chaos. Some elements sought to reach their objectives—virtually undefended high ground to the left of Suvla; others bivouacked on the beach and became easy prey to Turkish guns. Still others advanced into the scrub and became lost. A few headed up towards the rendezvous point with the Anzacs, but by then Kemal had recognised the Allied plan and had moved in his reinforcements.

Monash was ropeable. 'A whole army corps sat down on the beach while its leaders were quarrelling about questions of seniority and precedence; and it was just that delay of 48 hours which enabled the Turks to bring up their last strategic reserve from Bulair and render futile the whole purpose of the landing.'[5]

Still the Anzacs pressed forward and on 7 August at 7.30 p.m. the New Zealanders reached the Apex, an intermediate knoll only 400 metres from Chunuk Bair. Colonel Johnston, commander of the Auckland Battalion, signalled to Godley, recommending a halt until just after dark, but he was ordered to attack at once. The remaining

British cruisers bombarded the heights, then the Aucklanders and a company of Ghurkhas advanced into blistering Turkish rifle fire. This time they gained The Pinnacle, another knoll only 200 metres from the summit. There they dug in and waited for the British forces from Suvla Bay to reach them.

The 14th Battalion had continued pressing forward under fire. Wanliss reported:

> Night also brought its duties, as fatigue parties had to make their way to a gully about a mile in the rear to help carry tins of water to the front. A hot day was followed by a cold night—blankets and overcoats having been left behind—the men shivered through the dark hours. The conditions were such that for the second succes-sive night sleep was almost unobtainable.[6]

But now at 7.45 p.m. on 8 August they were ordered to join the New Zealanders the next morning for the final attack on Chunuk Bair.

At 2.30 a.m. Jacka and his D Company of the 14th joined with the 15th and 16th Battalions heading for the summit. Wanliss: 'After an advance of some distance across hills and valleys a turn was made through a stubble patch known as "the cornfield" without any cover whatever. Men were dropping everywhere and the air was alive with missiles.'[7]

The 14th's commander, Major Rankine, collapsed with illness and Major Dare took over. Now they were in direct confrontation with the Turks and gradually they pushed them back up the hill with Jacka's D Company in the lead. This is where the Suvla Bay force was scheduled to meet up and protect their exposed left flank. Jacka and his mates waited in vain. They simply 'failed to materialise' and, as Wanliss wrote, 'great numbers of Turks, deploying behind a hill, came out and enfiladed our left flank. Fire was now coming not only from the high slopes in front but also from left and right. In the confused and chaotic fighting that ensued, units got intermingled, men separated from their officers. It was impossible to push on with an unprotected flank.'[8]

Monash was forced to act. He ordered the whole brigade to withdraw from its perilous position. Major Dare and his men resisted. He sent word to Monash that if only they could get support for the left flank they could hold the line. Monash's staff officer Colonel Pope responded. The 14th should 'retire' immediately.

On Chunuk Bair the New Zealanders suddenly faced a swarm of Turkish troops over the whole crestline led by Kemal himself. In the action Kemal was hit in the chest, but the watch in his breast pocket took the full force of the bullet. He took this as a sign from above and redoubled his efforts. The Turks fell upon the New Zealanders and the result was a rout. The New Zealanders fell back. The 4th Brigade followed suit, then dug in to hold their forward positions.

On 16 August, Hamilton finally sacked Stopford. By then the original plan for the 'left hook' was in ruins. But still Hamilton persisted in ordering new attacks from the exhausted Anzacs and the new British divisions, who were being torn to pieces.

The 14th Battalion suffered terrible losses, not least with the death of Lieutenant Wallace Crabbe and the popular chaplain, Andrew Gillison, the first Australian clergyman to be killed during the war. 'His death on an errand of mercy sent a cold chill through the hearts of the whole battalion,' Wanliss wrote.[9]

Finally, on 27 August, the 14th was ordered to join a combined force of 1000 men to take the infamous Hill 60, from which artillery would have a clear field of fire to Chunuk Bair. An Allied bombardment of heavy guns began at 4 p.m. and the Australian machine-guns opened up to prevent Turkish movement from the trenches. However, the bombardment went astray and merely alerted the Turks to the coming attack.

Wanliss:

The moment our men showed their heads above the skyline they were faced by a terrific rifle and machine gun fire. Very few succeeded in getting out of the trenches; some fell back wounded at once; others were hit on the fingers trying to drag themselves over the parapet. With the exception of a handful on the extreme left who got some concealment in a shallow ditch running along a hedge, no one got forward any distance. The attack was stillborn; it was blotted out before it materialised.

It was the final major engagement for the 14th on Gallipoli and it left the Australians deeply disillusioned and fiercely angry with the British leadership. Jacka, who was promoted to corporal the following day, was unforgiving. 'Worst month we ever had,' he wrote on 31 August. 'Practically the whole Battalion wiped out in these stunts.'

Then and thereafter he was cured of any respect he might once have nurtured for the British High Command. He would fight the good fight. He would never lose sight of the real enemy that threatened his country and the Empire to which it belonged. But at the same time he would never forgive the incompetent bastards who had brought needless slaughter to his mates. And henceforth he would never again accept their orders without question.

10

WITHDRAWN

Though Hamilton tried to present it to the War Cabinet as a partial victory, the attempted breakout had been an abject failure. He had now lost more than 40,000 men for the gain of less than 300 square kilometres of useless territory. Ashmead-Bartlett was merciless: 'The blame for this, probably the greatest reverse ever suffered by a British Army in the field, must primarily rest with Sir Ian Hamilton and his Staff.'[1]

Others had contributed. 'Birdwood', he said, 'cannot escape his share of responsibility for a plan of operations which, to a soldier of his standing and experience, should have appeared impracticable from the start.' He was also hard on the newly arrived British troops, who had not performed well. Indeed, the only elements who truly distinguished themselves were the Anzacs, who fought 'with reckless abandon' against impossible odds but to no avail. The only sensible option now open, he believed, was to abandon the expedition altogether.

It was at this critical time that the Australian journalist Keith

Murdoch arrived and made contact with the Anzacs, then with Ashmead-Bartlett. Murdoch was stationed in *The Times* building in London as the editor of a cable service for the Melbourne *Herald* and the Sydney *Sun*. Arriving on 4 September, he spent a few days with the troops, then sought out his fellow journalists. He told Ashmead-Bartlett that the Australian officers believed that with the coming of winter their position would be untenable. 'He declares, and I think quite rightly,' Ashmead-Bartlett confided to his diary, 'that unless someone lets the truth be known at home we are likely to suffer a great disaster . . . He, therefore, begs me to write a letter which he will carry through uncensored, telling the plain truth, which he can hand over to the government.'[2]

The war correspondent hesitated. Breaking censorship was tantamount to an act of treason but, 'I am told that everyone is entitled to write to the Prime Minister without submitting a letter to the censor; but whether this is true I cannot say.' In the end he justified the action on grounds that, 'For the past month, ever since our disasters at Anzac and Suvla, every general I have met, and a great many sailors, have begged me to take some steps to make the truth known to the government.'

First he briefed Murdoch, then gave him a long letter to Prime Minister Asquith that chronicled Hamilton's folly and his misleading dispatches to the War Cabinet. 'The Army is in fact in a deplorable condition,' he wrote.

Its morale as a fighting force has suffered greatly and the officers and men are thoroughly dispirited. The muddles and mismanagement beat anything that has ever occurred in our military history

. . . The Commander-in-Chief and his Staff are openly spoken of, and in fact only mentioned at all, with derision . . . I am convinced the troops could be withdrawn under cover of the warships without much loss, far less in fact than we suffer in any ordinary attack.

Murdoch headed back to London with the explosive letter in his briefcase, but when he reached Marseilles—for reasons never fully explained—he was intercepted by British and French troops and forced to hand the letter over. The best suggestion is that someone— either a fellow journalist or a soldier who had overheard the plot—informed Hamilton of the breach of censorship and he cabled ahead to Marseilles. Ashmead-Bartlett was summarily expelled from the combat zone and returned to London.

By then Murdoch had briefed the new Australian prime minister, Billy Hughes, and his own version of Ashmead-Bartlett's letter had found its way to the War Cabinet, where it was given the unlikely status of an official Cabinet document. With Ashmead-Bartlett's arrival in London on 10 October, the forces were gathering against Hamilton. By then the pathetic Stopford had brought action against Hamilton over his 'unfair' dismissal. While the case was dismissed out of hand, it added to the sense of confusion and chaos in the Dardanelles.

Finally, on 13 October, Kitchener sent a cable that required Hamilton himself to decode. It took a roundabout way to deliver the blow but there was no denying its import. Hamilton was axed.

To the men in the field, such machinations meant little. According to Newton Wanliss:

The majority of the survivors on the Peninsula were worn and haggard with long hair and hollow cheeks, covered with dirt, vermin and sores, wearing brimless hats with uniforms torn and stained.

No one would recognise in the jaded handful of worn and weary men the remnants of that magnificent battalion—bronzed and bursting with vitality—which took part in the famous brigade route march through the streets of Melbourne on 17 December, 1914. The old spirit existed in the survivors but the flesh was very, very weak.[3]

Jacka himself had been given a 'spell' on Lemnos. Here he had his first taste of celebrity when he was presented to the French naval commander, Admiral Guepratte, who exclaimed, 'Le Caporal Jacka, qui a gagné La Croix Victoria.' He was still on the island when Hamilton's successor, General Charles Monro, arrived to report on conditions to Kitchener and the War Cabinet.[4] He would decide whether the Gallipoli expedition would continue, or the Anzacs and their British comrades would risk annihilation in a withdrawal that the textbooks said would cost at least one-third of the force.

On 31 October, Jacka was ordered to prepare to return to the peninsula with his platoon. Before he left, however, there was one pleasant surprise on the island for Jacka—his young brother Bill. Having enlisted in March, Bill trained at Broadmeadows and embarked on HMAT *Euripides* in May. Though assigned to the 23rd Battalion, in September he made the transfer to his famous brother's 14th Battalion. Now here he was, a fresh-faced young private lining up for the journey to Anzac Cove.

The two men shook hands. Bill had always hero-worshipped his elder brother and Albert had always looked out for him. Now, joined in the most hazardous endeavour, the bonds would be powerfully strengthened.

Another brother, Sidney, had joined up in August. He had rejected the opportunity to join his brothers in the 14th. 'I didn't want to climb on Bert's bandwagon,' he told his family.[5] Instead, he would spend the next four years as a driver and sapper in the Light Horse attached to units in the Middle East. While sickness sent him to hospital several times, he would survive the war without serious injury.

On Gallipoli, winter was closing in and the bitter winds kicked up a swell that prevented the Jackas' vessel from landing. For 24 hours they and the other men rode the bucking waves until they managed a landing on 1 November.

While on Lemnos Jacka had received his sergeant's stripe, but his authority among the men was not dependent on rank. He led by example and he quickly disbursed his section to bivouac in a nearby gully. The Turks, as usual, pounded anything that moved. He recorded on 2 November, 'Stayed in gully all day and were heavily shelled by the enemy.' The following day they climbed up to the front lines again, Jacka and his section moving into Durrant's Post, to the left of Courtney's and under less pressure from Turkish machine-gun and rifle fire.

Their main concern was not an enemy attack but rather the bitter cold. Monash, an engineer in private life, organised his forces to build a network of tunnels, and the work at least kept them warm. Wanliss: 'All available clothing was used to combat the increasing cold. There was a shortage of blankets and overcoats which gave rise to much discomfort and caused many evacuations to the hospitals. Storms at Anzac about this time sometimes seriously interfered with the unloading of stores.'[6]

However, the weather did not prevent the arrival of Lord Kitchener, who landed at Anzac Cove on 13 November with Monro's recommendation to withdraw in his briefcase. The hero of Khartoum wanted to see for himself the obstacles facing the Anzacs and the British on the peninsula. The commanders quickly assembled. The soldiers who recognised his tall figure left their dugouts and crowded around. Monash recorded his words: 'I have brought you all a personal message from the King. He wants me to tell you how much he admires the splendid things that you have done here.'[7]

Though he kept his decision from Monash and the other Australian officers, the dye was cast. Evacuation was inevitable. It would be scheduled for mid-December to give time for all the naval and medical logistics to be in place. Until then, the decision had to be kept a tight secret. The Anzacs would carry on as before.

Among the reinforcements to the 14th Battalion that had reunited the Jacka brothers was Edgar Rule, a 29-year-old farmer from the Shepparton district who supplemented his farm earnings with a job on the Victorian railways. He had already led an adventurous life, having been orphaned in his youth, and in his late teens roamed the world, at one stage becoming foreman of a work gang on the Panama Canal. Like George Mitchell, he was a brilliant diarist and his writings would be published after the war under the title, *Jacka's Mob.*[8] Happily for the biographer, his arrival in the 14th coincides with Jacka's own decision to abandon the rough diary notes he had been keeping.

When Rule reached the peninsula he was shocked by the condition of the Gallipoli veterans. 'They seemed to us more like sewer workers than soldiers,' he wrote. 'They were proud of their rags, their whiskers and the colour of the dirt which stained their clothes and helped to set off their grimy, hairy faces.'

Up in Durrant's Post, Jacka received news of another promotion. On 14 November he was made company sergeant major. The news reached Corporal Rule as he and his mates received their unit allocations on the beach. 'Those of us allotted to D Company felt a thrill of self-esteem,' he wrote. 'Our Sergeant-Major was no less than Jacka VC.'⁹

They began the climb towards Durrant's. ' "Have you seen him yet?" was on all lips. The man who could point out Jacka seemed to swell with importance. To me, Jacka looked the part; he had a medium-sized body, a natty figure and a determined face with crooked nose.'

Moreover, his unorthodox method of dealing with miscreants in the ranks was already well known. 'One characteristic above all endeared him to all the under-dogs,' Rule said. 'Instead of "criming" men and bringing them before the officers, his method was: "I won't crime you, I'll give you a punch on the bloody nose." '

The battalion had another practice that surprised the newcomer.

The C.O. [Major Dare] told us we would now have to revert to the ranks and start from scratch again. Most of the men in the battalion had this remarkable outlook on reinforcements. So wrapped up were they among themselves that they resented new blood coming among them and wanted to finish the war on their own, in spite of the fact that only a handful were left.

However, Rule did not remain a private long. 'We had not been in the trenches a week when Jacka came into our bay one morning and informed me that he had decided to make me a lance-corporal. He ordered me to take a party of six men and patrol the battalion frontage from dusk until midnight.'

At the appointed hour, Rule set out on his first venture into no-man's-land. He remembered every terrible moment.

Here with every bound forward the feeling of loneliness and uncertainty increased. Occasionally, lying flat on the ground with our ears to the earth we visualised parties of Turks in every clump of scrub. [Pte Sidney] Green, one of the survivors of the original battalion, was a bundle of nerves. Several times he crept up to tell me that he was certain he saw something move in the bushes ahead. He knew the Turks took no prisoners; they slaughtered the lot.

A hundred yards out we halted in the vicinity of a frightful stench. Granigan, who had been out before, whispered that about six dead men lay in a heap in the next clump of scrub. I had never realised before that dead men smelt like dead animals and the experience came as a shock to me. Away over the ridge in the Turkish lines, dogs were howling as if kept on the chain; it was a certainty that they were not howling for raw meat.[10]

Further on he found two dead Tommies. 'It was my duty to search for the identity disks that hung about their necks but the notion of searching their decayed bodies was too repulsive. We gathered up their rifles and bayonets and left them.'

Returning, the men almost ran into a Turkish patrol. It was nearly midnight when they approached what they believed were their own lines, but then there was a sudden disagreement. Some thought they'd gone in the wrong direction and wanted to make a detour to the right. The argument was settled by a gruff voice from the darkness. 'Well, you silly bastards, aren't you coming in? You've been kicking up a hell of a row out there.'

They were right on target and clambered over the parapet to safety. But before reporting back to Jacka, Rule was diverted by the image of a soldier sitting in a dugout holding a sheet of paper, tears running down his wrinkled face. Rule: 'He had received a letter that day containing bad news about his wife. The woman he loved was seriously ill and he kept repeating, "Oh God, what can I do?"'

In late November a wild storm struck and for three days the men in the trenches suffered. Like a number of others, Bill Jacka's feet were badly frostbitten and he had to be evacuated back to Alexandria on 8 December. Albert saw him off with a mixture of impatience and relief. At least he was out of the firing line. And as a company sergeant major he was so busy there was little he could do to look after the youngster. Bill himself felt he had let his brother down, but he had never enjoyed Albert's robust constitution even though they had a strong facial resemblance.

By then, rumours had begun to spread that Gallipoli was to be given up as a bad job. Jacka told Rule and others in the trenches they were to remain absolutely quiet for 48 hours. It was part of a scheme devised by the Australian staff officer Brudenell White to prepare the Turks for extended periods of inactivity to cover the retreat.

Monash was deeply concerned about the effect the decision would have on the Anzacs. 'I am almost frightened to contemplate the howl of rage and disappointment there will be when the men find out what is afoot, and how they have been fooled,' he wrote. 'And I am wondering what Australia will think at the desertion of her 6000 dead and her 20,000 other casualties.'[11]

Edgar Rule heard the reaction from the veterans first hand. His platoon sergeant, Bill Gayning, said, 'We are sneaking off like whipped curs. Why can't we have another bloody go at them!'[12] Others took the opportunity to tend the graves of the fallen. They gathered in small parties and with their rifle butts knocked in rough crosses where particular mates had been buried.

The one saving grace was that Brudenell White's scheme worked perfectly. During the day, a team of Australian and British soldiers played cricket on the beach where the Turks could see them. An Australian lance corporal, William Scurry, invented a 'drip gun' that used water dripping from one container to another to fire a rifle automatically from the trenches after the troops had departed. But it was the pattern of silences that really made the difference between success and a terrible tragedy—that and a smooth sea that allowed the nightly departures from 16 December.

Jacka and his men of D Company 14th Battalion withdrew two nights later. Rule recorded the scene:

At nine o'clock we filed silently out of the trench to make room for a handful of men who were to keep the great bluff going until the following night, to be here, there and everywhere, to give the impression of a larger force.

Once clear of the trenches, the head of the company lost no time as it wound its way along the saps and through the gullies; the rear had difficulty in keeping up. The night was dark and the whole place seemed deserted.[13]

When they reached the beach, the company sat on the sand and waited their turn to embark from the pier. Rule:

At the sea's edge planks were laid out over the water on trestles like springboards to assist men in getting into the boats if the expected attack came off. Up in the hills the occasional bursting of bombs and the rattle of machine guns intimated that the Turks were unaware of the departure of the bulk of the garrison. The guns which normally flung occasional shells on to the beach were silent, and men turned their thoughts to the graveyard on our left where some of the larger wooden crosses were discernible in the night.

When their turn came, they boarded their boats, and the next morning they steamed into Lemnos harbour. One of the battalion's bush poets, Private Charles Smith, had written a verse during the journey:

Landing in face of a terrible fire
Storming the cliffs that rose higher and higher
Determined to push on and never retire—
Withdrawn!

Stubbornly facing the bullets that rained
Paying in blood for each yard that was gained

A ghastly picture of shattered and maimed—
Withdrawn

Toiling and fighting for months in vain
In scorching summer, snow and rain
Trials endured, yet little gain—
Withdrawn

Making a page in the history of fame
Upholding Australia's glorious name
Of one accord, one heart, one aim—
Withdrawn

'Twas hard to leave ground so possessed
More so the graves where comrades rest,
But after all, 'twas for the best—
Withdrawn.[14]

In a British hospital, George Mitchell was returning to health. News of the evacuation came as a physical blow to him. 'All that sacrifice, all that labour, all that suffering for nothing at all. No advantage gained and the flower of Australia's manhood lies on and below the earth which is not even in our own hands. I feel bitter about it.'[15]

Typically, Jacka kept his thoughts to himself. His actions spoke for themselves. The battle may have been lost, but the war in Europe hung in the balance. And if he was going to make a difference it would not be as an NCO taking orders from 'the heads'—they who had made such a hash of Gallipoli that there were fewer than

50 fighting men left of the battalion's 1000 who had marched out of Broadmeadows just over twelve months ago.

He fronted his battalion commander, Major Charles Dare. 'Sir, I want to apply for the officer's training course,' he said.

II

QUARTER-TIME BREAK

Jacka and his mates spent the Christmas of 1915 on Lemnos. It was not a happy time. If the horror of the trenches was behind them, at least for the moment, the sense of failure persisted. And the irony of presents from the Comforts Fund was not lost on them—each man received his delicacies from home in a billy can decorated with a cartoon showing a kangaroo pitching a Turk off the peninsula with its tail; the caption read, 'This Bit of the World Belongs to Us'.

The most prized gift among the cakes, fruit mince pies, lollies and penny trumpets was the roll of toilet paper on which they rested, for dysentery had once again broken out and Jacka was among those hardest hit. Then the rain came and the men lounged about in their tents playing cards. A big poker school developed and Jacka joined in briefly. But his Methodist upbringing had not prepared him for gambling; he played badly then worried about the lads who lost heavily.

Occasionally the men ventured into the Greek town on the island, but there was very little to divert them and, by 6 January 1916, they were happy to board HMAT *Cardiganshire* for the journey back to Alexandria. They would remain in Egypt for the next five months. According to Newton Wanliss it would be 'a time of recuperation, organisation, absorption of reinforcements, and training'.[1]

For Jacka it began with the rejection of his application for Officer Training School. The grounds were never explicitly stated, but his brother Bill believed it was his working-class background and outdoor employment. Whatever the reason—and most likely was his lack of formal education—Jacka would not accept the rejection. He would use whatever means at his command, from the support of junior officers and the new chaplain, to threats of a transfer to another battalion, until he got his way. But this would take several months of unremitting pressure. In the meantime, as company sergeant major he was deeply involved in the reorganisation of the battalion. At their camps at Ismailia and Moascar beside the Suez Canal, then a few weeks later at Tel el Kebir, 40 kilometres along the road to Cairo, the Australian and New Zealand forces were being totally reformed.

First the New Zealanders were separated from their mates of the 4th Brigade to help create their own division. Jacka's 14th Battalion remained in the brigade, but half the 14th would be separated out to form the nucleus of the new 46th Battalion. There was great emotional resistance from the old guard to the thought of leaving the 14th 'family'. Jacka himself was deeply affected. The 14th was his emotional hearth and home. He had been stung by the charges of favouritism because of Monash's affection for the unit. His own fighting qualities had answered the critics and to an extent he had come to personify the battalion and all it stood for. And now it was to be torn apart.

Corporal Rule said, 'It was Bert Jacka's duty to draw up a list of men who were to be transferred to the new battalion. The duty was an invidious one. I have no doubt Bert endeavoured to be perfectly fair to both battalions but for a few days our lines were a seething mass of discontent.'[2]

Men gathered in small knots and cursed the higher-ups who were separating brothers in arms. 'It was common talk among the NCOs that Bert had submitted a list and it had been rejected,' Rule said. Jacka's response was typical. 'Again he sent in a list [for the new battalion] containing the names of all his old cobbers with his own name at the top.' This too, it seems, was rejected, as Jacka must have known it would be. The 14th would never willingly transfer its VC winner.

The upshot was a remarkable scene. A few days later we were all drawn up on parade and the final stage of the great separation began. I can still see Jacka standing in front of the company, his heels together, and disgust and rebellion written on his face as he called out: 'The following sergeants will fall out on the right . . . Sergeant Banyard, Sergeant Twomey . . .'

At that stage Jacka had to stop, for Twomey had the floor. 'By gum, Bert, no more soldiering for me! You can make out a sick report because I'm off to hospital. To think that a man has never left the battalion and been in every stunt, and now he's to be chucked out like this. Bah—I thought you were a cobber of mine!'

'So much from Twomey,' Rule wrote, 'Banyards's language would need recording on asbestos.'

Having finished with the sergeants, Jacka called out the names of the corporals. 'Anxiously we waited for each one', Rule said, 'but mine was not among them. With delight, I realised that I was to remain with the 14th battalion.'

As did Jacka himself; and from 4 March 1916 the 14th would become part of the newly raised 4th Division. The Australian Government wanted Monash appointed the division commander. But Birdwood, who was in overall charge of the Anzac forces, preferred his fellow Britisher, and Indian Army comrade, General Sir H. V. Cox.

Birdwood and Hamilton had brought the 56-year-old veteran of the Indian Army on to the Gallipoli staff where he failed signally to impress Monash, who wrote, 'Cox is one of those crotchety, livery old Indian officers whom the climate has dried and shrivelled up into a bag of nerves.'[3]

In fact Cox had suffered a nervous collapse after the disaster of Helles and would never again expose himself to enemy gunfire if he could avoid it. In Egypt he and Monash had a sharp disagreement centring on an unnamed 'sergeant' (most likely Jacka himself) over the man's ambition to be commissioned from the ranks. Cox maintained that 'you couldn't have working-class men leading businessmen and those with university degrees'.[4]

Monash responded briskly: 'The man concerned is a born leader. He has proved himself on Gallipoli as a fighter. He is responsible, popular and strong. He wants to lead, make decisions and inspire. That's how it is done in the Australian force.'

Still Cox was unconvinced. Monash took up the cudgels again. 'Men of humble origin can rise during a war from privates to command battalions. The major difference is that Australia does not have a caste system.' Soon the argument became a sociological lecture from the Australian on the code of behaviour that had come to distinguish the AIF. 'Officers have to dress like the men, to live among them in the trenches, to share their hardships and privations.' If officers came from among the lower ranks it was easier to gain their respect. If they saw to their own comfort before that of the men, the word would get around. The men would lose respect. Cooperation between the officer and his men would diminish.

Finally Cox relented. Very shortly thereafter Jacka was enrolled in the officer training course, from which he emerged third in his class of twenty with a very creditable 94 per cent pass. To add to his groundbreaking VC he had become one of the first men of the AIF to have risen from private to commissioned officer, and certainly the first from Wedderburn, where his every promotion made news. His new status was formally gazetted on 29 April.

By then the 4th Division had been assigned a section of the Suez Canal defences and on Cox's orders had undertaken a three-day march through the desert to their new post. Each man had to carry his pack containing clothing and extra boots as well as his souvenirs; about his person would be a food pack, water bottle, field dressing, rifle, bayonet, trenching tool and 190 rounds of ammunition. The heat was intense and every step was through heavy sand.

Lieutenant Harold Wanliss, the historian's son, had joined the battalion as a reinforcement in November. Like Jacka, the newly minted lieutenant was instantly accepted by the men as a natural leader. But they were a study in contrasts—young Wanliss the dux of his agricultural school, fair, handsome and an outstanding team sportsman; Jacka darker and much more reserved, though with the aura of command implicit in his bearing and demeanour.

At first, their relationship was formal, even awkward on Jacka's part. But soon they would become much more than allies, sharing a mutual respect and regard that was rare for both men.[5] Harold had missed the worst of Gallipoli. Now he suffered in the latest ordeal. The historian wrote, 'Many were tortured by new and badly fitting boots; the stifling desert wind drove the sand into their sweat-covered faces. Some, nearly crazy with thirst, lurched along with their tongues out like dogs.'

Monash urged them to greater effort from the back of his horse. 'It was the only time I heard the men curse him,' Edgar Rule said.[6] Second Lieutenant Jacka worked tirelessly to keep his men together and conserve their water. It was a matter of some pride that fewer from his platoon fell out than in the rest of the battalion.

The soldiers' morale was not assisted by the sight of empty trains passing in the same direction as the march. 'Some few fell out, absolutely prostrated,' Newton Wanliss wrote, 'but nearly all joined up with the battalion after dark.'[7]

The new camp on the Sinai Peninsula was about 3 kilometres from the canal and from time to time the men were allowed to swim in its cooling waters. It was on the banks of the canal that the diggers observed the first anniversary of the Anzac landing with a church parade in the morning and swimming races in the afternoon.

'It was enjoyed by everybody but General Cox,' Rule said. 'The old man was furious because someone had entered his tent and purloined his supply of whisky.' Cox threatened reprisals but to no avail. Mischievous members of the band marched around the camp 'in every conceivable state of undress' playing 'Hold Your Hand Out Naughty Boy'.[8]

The training continued. An NCO school was established and in the field the men practised with new weapons such as the light Lewis machine gun and Mills bombs. Leave was taken in Cairo, but Jacka seems not to have made the journey.

He was assigned to B Company under the provocatively named Major Otto Carl Wilhelm Fuhrmann, a former public servant in the Supreme Court of Victoria. Though of German extraction, Fuhrmann was born in Melbourne and had joined the militia. He had been with the 14th from the beginning, but as transport officer had remained in Egypt when they set out for Gallipoli. As his subsequent actions would show, he was not one to volunteer for the front lines, and there was fertile ground for a personality clash between the two men. Indeed, at this time Jacka developed a reputation for preferring the company of his men to that of his brother officers.

The men responded, even though Jacka was unremitting in his demands. 'His candid tongue left welts on men's memories,' Rule said. However, a platoon member, Arthur Tulloch, maintained, '[We] would have followed him anywhere.'[9]

They followed him on 31 May on the short march from camp to Serapeum, then across the pontoon bridge to the railway station where the battalion loaded itself into open carriages for the overnight journey to Alexandria. After breakfast at the dock they embarked on the 15,000-ton liner SS *Transylvania* together with the men of the 13th and 15th battalions for the voyage across the Mediterranean, through the Straits of Gibraltar then north across the Bay of Biscay to the French port of Marseilles.

According to Wanliss, 'The sea was calm, the weather delightful; each man had a bunk to himself.' The major hazard was the German submarine pack, but no submarines were sighted and on the morning of 7 June they entered Marseilles harbour. 'To me it was a glimpse of paradise,' Rule wrote. 'Probably this vision had inspired Dumas to choose Marseilles for the opening scene of the *Count of Monte Cristo*. I had just finished reading it for the second time and as we slowly sailed in I endeavoured to pick out the cliff over which the hero was tossed in a sack into the sea.'[10]

He was not alone in his appreciation of the undoubted charms of the French city. As soon as the *Transylvania* docked, Jacka and the other officers were mobbed by men seeking shore leave. 'The number who had dying mothers or fathers who imperatively must be cabled to, was countless,' Rule said.

> But our military chiefs knew their job and were taking no risks. A few must have managed to get loose because during the afternoon I was ordered to take a guard and proceed with an officer to capture several who were reported to be painting the town red.
>
> All we discovered were two Aussies surrounded by French civilians. The two were being killed with kindness, or rather beer and wine. It was the forerunner of the happy relations which always existed between the French and ourselves.[11]

Jacka and his company remained on the ship overnight, then at 10 a.m. on 8 June they marched through the narrow streets of the town as the locals hurried out of their shops and homes to cheer them. The experience was an affecting one, not least because it was so different from Gallipoli. Where previously they were invading a foreign country for some distant military goal, here they were defending people like themselves and who clasped them to their figurative bosom even before they had fired a shot. It was heady stuff for the young warriors of the New World.

Their journey by train up the Rhône Valley and through the gorgeous farmland of provincial France was a revelation. 'For sixty hours we forgot that we were on a deadly mission,' Rule wrote. 'Everything was so peaceful that the existence of a state of war was almost incredible. At the main French cities, maidens handed out refreshments, chatting and laughing the while. Few understood them, but what did it matter. Men had almost forgotten till then what decent women looked like.'[12]

Peasants left their work and waved to the passing troops; in the towns of Lyons, Macon and Laroche they tossed garlands and the Australians responded by singing 'The Marseillaise' and 'Australia Will Be There'. According to Wanliss, 'It was the trip of a lifetime and sent a glow of enthusiasm through the ranks of the 4th Brigade. Never will it be forgotten by those who took part in it.'

They passed though Paris but without stopping. By now the glow was beginning to fade and the weather darkened as they travelled north towards Calais and branched off to the east where they pulled into the station at Bailleul, about 70 kilometres from the Belgian border and facing the most powerful war machine ever assembled.

During the journey they had been told of the death of Lord Kitchener, who was drowned when his ship struck a mine in the North Sea as he was travelling to Russia to rally the troops. No tear was shed by the veterans of Gallipoli and none would ever be. To

Jacka and his comrades, Kitchener epitomised the 'heads' who had put them through hell on earth for no result. Platoon member Arthur Tulloch said it was clear to all Jacka's men that henceforth, whatever orders might come down from above, Jacka 'wouldn't do anything that he didn't want to'.[13]

It was an attitude that his Australian brigade commander, Monash, could understand, if not approve. However, once in France, Monash learned he was in line for higher duties. The demands of the Australian Government, combined with a guarded endorsement from Birdwood, meant that he would soon be given his own division. Nevertheless, when the 4th Brigade reached the front he was still in command. Before he departed he would lead his men into battle against the *real* enemy.

Jacka and his mates were ready for the fray.

12

HUNTING THE HUN

By July 1916, the war was going badly for the Allies. For the previous four months, the German offensive in the south to take the fortress of Verdun had chewed up no fewer than 78 French divisions and 65 German divisions in a mutual slaughter that produced more than 600,000 casualties. The fortress was of little strategic value but it had great symbolic meaning to the French. Their commanders poured a seemingly endless stream of soldiers into the killing machine until even the men finally threatened to mutiny. By mid-year the French supreme commander, Marshal Joffre, was desperate for the British to relieve the pressure by engaging the Germans in the north.

The British supremo, General Douglas Haig, had been fiercely critical of his predecessor, General John French, whose impulsive offensives in 1915 had crippled the British Expeditionary Force (BEF). But he now had 57 British divisions at his disposal—more than enough, he calculated, to attack the enemy in the north and 'roll up' the German lines. He willingly agreed to bring his offensive forward.

Haig was the heir to the famous whisky distillery that bore his name. He had spent his life among the minor aristocracy and the military establishment. Posted to India in 1886 aged 25 with his regiment, the 7th Hussars, he rose through the ranks and later fought in the Sudan and South Africa on the staff of General French. Back in India, Colonel Haig served on Lord Kitchener's staff and in 1906 he returned to London as director of military training with special responsibility to develop a British expeditionary force.

At the outbreak of the Great War he took command of the 1st Army Corps within the BEF, rising to full general, and finally, in December 1915, was given command of all British forces in France. With a broad, open face, a luxuriant moustache, and a bluff and hearty air among his peers, he epitomised the upper-class commander of his day. He would never see the ground on which his greatest battles were fought, either before, during or after the war. Technological innovations meant little to him. Even in 1926 he would write, 'I believe that the value of the horse and the opportunity for the horse in the future are likely to be as great as ever. Aeroplanes and tanks are only accessories to the men and the horse.'

Joffre suggested a joint offensive because he privately doubted that the British would fight hard enough unless he had them under his own hand. He indicated to Haig the area where their two armies joined: the Somme. Like Verdun, it too had no special strategic value. If the Germans fell back, they would simply shorten their supply lines. But once the British were committed, Joffre believed, they would be forced to stay the course. Haig assembled his staff officers and made plans.

On the Eastern Front, the Russians were also planning offensives, but without either the equipment or leadership to be effective.

On the contrary, they would plunge into a disaster that would kill more than a million men to no purpose whatever. In the south, the Italians were hard pressed by the Austrian army, which had been seeded with German regular officers and artillery units. They too would suffer terrible casualties. But all news of reverses and outright defeats were kept from the Australians on the Western Front. Instead, their fighting spirits were bolstered by well-honed propaganda that pictured the Huns as voracious baby killers and gloried in the prospect of imminent victory over the inhuman aggressor.

In the Flanders trenches, Jacka and his men felt they were well prepared. On 15 June, they had been issued with gas respirators and steel helmets. They were fit and well fed. It was time to confront the Hun.

Haig had decided on a series of raids along the entire front line to distract, wear down and mislead the German command about the place and nature of the Somme offensive. In Flanders, Monash's 4th Brigade was selected for the task; the Australian commander wanted to make a good impression so he chose what had become known as 'Jacka's Mob'—the 14th—for the task.

They spent a week settling into their billets—the barns and outhouses of French farms beneath overcast skies—and on 17 June the men of the 14th marched 20 kilometres to the front line where they relieved the 19th Battalion.

Monash briefed them personally before their first raid. The battalion commander, Lieutenant Colonel Dare, decided it would be led by Lieutenant Harold Wanliss, the young man who could be relied on to do exactly as ordered. Jacka was senior to Wanliss and there have been suggestions that he resented being passed over.[1] But there is little or no evidence to support such an idea.

The reason for the preferment of Wanliss is not difficult to discern. Lieutenant Colonel Charles Moreland Montague Dare, the scion of the Dares of 'Moreland Park', a property on the outskirts of Melbourne, had not been among those who welcomed Jacka into commissioned ranks. Moreover, he resented the loyalty the men of the battalion showed to the VC winner and regarded him as a 'handful'. However, there is certainly no suggestion from Rule, who was in the thick of the raid, that Jacka was at all concerned about who led the breakout from the front lines.

As it happened, it was a costly exercise. One officer was killed and most of the men were badly wounded. Wanliss himself was hit three times, most seriously in the jaw, and had to be carried back to the trenches by Stephen De Arango—now a sergeant—who had been with Jacka in the action that won him the VC.

A section of seven men under Edgar Rule, also recently promoted to sergeant, went forward across no-man's-land to establish a listening post as close as possible to the German lines. However, they were spotted and the Germans opened up with a furious fusillade. 'I could see streaks of fire curving through the air as their trench-mortar bombs fell on our wire,' Rule said. 'When they landed and burst the earth rocked, even 300 yards away.'[2]

Jacka and his platoon were under blistering fire. 'In the sector occupied by Jacka's men things must have been very lively,' Rule said. 'One of his Corporals, Charlie Smith, told me they had to lie in the bottom of the trench along with several dead men, but Jacka kept walking to and fro as cool as an iceberg. One of the company runners told us afterwards that Jacka came to the company headquarters where a man or two might be sheltering. He was not long in finding someone.'

Rule said those nearby heard Jacka's voice: 'Hello, hello, what the devil are you doing here?' A couple of shells crashed into the back of the trench, then Jacka shouted, 'Come on, get out of here before I pull you out of it by the legs.' Then from one of the shelters another voice was heard: 'What's all the trouble about?'

'Holy Moses,' Jacka responded, 'is it you? You're a damned disgrace to the battalion.'

Rule says, 'Two more shells exploded close by and Jacka strolled back to his men. We never knew to whom it was that he had spoken like that, but there were several malicious conjectures.'

Among the candidates, no doubt, was Major Fuhrmann, Jacka's company commander who had a predilection for avoiding the shot and shell of battle in favour of a safe harbour and assiduous politicking in the officers' mess. After the war he would find a congenial billet in the office of that Australian master politician, Billy Hughes.

When Jacka reached his own trenches, the Germans opened up with rifle and machine-gun fire. Jacka and his men responded with Mills bombs and a volley of rifle fire, killing some and wounding three Germans. Then, as the fighting died and without waiting for orders, Jacka leapt over the parapet with a small team and brought back the three Germans as prisoners for the intelligence officer. They proved to be members of the 231st Prussian Reserve.

The next day Rule was approached by Private Harry Danman. 'To some of the men, Harry was a joke,' he wrote. 'No doubt this was due to his well-bred bearing and evident shrinking from any coarseness. There was nothing effeminate about him though obviously he had not yet fully developed into manhood.'[3]

The young private needed to confide. 'I don't seem able to adapt myself to these awful conditions like the rest,' he said. 'And when I think of how Lieutenant Jacka abused some of us for funking in those shelters last night, I feel thoroughly ashamed of myself. I could not help feeling afraid, but Lieutenant Jacka seemed afraid of nothing.'

The sergeant sought to reassure him. 'I've not the least doubt that Jacka was not afraid,' he said, 'but don't think you're peculiar. I've not heard of anyone else going into raptures over last night's entertainment.'

In the section of the raid to the left of the 14th Battalion, John Monash had joined his men briefly in the front line. He relished the fight, his last action as brigade commander. On 13 July, he was officially withdrawn from the battlefield and given charge of the 3rd Australian Division being assembled at Larkhill in the south of England. Before he left he commended his men on the raid as 'worthy of the highest praise and reflecting the greatest credit on their offensive spirit'.[4]

Wanliss wrote, 'A brigade will always respond to a strong person-ality and the capable and vigorous leadership of its great chief gave the 4th a reputation second to none, even among the virile brigades of the AIF. His successor, Colonel Brand, was an energetic officer who had shown initiative on the Peninsula, but he lacked the wide range of mind of his famous predecessor.'[5]

Wanliss reflected the view of the officers and men, and not least the Victoria Cross winner to whom most looked for a lead when any newcomer appeared in their ranks. Jacka was aware of the influence he carried and said nothing that would undermine the new com-mander's authority. He preferred to make his judgements on the man's actions and to act accordingly. Until then his attitude was formal and correct.

Charles Henry 'Harry' Brand was 43 at the time. Born a Queensland farm boy, he attended Bundaberg and Maryborough state schools and became a trainee teacher. He also joined the militia as a member of the Queensland Volunteer Infantry, and at the outbreak of the Boer War enlisted as a sergeant in the mounted infantry. He served two tours in South Africa and by the end of the war had risen to captain.

In the peace that followed he returned to teaching in north Queensland while continuing his involvement with the Volunteer Infantry. Then in 1905, aged 32, he joined the permanent forces as a lieutenant and worked his way up the ranks in administrative posts in Adelaide and Melbourne. When war broke out in 1914, he immediately transferred to the AIF as a major in the 3rd Brigade of the 1st Division under General Bridges.

He was among the first ashore at Anzac Cove on 25 April and in later fighting was awarded the Distinguished Service Order when he remained on duty after a shell struck the 8th Battalion's head-quarters. Promoted to lieutenant colonel, Harry Brand took command of the 8th in July 1915 and held the hazardous Steele's Post until the withdrawal from Gallipoli. However, there was a concern among the troops that he was too inclined to bend with the wind, particularly in the face of orders from high command.

Soon after the appointment, the brigade bid farewell to Flanders, entrained for the Somme and from the station marched through the mud to Domart. 'Hard as we were', Rule said, 'we had men lying out all along the roads for miles, too exhausted to go further'.[6]

The new brigade commander did not help his cause when he addressed the men on arrival, claiming, perhaps with heavy-handed jocularity, that he had 'won the DSO on Gallipoli before the 4th Brigade had even landed'. The official historian, Charles Bean, later described the speech as 'an extraordinarily inept and egoistic oration'.[7]

It could hardly have been better calculated to put the VC winner off-side. Jacka kept his feelings to himself, but Edgar Rule wrote, 'When the parade was over the Brig was just about the most unpopular man in France as far as our brigade was concerned.'[8]

On Sunday 16 July, the battalion was on the march again, this time the 20 kilometres in full kit to Naours where their farm billets were replaced by tents and dugouts. Brand then set a rigorous training schedule and for the next nine days they route-marched, trained and practised exercises in abandoned trenches behind the lines. Edgar Rule was made second in charge of a new platoon of 'bomb fighters'—specialists in the use of the Mills bomb—and they trained other units in the use of the hand grenade.

Then, on 25 July, they marched south towards the Somme, billeting in farmhouses overnight and reaching Warloy at 3 p.m. on the 27th. By then the First Battle of the Somme had been raging for three weeks. Just ahead of them was Pozières, where some of the toughest fighting had taken place. On 24 July the town had been taken by the Australian 1st Division and now they had been relieved by the 2nd and were returning through Warloy.

'Those who watched them will never forget it as long as they live,' Rule said. 'They looked like men who had been in hell. Almost without exception each man looked drawn and haggard, and so dazed they seemed to be walking in a dream. Some companies seemed to have been nearly wiped out. In all my experience, I've never seen men so badly shaken up as these.'[9]

Slowly the ragged line trailed away. Now it was the turn of Jacka's Mob.

13

BRAVEST MAN IN THE AUSSIE ARMY

Just before the Battle of Pozières, Bill Jacka received his commission to second lieutenant. Albert sought him out for a handshake. Both men knew that they might not survive the 'big show' now in prospect, but there was little room for sentimentality on the battlefront. It was not the Australian way. As Lieutenant Walter Mann wrote home at the time, 'I'll do my best to return to you but if I do get a smack you'll have nothing to be ashamed of and nobody will be able to say you gave birth to a son who was afraid to die.'[1]

The Jackas were similarly stoic, at least on the surface. Young Bill would later admit that he gained strength from his elder brother's presence and feared what life would be like without him. But after a few brief words they parted and returned to their units. Albert, now 23, had been briefly assigned to C Company, commanded by the 24-year-old architect Captain Stewart Hansen, but now returned to B Company under Major Fuhrmann.

At 1.40 p.m. on 6 August the 14th was ordered to relieve the 26th and 28th battalions of the 2nd Division in the front line at Pozières Ridge. At 2.30 the battalion moved off in companies at ten-minute intervals. Their route lay through the village of Albert via Tara Hill, then through Sausage Valley and finally across 120 metres of open country to the firing line. Lieutenant Colonel Dare ordered Jacka's B Company into the front line with C Company in support. The other two companies remained in reserve.

The battalion moved forward, the men humping their heavy packs hour after tortured hour, as day darkened to evening, through the artillery, the transport lines, the cook houses, ammunition dumps, and the scurrying of vehicles, horses and men on foot. The roll and flash of guns lit up the sky as they approached the battle lines. They reached Albert at midnight and slept for a few hours in a paddock before being roused at 2.30 a.m. to continue the march.

A shell landed on the road no more than 20 metres in front of B Company, covering a dozen men in mud and dirt but leaving only minor casualties. In the lead, Jacka's platoon pushed on through Sausage Valley. By now the German guns were reaching a crescendo. When they arrived at the communication trench that would take them to the forward line, the jagged sap offered some protection from the cannonade that rocked the earth around them. The trench was littered with bodies partially buried in the soft ground; bloody hands and feet protruded, and the stench of death was mixed with cordite and human waste.

Still they pressed forward until they reached a dead end. Now there was only open ground between themselves and the firing line, and beyond that, the enemy. With Jacka leading, his 5 Platoon made the dash from shell hole to shell hole as shrapnel burst overhead, until they reached the line. Private Charlie Smith stuck close to his lieutenant. He told Edgar Rule he found his leader 'strangely suited' to the fierce battlefield.

Though they didn't know it at the time, Jacka and his men were at the forward point of a bulge into the German defences. The Australian attack had penetrated further than expected, and behind the German lines the commanders were furiously organising a counter-attack to prevent a breakthrough.

To one side of Jacka's platoon was 6 Platoon under Lieutenant Henry Dobbie, a former clerk from Footscray, and behind them was Lieutenant Frank Appleton's 8 Platoon 150 metres back, waiting in reserve. Major Fuhrmann remained a further 200 metres behind them at company headquarters in a capacious dugout.

About 9 p.m. the German artillery began a massive bombardment. According to Wanliss, 'The guns were innumerable and they were exactly ranged. The drum fire was incessant and continued all night with unabated fury.' The pounding seemed endless. 'There were shells from the big 12-inch Howitzers down to the little nerve-racking "whizbangs"; there were high explosive shells with sulphur fumes which burnt immediately overhead, and there were other shells with neither fumes nor smoke. Both the earth and the heavens seemed rent by this concentrated effort of man's fury.'[2]

As the barrage faded, the German command ordered a do-or-die effort to the infantry, threatening 'any officer or man who fails to resist to the death on the ground won, will be immediately court martialled',[3] and at 4.45 a.m. they attacked on a narrow front in waves 70 metres apart. The full force of it struck 5 Platoon and, despite enfilading fire from the 15th and 48th battalions, the

Germans charged into and over the Australian lines in the semi-darkness.

Jacka and one section had secured themselves in a deep dugout. He raised himself to the edge and looked out. As far as he could tell in the chaotic fury of the battlefield, the situation was 'just the same', he told his troops. But in the half-light he was unaware that two lines of German troops had actually charged past his position and were locked in combat with members of the 48th behind him. Then a German in the second or third line rolled a bomb into the wide entrance of the section's dugout. It exploded, severely wounding two men and stunning the rest.

Jacka was first to recover. He charged up to the parapet and fired his revolver at the advancing figure, who immediately broke off and disappeared in the pitted field. Turning to the rear he suddenly realised to his astonishment that the first German line had passed over his position and was now almost 100 metres behind him. The second line was also between himself and the men of the 48th on the left who, even as he watched, came out of their dugouts with their hands raised in surrender. Two Australian officers and about 40 men threw down their arms as the Germans surrounded them.

Jacka took stock of the situation. He signalled his men to stay down. Now the Germans were beginning to push their captives forward. 'Don't move,' he said.

To the right, Sergeant Edgar Rule had been preparing his bombers for action, but he was too far away from the battle to get an effective volley off. He was slipping a clip of cartridges into his rifle when a man came along the trench yelling out, 'Jacka is killed and the Huns have got the ridge.'

Rule's officer, Lieutenant Thompson, laughed at the idea. 'That man's gone off his head,' he said. But as the daylight grew stronger, Rule said, 'We saw a number of men running along the crest out in front of us about 500 yards away. Not one among us knew definitely where our front lay.'[4]

Jacka knew. He called his men to him. Only seven were unscathed but all gathered around. Quickly he explained the situation. By now there were more than 50 Germans shepherding the Australians back to captivity. 'This is no good, boys,' he said. There was no way they were going to let their mates be taken. He held his seven able-bodied men until the Germans were about 30 metres away then, brandishing a rifle, leapt up on the parapet with a guttural cry. 'Charge. Charge the bastards.'

Jacka raced at the leading officers, firing as he went. For a moment the Germans were nonplussed, then they fired back at the Australians charging at them from their own lines. Two of Jacka's men—Jack Finlay and Billy Williams—were immediately hit by a bomb and fell back into the trench. Each of the other five was hit by rifle fire, but most kept going. Some of the Germans dropped their guns, fearing that they had fallen into a trap; others fired their rifles at the Australian leader who seemed unstoppable. Four Germans had found a foxhole and began shooting at him.

Jacka said later, 'They hit me three times and each time the terrific impact of bullets fired at such close range swung me off my feet. But each time I sprang up like a prize fighter, and kept getting closer. When I got up to them they flung down their rifles and put up their hands. I shot three through the head and put a bayonet through the fourth. I had to do it—they would have killed me the moment I turned my back.'[5]

He rejoined the charge, taking out at least a dozen men before he went down again. The men of the 28th, taking advantage of the Germans' confusion, had by then turned on their captors and wrestled their rifles from them. From other parts of the battlefield Australians were drawn to the struggle in defence of their mates.

From the right, Sergeant Frank Beck arrived with a small party from the 48th Battalion. From the left, Lieutenant Alan Dunworth chimed in with a platoon from the 15th. Edgar Rule watched in amazement. 'Through my glasses I could see some of our boys standing up and firing point-blank at other men. Some figures I could see on their knees in front of others, praying for their lives, and several were bayoneting Huns. It was one of the queerest sights I've ever seen. Each Aussie seemed to be having a war all on his own.'[6]

Jacka went down again, this time for keeps. He had been wounded no fewer than seven times, one bullet passing right through his body beneath the right shoulder. Of the seven men who charged with Jacka, four were killed. A stretcher bearer found him, took off his tunic and dressed the worst of his wounds. The man then went for a stretcher but was killed before he could return.

Jacka lay on the battlefield until finally some of his men found him. Rule said, 'Pretty soon all the Huns who were left got into a communication trench and were brought through to us in the rear.'[7] Then as the last of the Australian wounded passed by, Edgar Rule called out to one of the bearers, 'Who've you got there?'

He replied, 'I don't know who I've got, but the bravest man in the Aussie army is on that stretcher just ahead. It's Bert Jacka and I wouldn't give a Gyppo piastre for him; he is knocked about dreadfully.'

Jacka had single-handedly turned a battlefield defeat into a rout for the enemy. Charles Bean later wrote, 'Jacka's counter-attack . . . stands as the most dramatic and effective act of individual audacity in the history of the AIF.'[8]

However, these were the least of Jacka's concerns as he passed through a regimental aid post where his brother Bill, who had been wounded in the arm, found him.

'He was just about to be loaded into the ambulance,' Bill recalled in 1974.

> I have never seen anybody look so terrible in all my life. He'd been shot through the nose—in fact, it looked as though he'd been shot everywhere.
>
> All through the years, when I've thought of it, I've thought of Albert's face as being like a lump of lard—it was absolutely bloodless.
>
> When I looked at him, I thought, 'By Jove, you've had it, Albert. I won't . . . I'll never see you again.'[9]

But even he underestimated his brother's fighting spirit. Though desperately wounded, Jacka rallied when he reached the 4th Australian Field Hospital in a village school behind the lines, and on 8 August was transferred to the 20th General Hospital in France. The following day he was carried aboard HMS *Dieppe* in Calais and in short order reached the 3rd General Hospital in Wandsworth, South London.

Almost immediately, word of his feat swept through the unit. All agreed that he had earned a second VC. And by any comparison with the deeds that were so honoured—including his own at Gallipoli—the highest award for bravery was justified.

Rule was in no doubt. 'He certainly deserved it,' he wrote. Wanliss was more emphatic.

This brilliant counter-attack against an overwhelming and triumphant enemy was completely successful—all the Australian prisoners were released, the whole of the German escort guarding them was killed or dispersed, and in addition 42 unwounded Germans (including two officers), the survivors of the German escort, were captured.

It was a marvellous piece of work, bold in conception, brilliant and heroic in execution, smashing and demoralising to the enemy, and fruitful in its results—a splendid piece of bluff carried to a successful and glorious conclusion by a handful of men who had already endured a nerve-racking bombardment of several hours.

The records of the AIF teem with successful exploits in the face of great odds, but they do not contain anything which surpasses (if anything quite equals) the work of Jacka and his seven on Pozières Ridge.[10]

However, before Jacka's action could be properly recognised, a report on it had to pass through channels. Here it confronted a major impediment in the form of company commander Fuhrmann, who was too far behind the lines to gain any understanding of the action. In fact, in his initial report in the 14th Battalion war diary he placed himself at the centre of events. He told the official historian who was behind the lines at the time that 'when Jacka saw the Germans attacking he reported to [Major Fuhrmann who] sent Appleton up with the reserve platoon of B Coy . . . As soon as Appleton's platoon arrived the three platoons went into No Man's Land and counter-attacked to the right front.'

This was plainly self-serving, not to say flagrantly untrue, and Bean later corrected it.[11] But it was Fuhrmann who reported to Dare, the man responsible for making recommendations, and his report was at best tepid in its description of the action. Dare's final recommendation read, 'For conspicuous gallantry. He led his platoon against a large number of the enemy who had counter-attacked the battalion on his right. The enemy were driven back, some prisoners they had taken were recovered and 50 of the enemy captured. He was himself wounded in this attack.'

This is not the kind of stirring prose that would have inspired those higher up the chain to award a bar to Jacka's VC. And this time there was no John Monash to take his own soundings from the men. It may well be that Brand, recently promoted to brigadier, had already become aware—like Colonel Dare—that Jacka attracted a loyalty and influence among the men that contrasted with their attitude towards himself.

The commander of the 48th Battalion, Lieutenant Colonel Raymond Leane, who would become a highly decorated brigadier general, gave full credit to Jacka in the 48th's war diary, despite coming from another unit. (The 48th was known as the Joan of Arc battalion as many of the officers were of the same family as the commander, hence it was 'made of all Leanes'.) The 14th's war diary, compiled under Dare's authority, did not mention the action at all. In the end, Jacka was awarded the Military Cross. Bean later wrote that 'no action ever performed in the AIF quite so thoroughly deserved the higher award'.[12]

But though his own chain of command had under-reported Jacka's action at Pozières, word soon spread through the informal grapevine of war correspondents, and he was overwhelmed by the attention of the press. After the first couple of days in the spotlight, Jacka retreated, finally pleading with his nurse to 'tell them I'm dead'.[13]

She was more convincing than expected and a week after his arrival *The Times* reported that the Australian hero had died of his wounds. Jacka was amused, but only until the news reached his mother in Wedderburn. It took an exchange of urgent telegrams to calm Elizabeth Jacka's maternal fears.

Her son's fears were of a different order.

14

ACTION AND REACTION

Shell shock, as post-traumatic stress disorder was then termed, takes many forms. It appears that in the weeks immediately following the action Jacka was in good spirits. Only later in his convalescence did he struggle at the brink of a terrible pit of nerves.

At first, he underwent several operations, from which he recovered well. Then came news of his promotion to first lieutenant on 18 August and with it a bundle of cards and letters from Australia and his mates in the battalion. They were full of congratulations and anticipation that he'd get a bar to his VC. General Birdwood and his divisional commander, General Cox, also wrote, heaping praise and wishing him a quick recovery. Brother Bill, who was recuperating in the 4th London Hospital at Denmark Hill, near Wandsworth, visited and told him that news of his action at Pozières Ridge had 'spread like wildfire'.

Jacka's response was typical: 'I was a VC—what else could I do?'[1]

In September, Jacka responded in a letter to a mate from the 15th Battalion, Captain John Corrigan: 'I was hoping to get out of here early next week but some cook had to get scarlet fever in our ward and we are in quarantine again.' He wrote in a firm hand and, despite the restrictions of the hospital, his morale seemed excellent. 'I am getting fairly well again', he said, 'but feel a bit weak at times. I had General Cox out to see me yesterday and I do not know if he was pulling my leg or not, but he told me that I have the D.S.O. and that it would be officially published next week.'[2]

Jacka was particularly delighted at the prospect of receiving the Distinguished Service Order. Though it was a step below the VC, the DSO was usually reserved for senior officers and was greatly prized by the military establishment. Cox then brought a surprise into the ward—his wife and daughter who wanted to meet the famous Australian hero. Jacka told his mate, 'He said to his wife that I had now won the DSO too, so I am beginning to think I must be getting something alright.'

Then he confided to his friend in terms that say much about his consciousness of his humble background and the divisions within the army: 'I tell you, Jack, I earned a DSO right enough. If I get it I will look sideways at Dare and some of his mob.'

Only at the end of the letter did he mention that the following day he would be 'going down to Windsor Castle to be decorated and I am staying to luncheon. A man will be amongst some class then, won't he?'

At the time, Corrigan, a Queenslander, was himself recovering at Edinburgh from wounds sustained at Pozières. Jacka promised to join him for a few days if he were given furlough. He signed off with the words, 'Hoping to see you soon. I am, Your Sincere Friend, Bert Jacka.'

The investiture of his Victoria Cross by the king himself at Windsor Castle on 29 September 1916 more than a year after it was earned was a highlight, even though photographs taken at the time show Jacka to be very thin and with an eye patch covering one of his facial wounds.

At the luncheon, all the Australians sat together and found themselves confronted by more eating utensils than they knew what to do with. They decided to follow the lead of the British equerries and other courtiers and all went well until drinks orders were taken. 'Make mine a beer,' said the Australians, only to be told that the palace was 'dry' for the duration, King George V having sworn off until the enemy—led by his cousin the kaiser—had been defeated. Happily, Jacka's teetotal pledge saved him the embarrassment.

Jacka made a firm and favourable impression on the king, and he would receive a number of invitations to Buckingham Palace when he was recuperating from later wounds.

Back in France, Edgar Rule had been slightly wounded and, on recovery, found himself passing through the famous 'Bullring' at Etaples, the enormous camp near the Channel coast where troops were trained before being posted to the battlefield or toughened up after a spell in hospital. When he found the 14th Battalion's lines he discovered the newspaper report that Jacka had died of his wounds. It was the first thing he mentioned when he saw his mate George Ross. To his astonishment Ross began to laugh.

'I can see that you don't know the sequel to Bert's death,' he said.

'What do you mean?'

'Well, Bert has been killed in a way. But what has finished him has been the kind attentions of all the old ladies in England—and not only the old ladies by any means; some very attractive girls found their way to his bedside.'

Rule was both relieved and amused. Jacka was never a ladies' man. On the contrary, he was always rather shy with the opposite sex.

'Bert's far from dead, don't worry,' Ross said. 'We'll have him back with us yet.'[3]

In fact, his return was touch and go. Whether he was feted by the ladies or not—and Rule's exchange might well owe more to the troops' imagination than to reality—on 11 November he faced his medical board in London and they decided he would not be fit to return to the front for three months. He would recuperate at a training camp at Perham Downs, Wiltshire—a bleak, depressing establishment, where he would be assistant adjutant. A photograph taken at the time shows him shaking hands with another Australian VC winner, and Perham Downs inmate, Private Martin O'Meara, a stretcher bearer in the 16th Battalion who had done outstanding work at Pozières and on the subsequent advance on Mouquet Farm. O'Meara would stick out the whole war, but on his return to Australia in 1919 would suffer a total collapse and spend the rest of his life in a mental institution.

By then Jacka had heard that the promised DSO would not be awarded. He would get a Military Cross instead. There was no explanation and he asked for none. But clearly, the combination of disappointment over the decoration and the prospect of a long period of inactivity affected the man's frame of mind at this most vulnerable time. The MC was an admirable decoration, but it carried little of the prestige of a DSO, and nothing of the mystique of a VC.

To anyone else, the MC would have been received as a genuine honour. But in this respect, Jacka was not like other men. The standards by which he judged himself were of a different order. The MC was not quite an insult from the snobbish Dare and the military establishment, but it was a rejection and to Jacka it must have felt like a calculated slap in the face.

Once he let his guard down, he was swamped by a terrible wave of depression. Rule had a friend at Perham Downs, a sergeant typist, who told him of Jacka's fight against a breakdown. Jacka's first response was to turn his back on his 'family' in the 14th and apply to join the Flying Corps. He had watched the development of the biplanes since the primitive reconnaissance versions at Gallipoli gave way to the attack aircraft that duelled in the skies above France. This was man-to-man combat with no ties to a system that valued men by their wealth or family background. It would free him from the Dares, the Fuhrmanns and the Brands with their jealousies and their incompetence.

But then came the second thoughts—he would be walking out on his mates in the 14th; more importantly, he would be leaving his men to the mercy of an officer corps that would put them in jeopardy with foolish orders and careless planning.

He was torn; and according to Rule's friend, 'the iron will was so badly shaken that the noise of a box-lid hurriedly closed would set up a physical shaking that would continue for hours at a stretch'. On these occasions, 'He was incapable of signing his name to an order or memo.'[4]

Half an hour on the Perham Downs rifle range would produce a similar effect. He took up riding the camp's motorbikes at great speed. 'On two occasions this lack of nervous control led to severe motor-cycle smashes on a level road,' Rule said. 'Of all these trials we saw not a trace, and few men ever knew of them.'

At the same time Jacka found himself under siege from the government of Billy Hughes, who had embarked on a campaign to introduce conscription and wanted the Australian hero home to speak on behalf of the cause. Jacka would not have a bar of it. In the first place, he agreed with the great majority of his comrades in arms who said: 'If they don't want to volunteer, we don't want 'em here.' Conscripted forces, they believed, would be unreliable in the trenches. Second, he was no soapbox orator; the whole idea was anathema to him. Third, he didn't believe the VC should be used in a way that would tarnish it politically. Finally, he knew that Hughes was breaking Labor Party policy and that meant his father Nathaniel would be totally opposed.

However, senior officers like Haig, Birdwood and Cox were thoroughly in favour of the proposal and made it clear that, should he accept, arrangements would be made to return him to Australia. The pressure mounted. Jacka's response was as singular as it was predictable—he demanded to be returned to the front line. He would forfeit the three months' recuperation time at Perham Downs if only they would send him back to the 14th in France.

The authorities knew they could not keep a VC winner from returning to his unit, so after only two weeks at the depot he signed out. Jack Corrigan later claimed Jacka spent a few days with him in Edinburgh on his way back to the battlefield. But in any case Jacka resumed duty officially on 9 December 1916.

Also at Perham Downs after a long recuperation was George Mitchell of the 15th Battalion. He reported to the Bullring at Etaples before heading back to his unit. Mitchell would soon transfer to the 48th, the Joan of Arc battalion.

Jacka was on his way back to the 14th when he recognised the colours of a young 13th Battalion second lieutenant, Tom White, who was taken aback when the VC winner approached him. White later wrote:

I was crossing the Channel when I heard, 'Hullo Thirteen, just joining them?'

'Yes.'

'Rough mob.'

'Got a great name,' I replied.

'Earned it too. I'm Jacka, 14th Battalion. How's Aussie?'

We yarned about districts known to both before he introduced me to a few he knew. I noticed that he refused every invitation to drink or smoke. I was expecting him to be a good swearer, but, except for an occasional expressive adjective, I never, in two years fairly close acquaintanceship, heard an obscenity from him. Awaiting disembarkation at Boulogne, Jacka took charge of me.

'You don't want to go to the Bullring, do you?'

'Can I dodge it?'

'Yes; we're at war now—or nearly there.'

'I've never even seen a bomb, gas mask or cannon.'

'You'll soon see enough of them. But the Bullring's a hell of a place!'

As the troops began descending the gangway, Jacka pointed

out the Landing Officer. 'He's separating the sheep from the goats—sheep to the Bullring, goats to the Somme. See if we can't be goats together. He's asking them questions and sending them left or right. Keep close to me and say what I say.'

'Returning to unit?' questioned the officer, saluting the VC ribbon.

'Too blanky true! *Both* of us, Fourth Division.'

I was at liberty in Boulogne with Jacka, awaiting a train to Amiens. Two evenings later we detrained near Albert, and wandered for hours looking for the Fourth Brigade among ruins, great guns, terrific noise, and troops moving in all directions. It was bewildering to me and I felt ashamed at jumping into a hole as a long range shell crashed, especially as Jacka did not notice it.

The Brigade had recently moved and no one knew where it was. At last, after returning some miles, he said, 'There's your mob. Good luck. See you later. Cheerio.'

I was immediately miserable, lonely; lonely among thousands of digging, marching and carrying men. Stumbling down some steps, I saluted the Colonel and Adjutant, working by candlelight.

'Come to join the 13th, Sir,' I stammered.

'What name?'

I told him.

'Haven't been notified to expect you. Where have you come from?'

'Australia.'

'I know. When did you leave there?'

'Seven weeks ago.'

'Seven weeks? You haven't been through the Bullring then?'

'No, Sir.'

'How did you manage it?'

'I met Jacka crossing the Channel.'

He smiled. 'Just what Jacka would do!'[5]

When Jacka rejoined the 14th at Ribemont he was immediately appointed assistant adjutant and sports officer to Adjutant-Captain Arthur Blainey, a regular soldier born in England but living in Melbourne at the outbreak of war. Blainey had been with the 14th from the beginning. Though Jacka didn't fully appreciate it at the time, the best news for the returning hero was the imminent departure of Lieutenant Colonel Dare, who would return to Australia in February and take no further part in the war. His replacement as battalion commander was an officer Newton Wanliss described as 'perhaps the ablest man who commanded a battalion of the AIF in France', Major John Henry Peck.

Peck, a nuggety, dark-haired man, with a direct and open manner, was a regular soldier who had landed with the 3rd Brigade at Gallipoli as a lieutenant and six months later had been promoted to brigade-major.

Edgar Rule was an immediate convert. 'He held an inspection [at Ribemont] one day and it was the funniest inspection I've ever seen. In his cheery, witty way he had everyone rocking with laughter, yet when he wanted the men to do any particular movement, they would move as one man. As time went on our regard for him grew . . . until we just about worshipped him.'[6] However, this was no guarantee that the irascible and easily provoked Jacka would fall into line.

Soon after his return, Jacka was with the men in a billet near the Somme, a commodious barn with tiers of bunks, walls of plastered mud and an earthen floor. Rule overheard one of the new officers asking about the 'retiring-looking chap sitting on a valise' in the corner. Rule looked across. It was Bert Jacka. The new officer was Lieutenant Ernest John Edmonds, a former commercial traveller from St Kilda. A couple of days later Jacka called on Edmonds, and another reinforcement, Lieutenant Herbert Anderson, to accompany him to the 'hopping-off' position for the battalion in their next action. It was important, he said, to familiarise themselves with the terrain prior to the 'stunt'.

As they made their way forward past dugouts and ditches containing reserve units, two fearsome 5.9-inch shells exploded nearby. It was Jacka's first close encounter with enemy shelling since his return to the unit. He turned to the new officers. 'They say a man is never the same after he has been wounded,' he said. Then he grinned, 'I'm damned if I notice the difference.'[7]

However, while Major Peck was generally regarded as a great improvement on Dare, the brigade commander, Charles Brand, remained a thorn in the battalion's side. And Jacka's attitude to him reflected the view held by the men.

In the mud and slush of the front line, diplomacy was at a premium. Jacka was with his platoon in a trench a metre deep in mud when Brand made a 'morale raiser' visit. 'I have great news for you, boys,' he announced. 'I have just received from Division a report that the French attacked last night and captured many thousand prisoners.'

This was received in total silence. They had heard this sort of thing many times before. However, Brand mistook their silence for 'front line deafness' caused by the constant shellfire, and repeated his news.

In the pause that followed, one fed-up digger turned to him. 'Do you think we are winning, sir?'

'Of course I do—am I not telling you what the French did last night?

The digger looked down at the metre of mud in the trench. 'Well, if we're winning, God help the bloody Germans.'[8]

Every time Jacka told the story he roared with laughter.

15

FAIR AND FOUL

After nine days at Ribemont the 14th was withdrawn from the front and marched out to Rainneville, 30 kilometres west of Pozières, where they spent a glorious Christmas. 'We had been promised a good long rest and everyone set themselves to make the most of it,' said Edgar Rule. 'Christmas dinner was something to be remembered—we even got sauce to our pudding.'[1]

This was followed by a sports day organised by Jacka, and the distribution of letter and parcel mail from Australia. Bill Jacka had also returned to the battalion and the two brothers shared their news from home.

The battalion remained in the area, training for both combat and sports competitions against other battalions of the 4th Brigade. Wanliss: 'During these athletic contests all temporarily forgot the war and felt as if they were back in Australia again.'

It was here that Jacka and the recently promoted Colonel Peck made their acquaintance. It was perhaps the most valuable of Jacka's wartime relationships. The battalion commander clearly recognised

Jacka's value as an ally, not only through his influence among the men, but in his raw intelligence and dedication to running an efficient operation. He went out of his way to draw him into his circle.

Peck encouraged all the officers and NCOs to take classes, and Jacka responded to the opportunity. The colonel began a debating society among the officers and made sure Jacka took part. The effect was almost immediate. Jacka found a new understanding and respect for men he had previously regarded as snobs. And as he gained the confidence to express himself in formal debate and informal discussion, a new sense of mutual respect developed.

He found a particular interest in the off-duty activities of Harold Wanliss, who had also returned from hospital in England, and at every opportunity was studying new agricultural methods in the British and French countryside. Some would have application to Australia on his return and the two young men worked closely together, particularly after Wanliss replaced Adjutant Blainey, who was given his own training battalion in England.

Peck simultaneously made Jacka the battalion's intelligence officer. The appointment not only forestalled any concerns Jacka might have that he was being passed over as adjutant, it made the most of his planning skills and those 'shepherding' qualities of childhood that found expression in his determination to minimise casualties among the men.

When asked what he thought of the new commander, Jacka was in no doubt: 'He'll do me,' he said.[2] The feeling was mutual. Peck recommended his 23-year-old intelligence officer for promotion to captain, and the new rank would be confirmed in due course. Moreover, Peck 'kicked Fuhrmann upstairs', recommending him as brigade-major of the 4th Brigade, a promotion that ensured he would thereafter be concerned solely with administration.

Wanliss: 'Under the virile leadership of its new and capable chief, the 14th attained the high-water mark of discipline, efficiency, reputation and contentment.'[3]

On 2 January 1917, they left Rainneville in full marching order for the return journey to Ribemont. After ten days of combat exercises they moved closer to the action at Mametz, a few kilometres behind the Somme battlefield of 1916. The next move, five days later, was south to Bazentin where they did their share of 'fatigue' duty, mostly repairing roads and clearing away the detritus of battle.

On 23 January, two companies of the battalion went forward to take over the reserve line from the 47th Battalion near Fleurs. Jacka accompanied them. As intelligence officer he was entitled to deploy himself in the front line as an observer, gathering background for subsequent 'stunts'. But on this occasion he had a deeper motive—it had been months since he'd faced the enemy in no-man's-land and after the 'shell shock' of Perham Downs he needed to know whether his nerve would stand up under fire.

Leaving the troops in their dugouts at dusk, he made his way forward over the pitted ground. Both sides were securely entrenched. Rifle and machine-gun fire was sporadic but sufficiently threatening to provide a genuine test. After an hour he returned, then made his way back to battalion headquarters. He was satisfied. He later told Rule that when the bullets started flying he 'didn't flinch'.[4] He was ready for battle.

A week later, C Company, under Captain Stewart Hansen, received orders to join a brigade action to capture a position known as Stormy Trench. Two days earlier the 15th Battalion under Colonel Durrant had attacked and captured it at night but ran out of bombs and had to retire before dawn. The Germans moved back in. Now Brand offered Durrant the pick of any company in the brigade to assist. He chose Hansen's unit.

Edgar Rule said, 'It was a high compliment and the boys responded with pleasure. Others have told me how our boys cleaned and oiled their rifles and bombs, and made all preparations to live up to their name as the picked company of the 4th Brigade.'[5]

The night was bitterly cold, 'the sort of night on which a man dreads a wound more than on any other' and, as they moved out, barrages from both sides lit the battlefield and rocked the ground beneath their feet. As Hansen was leading his men in he said, 'Well, the only way to glory is through blood and guts.'

In the rush across the frozen snow towards Stormy Trench, the Australians overwhelmed the defenders with their accurate fire-power; they took the trench with only light casualties. But no sooner had they occupied it than the Germans prepared a counterattack.

Wave after wave of bomb throwers materialised from the darkness in three separate attacks. The 13th Battalion's A Company took the brunt of it, but, led by Captain 'Mad Harry' Murray, they staged their own attack with twenty bomb throwers. On one occasion the company gave up a short section of ground. Murray then rallied his command to take it back.

From midnight to 3 a.m. the Australians kept up the pressure with bombs every time there was movement on the other side. Then, as they spotted preparations for yet another attack, Murray called in the artillery. The German advance collapsed.

Hansen had charge of the right side of the trench, which came under heavy fire. His casualties numbered 95 out of the 120 who started out and at a crucial moment Hansen himself took a hit that ripped his forehead open. He never regained consciousness and died three days later.

However, the Australians remained at their posts and by 8 p.m. that evening Murray's company held the ground and the Germans abandoned all plans to recapture the position. Murray won the VC for his actions and, when he was relieved, Jacka was one of the first to seek him out. The two men would meet again many times and would share a mutual regard throughout their lives.

The 4th Brigade came out of the line after the Stormy Trench fight and retired to Mametz, then to Ribemont, where they settled in to see out the rest of the winter. Haig's great offensive had failed miserably. The positions held by the opposing forces were little changed from those occupied in July 1916. But in the eight months of fruitless battle, hundreds of thousands of young men on both sides had been killed or seriously wounded.

George Mitchell wrote, 'War of attrition! To us it was the last word in ineptitude. The higher command seemed to say, "We will give you three dead British for two dead Germans." Many a long and bitter day was to dawn before the genius of Monash would light the way to victory.'[6]

Behind the scenes, politicians on both sides were raising the possibility of a negotiated peace. But they were quickly drowned out by those who were still confident the war could be won. The German admirals promised to bring Britain to her knees within six months if their U-boats were allowed to 'sink on sight'. Ludendorff, the power behind the compliant Field Marshal Hindenburg, backed them. It was a good tactical decision—soon British shipping would suffer appalling losses—but very bad strategy, since it would undermine the isolationists in America.

In Britain, the new prime minister, Lloyd George, was in no doubt of his capacity to organise the country's war effort. British shipping was put under government control. Labour was directed to munitions factories. Country agricultural committees supervised the growing of foodstuffs. In time, he would single-handedly develop the naval convoy system that would eventually neutralise the U-boat menace. But he was continually at odds with Haig and the army chief of staff, General William Robertson.

From France, Haig trumpeted his certainty that victory was just around the corner. In Paris, the French government declared their confidence in their new commander-in-chief, General Robert Nivelle, who had a plan for a massive Allied offensive in the spring of 1917. With Lloyd George's agreement, Nivelle would be given command of the entire Allied force on the Western Front.

In Russia, supply lines were in chaos and in the capital Petrograd there were food riots. Soon, sections of the military joined in, and when Tsar Nicholas tried to return to the capital from headquarters, railwaymen stopped the train. Faced with widespread mutiny, the tsar accepted his generals' advice and, despite the wails of his wife and courtiers, abdicated the throne in February 1917.

Russia's new rulers—the Council of Workers' and Soldiers' Deputies—promised to wage the war more effectively. For the moment, the leaders of the West were encouraged by the turn of events.

In the United States, President Woodrow Wilson had promised in his re-election campaign of 1916 to keep the United States neutral. However, the German sinking of US shipping and some ham-fisted Teutonic diplomacy in Mexico were about to change his mind. A formal declaration of war against Germany would be made on 6 April 1917.

In Australia, the conscription referendum was lost and Billy Hughes had been expelled by the Labor Party. But he had now formed a new government with the conservative opposition and created the Nationalist Party. Hughes had so identified himself with the war that he assumed the role of the 'Little Digger'. In his view, all thoughts of ending the conflict before total victory were unpatriotic and possibly treasonable.

Meanwhile, in the trenches, George Mitchell was in a philosophical mood. 'Our thoughts of the war were not good company', he wrote,

> though none of us doubted eventual victory, or ever lost his feeling of personal superiority over the enemy. But the human mind, that unexplored and wonderful thing, is full of resource.
>
> When actuality becomes too depressing, it creates for itself a pleasant and romantic dream world. And so, in those nights when time seemed to have halted, bogged too, in this deadly mud, my mind ranged over all the beautiful things I had seen or heard.
>
> Hours would I search for the lilt of a song I had loved, the words of a stirring poem, or to recreate a remembered face. I am convinced that the front-line soldier developed an extraordinary power of appreciation of the beautiful in all its forms. Those naked

hours of watching, enduring in the teeth of man-made horrors, rain, sleet and bitter cold, could leave no man unchanged.[7]

Jacka and the 14th Battalion were taking a break from the horrors and enjoying the relative comfort of their billets at Ribemont where they were stationed through late February and March. The billets—mostly huts and farm sheds—were cheerless, draughty, congested and vermin-infested. The officers' quarters were little better, though not so crowded. However, both officers and men were drawn to the *estaminets*—village cafés that were generally warm and clean and open for most of the night. There they could buy coffee and wine and release the fierce tensions of combat in endless conversation and the mateship they held so dear.

Newton Wanliss said, 'Their discussions were interspersed with the consumption of chips and fried eggs and innumerable cups of coffee, sometimes flavoured with rum. French women are perhaps the world's best cooks and it was generally a woman who presided at the estaminet, which became in reality a soldiers' club.'[8]

Most nights, Colonel Peck led his off-duty officers to a tea room where they discussed the day's activities and did their own share of bonding. These were memorable occasions to all those involved, and Jacka was a regular participant.

Among the local identities was 'Incinerator Kate', a bag lady who kept all her goods in a barrow and whose eccentricities were a perennial source of amusement. However, when the CO's batman, 'Sailor' Day, was caught by the commander taking advantage of her in the officers' quarters, Peck blasted the man up and down the camp.

HMAT *Ulysses*, the ship carrying Jacka and other members of the 4th Brigade to war, just prior to departure on 22 December 1914. Colonel John Monash, who also travelled on the *Ulysses*, would command the 4th Brigade with great distinction and recommend Jacka to be awarded the first Australian VC of the war. The two men would develop strong bonds of respect and friendship. *Courtesy AWM, neg. no. PB1086*

Corporal Jacka VC outside a tent on Mudros Island in the Aegean during the later days of the ill-fated Gallipoli campaign. *Courtesy AWM, neg. no. P02141.003*

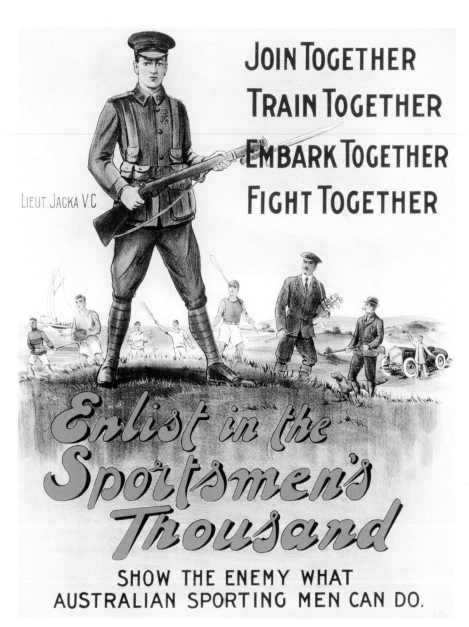

JOIN TOGETHER
TRAIN TOGETHER
EMBARK TOGETHER
FIGHT TOGETHER

LIEUT. JACKA V.C

Enlist in the
Sportsmen's
Thousand

SHOW THE ENEMY WHAT
AUSTRALIAN SPORTING MEN CAN DO.

Government poster using Jacka as a role model in the big recruiting campaign following the award of his VC won in the action at Courtney's Post on 19–20 May 1915. His sporting deeds as a boxer and cyclist helped to create the image of Jacka as the quintessential Australian digger. *Courtesy AWM, neg. no. ARTV00026*

Studio portrait of Second Lieutenant Jacka VC taken in 1916 prior to the battle of Pozières, where he received severe facial injuries. *Courtesy AWM, neg. no. P02939.001*

General Sir William (later Lord) Birdwood, centre, shakes hands with Jacka after presenting him with a Bar to his MC for bravery during the first attack on Bullecourt, near the Hindenburg Line. The ceremony took place at Ribemont. Standing in the background at right is General William Holmes. *Courtesy AWM, neg. no. E00438*

Studio portrait of Captain Harold Wanliss, the son of the 14th Battalion historian, Newton Wanliss. Harold, the much admired former dux of his agricultural college, was a very different character from the relatively uneducated Jacka yet they became good friends. Harold Wanliss was killed in action in September 1917. *Courtesy AWM, neg. no. DASEY1210*

Captain Jacka, holding the map, studies the big model of the Messines area ordered by Monash prior to the Battle of Messines. The next day, 7 June 1917, Jacka would lead his company into battle. *Courtesy AWM, neg. no. E00631*

Major General John Monash at his headquarters in the Villers-Bretonneux sector on 25 May 1918. *Courtesy AWM, neg. no. E02350*

Group portrait of the officers of the 14th Battalion. Left to right, back row: Lt G. Huse, Assistant Adjutant; Lt F. Larter; Lt W. E. Manie; Lt A. King, Lewis Gun Officer; Lt J. H. Johnson MC and Bar, Intelligence Officer (killed in action 2 May 1918); Lt R. Roxburgh; Lt R. Wood (killed in action 4 July 1918). Middle row: Lt F. G. Griffiths; Lt J. Chubb; Padre Rolland MC; Lt Thomas; Lt J. Garcia DCM MM; Lt L. Stevens, Transport Officer; Lt S. Garton DCM; Lt T. H. Griffiths MC; Lt W. Boland MC and Bar; Lt G. Wilson; Lt G. Trewheela MC. Front row: Capt J. Craven DCM, Signals Officer; Lt L. Bain; Capt N. C. Aldridge MC and Bar; Capt C. R. T. Cole MC, Officer Commanding A Company; Major W. R. Wadsworth DCO MC, Officer Commanding C Company; Lieutenant Colonel C. M. Johnstone DSO, Commanding Officer of the Battalion; Capt R. Jones MC MM, Officer Commanding B Company; Capt A. Jacka VC MC and Bar, Officer Commanding D Company; Capt W. Beamond MC; Capt J. A. Mitchell MC, Adjutant; Capt Spargo; Capt R. E. Hayes, Quartermaster. *Courtesy AWM, neg. no. E01725*

Jacka organised the Anzac Sports at the 1st Australian Camp Hospital, Sutton Veny, and is pictured with the Divisional Boxing Champion, believed to be Sergeant Dave Alexander. *Courtesy AWM, neg. no. P00563.001*

Captains Albert (left) and brother Bill Jacka on leave in England in 1919, taken probably just before Bill's wedding to Joan Jacka. By now Albert's facial wounds from the battle of Pozières in 1916 had healed. *Courtesy Port Phillip City Council*

The wedding of Bill and Joan Jacka with Albert as best man, 11 June 1919. *Courtesy Josephine Eastoe*

Framed print of the HMAT *Euripides* that brought Jacka and his compatriots home to Australia in September/October 1919. Jacka's signature is on the far left. *Courtesy AWM, neg. no. P03987.001*

Welcome home party for Jacka at the Clifton Hill house of his maternal aunt and uncle, Mr and Mrs Ted Waldron (standing behind the gate). Jacka's mother Elizabeth is on one side of the gate, slightly turned towards Albert on the other. Brother Sidney is to the right of his mother. *Courtesy Josephine Eastoe*

Vera and Jacka at an official mayoral function on 21 April 1931. *Courtesy Port Phillip City Council*

By now, Jacka had become one of the stalwarts of the debating club. The chaplain, Captain Francis Rolland, had been given charge and the debates were a popular part of the after-hours activity. Hundreds of troops from the surrounding camps attended. Moreover, Peck maintained and expanded his educational program. Jacka was invariably among the first to sign up for the new courses, ranging from hardcore military tactics to the principles of book-keeping.

Then in March, Jacka's captaincy was confirmed. The 24-year-old country boy felt for the first time that he was embarked on a career path that had real possibilities. With senior officers like John Peck to protect the men from the foolish incompetence of 'the heads', the path through the military profession was not just open, it was damned attractive.

Edgar Rule had left the 14th Battalion briefly to work on a light railway behind the lines. It was his way of recalling happier times in sunnier climes. But soon he found himself 'homesick' for the 14th and made his way back to his unit. 'I set out for its camp about 4 p.m., along with another boy who was returning from the hospital,' he wrote. 'Before we left we saw Lt [William] Shirtley of the 13th who told us that we were just in time for the biggest battle that had ever been fought. He was a bit out in his reckoning. But if he had said "the biggest butchering for us" he'd have been right.'[9]

16

'INSPIRATION'

The German High Command had finally reached the conclusion that the best method of attack was defence. The terrain, the weather, but most particularly the machine gun, with its capacity to cut down an advancing enemy in crossfire, had made a mockery of the great offensives on both sides. Time and again, from Gallipoli to Mons to Verdun and the Somme, it was the infantry charging over open territory that suffered the greatest casualties. The old military maxim that defence was 'bad for morale' no longer applied. It was a lesson hard learned but at last it had penetrated the Teutonic consciousness.

Accordingly, Hindenburg and Ludendorff decided to withdraw their forces from the salient they held in the Somme, back to a much more defensible position, celebrated in song as the Siegfried Line but better known to the British as the Hindenburg Line. They did so in the greatest secrecy and it was not until the British made tentative advances on 17 March that the Allies realised the extent and manner of the retreat. The Germans had laid waste to the area, polluting the water supply, destroying the bridges and roads, and levelling the villages.

After a final sports day on 15 March, the 14th prepared for battle. Seven days later, thoroughly rejuvenated by their rest and recreation, they began their advance to the new front line. Wanliss wrote, 'After nine months of the misery and monotony of trench warfare, the battalion seemed to be coming into its own again.'[1]

However, they soon discovered that not only had the Germans smashed the infrastructure in their withdrawal, they had left behind a series of booby traps that would take a heavy toll on the advancing troops. On the night of 29 March, a delayed-action detonator triggered a mine in a roofed stable which had been used as a battalion headquarters, killing five and severely wounding another three. Fortunately, most of the officers and men had left the previous night.

Still they pressed forward, their heavy packs carried ahead in trucks, the men marching to the band playing the battalion's signature tune, 'Swanny River'. On 3 April, as they tramped across open countryside, they were diverted by a flurry of aircraft activity overhead—German planes were attacking Allied observation balloons. Then into the slate-grey sky flew Baron von Richthofen's unmistakable red triplane. Wanliss reported, 'Hundreds of our rifles and machine guns were turned on it.' A wild fusillade echoed across the battlefield. However, it escaped 'to the accompaniment of loud Australian cheers, the admiration and sporting instincts of our men overcoming all political animosity'.[2]

On 7 April the battalion moved into the forward lines at Noreuil, relieving the 51st Battalion, which came under shellfire as they retired. That evening John Peck was called to divisional headquarters to be briefed on the proposed Allied advance, the great Spring Offensive that would mark the beginning of the end of the war.

In two days, British and Canadian units at Arras and Vimy Ridge would engage the enemy to draw off German forces from Nivelle's main attack on the Aisne in the south, scheduled for 16 April. The Australian 4th Division in the north at Bullecourt would also be part of the feint to confuse the enemy about the location of the major French penetration.

The 4th Division was now commanded by an Australian, Major General William Holmes, who had replaced Cox in January after Jacka's hospital visitor suffered a nervous breakdown. Holmes, whose father had been a regular soldier in England and Australia, had joined the NSW 1st Infantry Regiment as a bugler at only ten years of age. In civil life he worked as a public servant, but at the outbreak of the Boer War he enlisted as a commissioned officer and rose to the rank of lieutenant colonel, winning a DSO on the battlefield.

Early in 1915, he commanded the small Australian force that ousted the Germans from their New Guinea colony at Rabaul, and by August he was leading the 5th Infantry Brigade in Gallipoli. There he developed a reputation as a conscientious commander who scouted the battlefield personally before sending in his men. However, his division, under Anzac chief Birdwood, was part of the 5th Army commanded by the British general Hubert de la Poer Gough, who, like his superior, Haig, was frustrated that in this war there seemed no opportunity for a good old cavalry charge.

Gough chafed against his instructions simply to draw the Germans away from the main French advance. This was not the sort of operation that appealed to a man who, against orders, led the relief of Ladysmith in South Africa to the applause of a grateful nation. Nor did it sit easily with his ambitions to replace Haig in the top job.

However, at the divisional command, Peck and Brand were unaware of the personal forces at play among the imperial general staff. They reported that their units were fully prepared and at the peak of their fitness. This was plainly true. All they required was a clear plan of attack from a thoughtful and conscientious high command and they would deliver the best possible outcome. Instead, through mismanagement, hubris, arrogance, vanity, hauteur and bloody-minded incompetence, 'the heads' were about to consign many thousands of eager young men to a needless death.

When Peck returned and briefed his officers, it was apparent to Jacka that the first essential to a successful operation was good intelligence. Accordingly, on 8 April, three days before the opening shots were to be fired, he set out through no-man's-land, alone and lightly armed, to survey the battlefield. He soon discovered that a sunken road 300 metres ahead of the battalion's position had been abandoned by the enemy, which had retreated all the way to the defensive line at Bullecourt. If they moved quickly, the 14th, 16th and 46th battalions could take it unopposed.

He made the case to Peck and Brand who responded immediately, and by nine o'clock that evening, the units had quietly taken up their new position. When the inevitable German barrage took place, the shells would overshoot the brigade. In a single stroke Jacka had saved the lives of many of his comrades. And despite his spectacular feats of combat, this one act would be among his proudest moments.

However, in the annals of the Great War this success paled into insignificance by comparison with the disaster that was about to be visited upon the troops at Bullecourt. On 9 April, Gough was seized by the 'inspiration' to abandon the diversionary role assigned to his 5th Army and instead to attack the massively defended Hindenburg Line itself.

In fact, he decided, he would spearhead the attack with twelve newly arrived British Mark I and Mark II tanks—the modern-day equivalent of a cavalry charge. The tanks were essentially a training squadron. They had never previously been used in combination with an infantry advance. Their armour was vulnerable to relatively light shelling. Their mechanical reliability was in question. Yet he would not only use them in concert with the Australians of the 4th Brigade, he would forgo the covering artillery barrage so as to take the enemy by surprise.

If all that were not enough, the tanks and their half-trained crew would travel all night to reach the rendezvous point, while the Australians would have to remain silent and unseen in the trenches for 24 hours in freezing conditions until they arrived.

The Australian command, from Holmes to Brand and down to Peck, were taken by surprise. When they protested, Gough would brook no resistance and there was no court of appeal. The 14th Battalion's intelligence officer was no less surprised, but his capacity to protest was nullified by the demands for more information about the enemy's disposition. Brand sent him and his counterparts in the 16th Battalion, Lieutenants Bradley and Wadge, to report on the barbed-wire entanglements they would face in the advance.

Typically, Jacka not only reached the first line of wire, he went beyond it to where German patrols were mending and reinforcing it. Leaving the others behind, he narrowly avoided capture by a patrol in an area where some breaks had been made by British artillery. 'How they failed to see me was a puzzle,' he told Edgar Rule later. 'They almost trod on me.' When someone asked if he was afraid, he said, 'Oh no, I was quite calm, because I knew what to do. I was watching them and if they had discovered me I was going to get in among them and shoot the lot before they knew what had happened.'[3]

The second line, he discovered, was almost undamaged and clearly remained an almost impenetrable barrier to the infantry unless hit by a massive barrage. Undoubtedly, it would be a gross impediment to a combined tank and infantry advance.

He returned to his patrol and they made their way back over the churned-up no-man's-land. Jacka went directly to battalion head-quarters to report his findings to Peck. There he discovered Brand and immediately confronted the brigadier with the view that the planned operation was 'pure murder'.[4]

Brand was in a cleft stick. His orders from above brooked no possibility of alteration. Yet now the man he had sent to gather the vital information needed for the operation was telling him it was folly to attempt it. And worse, his battalion commander had every confidence in Jacka's military judgement. Brand hesitated. The Jacka he confronted was no longer the brusque, monosyllabic fighting man of Gallipoli and even Pozières, but a newly eloquent and assertive captain whose personal courage was legendary.

It may well be that Jacka had made his points too forcefully, that he had backed the brigadier into a corner and threatened his personal authority. He may well have won the debate, but in doing so, lost the argument. Brand turned to the other members of the patrol. Since they had not accompanied Jacka through the wire, they could not be as positive about the state of the second line of entanglement. Brand grasped this straw and ordered that the operation proceed as scheduled. Jacka stormed out. Peck had no choice but to fall into line.

Still furious at the rebuff, Jacka, with Bradley in tow, returned to no-man's-land at 2.15 a.m. to lay down tapes that would provide his men with their jumping-off point when the tanks arrived and they assembled for the attack. If he couldn't stop the engagement, at least he could ensure everything possible was done to minimise casualties.

They were almost finished when he spied two Germans heading directly for the markers they had just put down. Bradley was too far away to see his signal and the enemy soldiers were themselves so separated that he couldn't risk taking one without the other escaping to raise the alarm. So he slipped back in the darkness until he found a Lewis gunner and together they circled the pair who had now come together.

Jacka rose behind them, his revolver at the ready. 'Halt!' he shouted. The two men stopped momentarily and he could now see that one had a cane—it was an officer accompanied by his orderly. The officer stood his ground then made to leave. Jacka pulled the trigger, but the revolver misfired. The German orderly raised his rifle, but before anyone else could move, Jacka covered the five metres between them and knocked the man down. Then he pushed both men roughly towards the Allied lines. 'Get moving!'

They had only covered a few metres when another German patrol loomed from the darkness. The officer hung back, but before he could make a sound Jacka cracked him on the side of the head. He gave no further trouble.

When they reached battalion headquarters, the officer complained to Peck that he had been roughly treated. The colonel smiled. 'You may not know the identity of your captor,' he said, 'but you can count yourself bloody lucky to be alive.'[5]

Just before midnight, Jacka joined his A Company in the field for the interminable wait for the tanks. Soon snow began to fall. George Mitchell was in a trench nearby. He later wrote:

> By the edge of a ploughed field we lay in our rows, dark blots in the snow. My [Lewis] gun rested on its bipod, snout raised as if snuffing the battle. The moon went under a snow-cloud and the falling flakes made into white heaps the line of prone forms. Cold in the snow-laden wind we lay, hoping for the order to advance.
>
> Away on the left, artillery pounded heavily, but ahead and behind us might have been dead polar regions for all the sign of life we could see or hear. A light rocketed up, perilously close. Four Maxims commenced to jabber fiercely and strings of bullets hissed overhead. Lady Death was ready to take the stage.[6]

But then all movement died away and soon dawn streaked the sky, and the snow cloaked the battlefield with its pristine beauty. Adjutant Harold Wanliss could be seen hurrying from the direction of headquarters. His message flashed around the battalions: the tanks were held up; the attack was cancelled.

His father wrote, 'Cold, cramped and stiff, feeling the reaction after being keyed up for hours to a concert pitch of expectation, all started back to the Noreuil Valley cursing the tanks and everybody connected with them. The bungling that had resulted in this grotesque fiasco was evident to everyone and confidence in the higher leadership was badly shaken.'[7]

17

BUTCHERING AT
BULLECOURT

The Germans facing the 4th Brigade had a perfect view of the hundreds of dark figures suddenly rising from the earth and tramping back across the white background. They resisted the temptation to mount a barrage—far better to use the intelligence so handily obtained. If the area around Bullecourt was to be the point of attack, that was fine. They had reserves aplenty. They would be waiting.

In fact, they would not have to wait long. Almost incredibly, General Gough ordered that the attack be carried out the next night. And once again it would be without the protection of an artillery barrage. 'Surprise' was still the keynote of the occasion.

John Peck vigorously protested but to no avail.[1] It is doubtful whether his view went beyond Brand. At general headquarters, Birdwood objected that the tanks were unreliable. Gough responded with the assertion that experience had shown that '75 per cent' of accompanying troops would reach the enemy lines. Holmes's view is not recorded, but the fact that the issue was referred up the line to Haig suggests that he too opposed it.

Haig backed his fellow cavalry officer. A formal order was issued at 11.15 p.m. and the 4th Brigade's battalion commanders met at midnight to make final preparations. The exhausted troops who had spent half the second night lying out in the snow were again ordered forward.

Without waiting for orders, Jacka once again made his way alone into the forward area where he had laid the tapes the night before. They were covered with snow and he ran and crawled the length of them, passing them through his hands to bring them to the surface. Then came the growl of tank engines and everyone looked in their direction. So much for Gough's 'surprise'.

George Mitchell said,

We saw the tanks over on our right—big black blurs outlined sharply against the snow. They lined up and moved forward, slowly. They would stop, move on, then stop again. Their exhausts flared red in the night. Their droning noise aroused the German lines. Big shells smashed among us. Our platoon commander, Caldwell, got it first. Others staggered back looking like snowmen save where the blood showed black.[2]

Out among the tanks there was no one with overall authority since the Tank Corps was independent of the Australian command. Jacka solved this problem by taking charge himself. It was an extraordinary act, stepping outside the chain of command to meet a totally unforeseen situation. In doing so, he exposed himself to rapidly growing fire from the German lines. But without his initiative the battle would have quickly descended into chaos.

He began assigning the leviathans their positions on the tape among the two forward battalions of the brigade. Ignoring the sniper fire, he walked ahead of the first arrival, placing it in front of the 16th Battalion, then arranged two others in front of the 14th. However, the commander of the fourth would not listen. In the imbroglio that followed, the tank became hopelessly bogged, the crew abandoned it and Jacka threatened to shoot them all on the spot. They ran for cover and were not seen again until after the battle.

Jacka reported to Peck at 3 a.m. that even if he were able to position the three additional tanks that had just arrived, the creaking monsters 'could not traverse no man's land in the time allotted'.[3] The infantry would reach the German wire well before the tanks. The result would be catastrophic.

Peck concurred, but what was the alternative? Jacka urged him to go over Brand's head and contact Major General Holmes. Peck accepted the charge and sent a message to divisional headquarters. Holmes responded at 3.40 a.m.: there was no choice—the plan must go ahead as scheduled.

Once again Jacka returned to the front lines to position the last of the tanks. By now the air was thick with machine-gun fire. George Mitchell saw 'a fierce panorama—on the right flank a gas-wave was billowing over the German lines. Showers of sparks rose out of the gas cloud as enemy countering shells fell.'[4]

It was 4.17 a.m. as Jacka struggled to place the final tank in position and give them their objectives. Almost immediately the German guns found their range and high-explosive shells fell around them.

The tank crews began to panic and one loosed off shells in the wrong direction, cutting down some Australian infantry.

A German shell exploded between Jacka and his assistant intelligence officer, Lieutenant Harry McKinley, who was mortally wounded. Jacka was blown off his feet but was otherwise unharmed. Finally at 4.45 a.m. the 14th Battalion went over the top on schedule, Jacka among the leaders.

Edgar Rule wrote:

> The Hun commenced to put up lights and during one lot that lit up the place like day, I saw a sight that I'll never forget. Advancing along the side of the spur as if they were on parade, with their rifles held at the high port, was a line of our boys. There were gaps, and in one or two places big spaces. With such intense machine gun fire, there was no need to inquire what was happening.[5]

The Germans were waiting for them. The German riflemen allowed them to almost reach the wire before they opened up. The tanks were worse than useless and soon the infantry had no protection. Jacka's report on the entanglement proved all too accurate. It was 25 metres deep and rose to a man's waist with razor-sharp cutting edges. Men were blown to pieces by the torrential force of the machine-gun fire, their body parts piling up against and within the wire. Wave after wave of young men flung themselves at the barrier.

Some made it through and they savaged the German defenders. Jacka himself waited for the last wave at 5 a.m. and fifteen minutes later sent a message back to Peck that the first trenches had been taken. For the first time the Australians had penetrated the Hindenburg Line.

Jacka left the fighting momentarily and reported back to Peck. Not only was the first trench in Australian hands, the second had also fallen. But the tanks were gone and casualties were too heavy for the advance to be sustained. Three of the four battalion company commanders had been killed. The situation was desperate.

Peck and Jacka contacted Brand, who ordered a barrage into the defenders' lines. However, confusion reigned among the artillery observers and the barrage was not forthcoming. In the trenches, Jacka's mate, Harry Murray VC, rallied his men and sent yet another message seeking artillery support. Brand appealed to Birdwood, but he refused to overrule the artillery officer, Lieutenant Colonel Reginald Rabett, who insisted his observers had spotted Australians well beyond the Hindenburg Line.

Jacka rejoined his men as the Germans counterattacked with bombs. For six hours the Australians held their own, but as their ammunition ran out they were forced to retreat.

In the Joan of Arc battalion, George Mitchell was in the thick of the fighting. With 60 men, his unit was the last to leave the Hindenburg Line. 'Back to the old front line,' called an officer as a bloodied messenger raced in. Mitchell swung his gun onto his shoulder and prepared to leave the dugout. He wrote, 'A dead sergeant still lay massive on the parapet. Other dead lay limp on the trench floor. Wounded sprawled or sat with backs to the parapet, watching us with anxious eyes. "You are not going to leave us?" asked one of them. I could not answer him or meet his eyes as I joined the party moving down the sap.'[6]

Murray shouted the order, 'Everyone for himself.' According to Edgar Rule,

There were lots who never heard it and fought on until surrounded by Huns who came in on them from rear and sides. Those who tried to break away were killed like flies. Numbers leapt out and lay in shell-holes until darkness set in, but those who lay doggo too close to the German lines were collected by Hun patrols and sent back to Germany. Of course, there were no end of wounded . . .[7]

The 4th Brigade had been shattered. The stragglers slumped back into the original front lines, and in the afternoon the 13th Brigade relieved them. They had attacked with a force of 3000 young men; they had sustained 2339 casualties. The whole 4th Division was crippled as a fighting force for the next three months.

The 14th Battalion survivors assembled behind the lines to march the 8 kilometres to Beaugnetre. Wanliss wrote, 'There has seldom been a more melancholy march. It was snowing all the time; officers and men had had two successive nights without sleep; and had just survived a bloody and disastrous battle. Everyone was absolutely exhausted and it was only by the greatest effort of will that the destination was finally reached.'[8]

In retrospect, Wanliss called the battle 'the most disastrous, the most bloody, yet perhaps the most glorious day in the history of the 4th Brigade'. After two sleepless nights, four Australian battalions with only rifles and hand bombs to defend themselves advanced more than a kilometre over completely open country under hellish frontal and enfilade fire, forced their way through a nightmarish wire entanglement and seized the famous Hindenburg Line. Then, despite being cut off from reinforcements or assistance of any kind, they held it for seven hours, repelling repeated enemy counterattacks backed by powerful artillery.

'Bullecourt', Wanliss wrote, 'will ever remain an imperishable monument to the heroism, the fortitude and the unflinching hardihood, of the Australian race.'[9] And no one had contributed more to the battle than Jacka and Murray.

Rule recalled, 'The tramp out that night was a heart-breaker. We were robbed of almost every ounce of energy by the thick mud that we had to get over, even before reaching the road.'[10]

When they arrived at Beaugnetre, acting quartermaster Lieutenant Anderson had hot tea and sandwiches ready. 'For those who wanted rum, there was plenty,' Rule said. 'In the AIF the rule was, no rum before a fight; the rum was given afterwards when the boys were deadbeat. But this feast looms as one of the best I ever had. Standing out in the open and with a couple of old lanterns to drive away the blackness of the night, we fairly gorged ourselves like beasts. It was just on twenty-four hours since anyone had had a hot meal.'[11]

When they had eaten they were told to continue down the road for about a kilometre to the camp where they threw themselves down and slept until well into the next day. 'In the afternoon we were formed up and marched into Bapaume,' Rule said. 'All that was left of our battalion was here now and, as the little handful marched by, Brigadier-General Brand and the C.O., Colonel Peck, were sobbing like little schoolgirls, the tears running down their faces. The pick of our battalion was gone and it was a long time before our unit recovered from this blow.'

Jacka marched beside the men all the way. Rule noted, 'For the good work he did at this stunt he received a bar to his M.C. Most of us considered that it should have been a bar to his V.C.' In fact, after the war Brand said he recommended Jacka for a VC but it was declined 'because VCs are rarely awarded when enterprises fail'.

In his 'Some Reminiscences', Harry Murray wrote, 'I was given a bar to my DSO. Birdwood personally told me it would have been a bar to my VC had we won the battle.'[12]

18

TANK ATTACK

In the wake of Bullecourt there was a terrible bitterness directed towards General Gough from the Australian camp but no public recriminations whatever. He continued to command the 5th Army and Haig called him 'one of my best officers'. When Birdwood addressed the remnants of the 4th Brigade in a speech that Wanliss called 'peculiarly misappropriate',[1] he was heard in stony silence. Edgar Rule said, 'Not a word did he utter in condemnation of those in higher authority, but it was plain to me that he shrank from being contaminated by the bloody fiasco.'

In fact, 'Birdy' was almost as culpable as Gough and Haig for permitting the attack to go forward under conditions that virtually guaranteed the Australians would be massacred. He escaped the survivors' most violent censure only because of his willingness to face them man to man. 'Boys, I can assure you that none of your own officers had anything to do with the arrangements for the stunt,' he said.[2] But even that was not true. Jacka knew that his failed confrontation with Brand had a significant impact on the outcome, and the relationship between the two men would never recover.

Moreover, everyone knew that the reason the brass were so niggardly with the subsequent decorations was that no one wanted to be seen rewarding a defeat, even though the acts of gallantry under fire were no less worthy than those of a victory. However, while the staff officers might gloss over the appalling misjudgements and high-handed stupidity, Jacka would not.

His reaction was twofold. He had been engaged first hand with the new tank weapons and while they had been an unmitigated disaster, he recognised that properly handled they could become a very effective addition to the battlefield armoury. He decided to write a report and he was not about to excuse the attitude and actions of the tank crews. When the battalion withdrew to its old 'home' at Ribemont he set about writing a 'Special Report on the Tank Operation in Attack Nights of 10/11'.[3]

Its description of the Tank Corps could hardly have been more scathing. 'The tank co-operation in the attack made on the Hindenburg Line on the night of 10–11th April, 1917, was useless, or worse than useless,' he opened.

Then he unloaded both barrels.

Tanks were late in arriving at rendezvous, which meant they were late in getting to the jumping off place. In fact, only three reached the latter place at all.

Of the six tanks allotted to the brigade, five reached the rendezvous; one being out of action before that place was reached. Of the five: One, disregarding guidance [from himself], tried to cross a deep, sunken road, and in consequence got in and could not get out again. A second one was out of action through engine trouble before jumping off place was reached, leaving three only to co-operate in the attack.

The tank crews seemed to know little or nothing of an attack by infantry, or nothing whatever about the particular operation they were to participate in. For instance: In the case of No 2 tank, the tank commander had not even synchronised his watch, his time being five minutes behind time as given to the infantry. Further: Tank crews did not even know the direction of the enemy. This is verified by the fact that they opened fire on our troops, thereby causing us many casualties. One tank in particular opened fire on our men at jumping off place, killing four and wounding others.

The organisation seemed to be bad and no one appeared to be in direct command of the show. This was shown by the fact that tanks wandered aimlessly about in every direction, thereby drawing enemy fire on us and on all our trenches.

One tank only reached the objective and did good work, but was almost immediately put out of action by direct hits from a gun in Riencourt. Commanders and crews of other tanks seemed to make no effort to reach their objectives and although [some] tanks were in no way damaged, even after the attack was well under way and tanks could have given great assistance in helping to connect up betweeen us and the brigade on our left, they made no effort to go forward, and wandered back, moving along the front of our jumping off place and finally pulling up alongside one of our dressing stations. Other tanks which had made no effort to get up to their objectives were found in various places on fire, although they had not been hit by shells.

One crew in particular, [when] asked why they had vacated their tank, stated that it had caught fire, but gave no reason for same. This same crew returned carrying two sandbags, one containing enamelware and the other food. Personal safety and comfort seemed to be their sole ambition.

Another crew was asked why they did not go forward to help clear a communication trench. They replied, 'They had no officer so could not do so'. This showed a great lack of initiative and that the whole affair, so far as this tank was concerned, to be the responsibility of one man, and that man gone; the tank could do no more though undamaged.

One tank returned almost to Reserve Battalion Headquarters, pulled up right on the skyline and in full view of Bullecourt, thereby making a splendid aiming mark and drawing severe enemy gun fire which made the route very dangerous for troops.

The whole outfit showed rank inefficiency and in some cases tank crews seemed to lack British tenacity and pluck, and that determination to go forward at all costs, which is naturally looked for in Britishers.

Having thoroughly damned the Tank Corps as represented by Bullecourt bunglers, Jacka then offered a more positive view. 'In my opinion,' he wrote,

manned by the bravest of crews and placed directly under infantry officers concerned in operation, they would be of great help. But they should never be relied upon as the sole arm of support in an attack by infantry. Further, when tanks are being got into position, we think it absolutely necessary that a heavy barrage be put up by our guns to deaden the sound of the tanks.

In our case, not a shot was fired when tanks were taking up their position, and so the whole operation was given away to the enemy.

He signed the report and presented it to Colonel Peck.

In the military bureaucracy, Jacka's report was the hottest of hot potatoes. It not only charged the tank crews with cowardice and dereliction of duty under fire, it called into question the whole foolish enterprise. Gough's 'inspiration' had not only led to the unnecessary exposure of Australian troops to enemy fire and contributed to a disastrous defeat, the tanks had actually killed four men and wounded others. If accepted, Jacka's charges could only lead to court martials and the exposure of Gough's (and Haig's) appalling blunder.

John Peck, no doubt with some misgiving, forwarded it up the line. When it reached the senior Australian commander, Major General Holmes, he forwarded it to Birdwood and Gough with the official report on the battle but in a separate 'secret dispatch'. The corps intelligence officer passed it to Gough, whose reaction was predictable. He ordered that the report 'should not enter the record'.[4]

According to the Australian general H. E. 'Pompey' Elliott, writing after the war, 'General Birdwood ordered that Jacka's report should be expunged from the records of the AIF and Jacka himself was thence onward systematically ignored both in regard to decorations and promotions.'[5]

However, both Elliott and later General Monash were privy to the report. Monash in particular would put all its recommendations into practice when devising his meticulously coordinated plans for a new form of offensive in 1918, one that combined all the offensive elements of warfare.

Other voices were later raised against the perpetrators of the Bullecourt disaster. Murray called it Gough's 'worst stunt' and attacked him for 'the use of unproven tanks, an infantry assault without artillery . . . and under-estimating the enemy'.[6]

Charles Bean was scathing in his denunciation of Gough:

With almost boyish eagerness to deliver a death blow, the army commander broke, at every stage through, rules recognised even by platoon commanders.

When, despite impetuous efforts, he was unable to bring forward his artillery and ammunition in time to cut the wire, he adopted, on the spur of the moment, a scheme devised by an inexperienced officer of an experimental arm [the tanks], and called the attack on again for the following morning.

Finally, after the tanks on the first trial had confirmed the worst fear of his subordinates, he insisted on repeating the identical operation the next day. Within two hours of the attack being delivered, every one of his impetuous predictions [sic] were being paid for by the crushing of the magnificent force which had been given to him to handle.[7]

However, these criticisms were made after the war. By contrast, Jacka stood ready for a confrontation with 'the heads' if called upon to justify his stance. He demanded the same level of dedication and efficiency from those above him as those he commanded. He was outraged at the needless death of so many comrades. But, as loved ones in Australia mourned the terrible loss of sons, husbands and brothers, the damning report simply disappeared. In the rarefied circles of the imperial staff, Jacka's cry of anguish and rage on their behalf was smothered.

No one to whom it was addressed ever responded to the report, at least not to Jacka's face. However, it is clear that his charges stung, and from that moment the attitude of the senior commanders towards him changed abruptly.

Where once he had been paraded before visiting VIPs as the exemplar of the Australian fighting man, where promotion through the ranks followed a steady path towards ever higher responsibility and command, and where every act of outstanding valour produced yet more honour and decoration, now a new perception was brought to bear from above. He was the lone wolf, the individualist who bucked the system and accused his superiors of gross incompetence.

It simply would not do.

On 16 April, Nivelle's main thrust against the German lines took place on schedule. It was a monumental disaster. The Germans were once again perfectly placed to inflict heavy losses on the advancing force. On this occasion a French sergeant major had been captured with all the details of Nivelle's plan in his possession. The Germans moved up fresh troops; the French went forward and into the arms of George Mitchell's 'Lady Death'.

By the evening, the French had advanced 500 metres instead of the 10 kilometres Nivelle had promised. The defenders simply tore the French lines to pieces, and all Nivelle could offer in response was more of the same. For two weeks, he threw the flower of France into the German guns until finally the army revolted. Soon 54 divisions were refusing to obey orders. At the end of April he was fired.

His successor as commander-in-chief, Henri Pétain, was from the other military extreme. Long an apostle of the defensive, his guiding slogan was, 'We must wait for the Americans and the tanks.'

It is highly unlikely that the new French commander ever saw Jacka's disquisition on tank warfare. But by then the author was concerned with new imperatives. The battalion was rebuilding itself. Promotions were notified, including a commission for Edgar Rule and, over at the Joan of Arc battalion, George Mitchell, who won the Distinguished Conduct Medal and rose from lance corporal to second lieutenant in a single bound. Jacka was not promoted, but at least John Peck ensured he was given command of D Company, to the unabashed delight of his men.

The second Anzac Day was celebrated with due ceremony—a church parade in the morning and later a battalion sports competition, once again organised by Jacka. It was a lively affair made much the more so by the sudden appearance of Incinerator Kate pushing her barrow at top speed through the battalion athletes with another French virago in hot pursuit. The lady chasing Kate (whose shawl was pulled tightly over her head and tucked under her chin, her jacket cinched by a piece of string around the waist, and whose skirt jutted like a tutu) was similarly arrayed except that she wielded a lump of firewood that she threatened to break over Kate's broad rump. The athletes stopped and stared, then roused their favourite to greater effort. Faster and faster went the wheelbarrow; but the firewood gained steadily.

Edgar Rule joined in the rising laughter. 'The driver of the barrow suddenly tripped and went headlong,' he said, 'clothes well up to the waist, revealing a dirty pair of khaki breeches. Then the billet of wood came into its own. Several of us were standing yarning to Bert Jacka and I thought he would never recover from his laughter.'[8]

However, when the hubbub settled, Jacka said to Rule, 'You and [Second Lieutenant Lloyd] Gill come over and have tea with us,' and led the way to the officers' mess.

Inside, he welcomed the newly commissioned duo. 'This is the first time we have had the pleasure of entertaining you newlyweds, and I wish to welcome you to the brotherhood,' he said. 'In being chosen by Colonel Peck to fill the places of those who have gone out, you have been given a great responsibility. It's a great battalion; let us see to it that we make it greater. That's all I have to say; spread yourselves and make yourselves at home.'

'That's right,' chipped in one of his subalterns, 'spread yourselves but don't make yourselves at home with the skipper's girl. That's all I have to say.' Jacka picked up a haversack and threw it at the speaker's head while the mess joined in the laughter.[9]

Later Rule wrote that the girl in question was the little schoolmistress of the village:

She was pretty, clever, and had a charming personality to which her broken English added charm. Jacka and several of his officers were billeted in her home, and so they saw a great deal of her. One had only to sit around and watch the hungry glances cast in the girl's direction to see the intense attraction she had for them. However, she was a good judge of men, for she kept them all at arm's length and reserved her eyes and smiles for Bert.

But Jacka was in love with his Company. Not many of us looked forward to fighting, but we all knew Jacka's ambition. He was longing for the day when he could lead D Company into battle.

He would get his wish, sooner than expected.

19

WITH MONASH AGAIN

On 7 March, John Monash, now head of the 3rd Division in II Anzac Corps, was called before his British commander, General Herbert Charles Onslow Plumer, a squat figure with a ruddy face and white moustache. Plumer's rather comical appearance belied a man whose dealings were characterised by an iron will and a meticulous attention to detail, traits he shared with Monash.

They also shared a wariness of men like Haig and Gough with their propensity for the cavalry dash, and in Plumer's case the aversion was reciprocated. On several occasions, Haig had threatened to remove him. However, Plumer now had charge of an operation that, it was hoped, would bring an end to the reverses suffered by the Allied troops, and he had selected Monash to help him plan it. The objective was the capture of a vital strategic feature of the Western Front, the Messines Ridge, which commanded the heights of the area around the battered Flanders town of Ypres, 25 kilometres north of Armentières, the defensive base of Monash's division.

The Allied force, backed by the British IX and X Corps, would

171

also include three other divisions in the front line—the New Zealanders, the British 25th and the Australian 4th Division. Monash and Jacka would be back in harness again. It was a prospect that Jacka, the newly minted company commander, relished. Monash was the one 'head' he could genuinely respect.

Jacka's comrades at arms were less enthusiastic. Edgar Rule said, 'Somewhere about the end of April we had a big divisional parade and march past. General Birdwood said goodbye to us as we were being sent away from the I Anzac Corps to operate with the II Anzac Corps up at Messines. This is where the 4th Division had such a rough spin. The rest of the Aussie divisions were allowed to rest until the Passchendaele battle came on in September, but we were kept hard at it.' Rule consoled himself that 'the heads' had promised that once this stunt was over they would be given a decent rest.[1]

However, even Jacka was 'knocked for six' when suddenly in May, Colonel Peck was transferred and promoted to Monash's staff in the 3rd Division. Wanliss wrote, 'Regret at his departure was universal.'[2] For Jacka it was doubly so when his temporary replacement was announced as the reluctant warrior, Major Otto Fuhrmann.

This was Brand's decision, and Jacka believed he had been wrongly passed over. The sense of injustice permeates the attitudes of those closest to him, such as Edgar Rule and his brother Bill. It is not known whether he confronted the brigadier personally, though it would have been perfectly in character, but in any case it was unsuccessful. After the war, Brand would write, 'A company under his leadership was as good as an extra battalion to me in a scrap.'[3] But whether he preferred a battalion commander who would take orders without question, or whether he received the signal from above that Jacka would not be acceptable, Brand took the path of least resistance.

Monash planned so meticulously that by the middle of May he called the massive operational battle plan—by now some 15 centimetres thick—his 'Opus Magnum'. It contained notes on farms in the area, ruins, rivers and all other significant geographical features. The German defences, ascertained from reconnaissance flights, were covered in the minutest detail, from wire entanglement to mortar emplacement, gun-pit, signal station, machine-gun post, dump, buried cable, tramway and trench. Then he ordered the building of battlefield models 10 metres across which he allowed unit commanders—right down to company and platoon level—to study prior to the opening salvo scheduled for 7 June.

However, the key to success was a ploy that appealed directly to Monash's engineering background—teams of tunnellers were working non-stop to undermine the ridge and pack some 130,000 pounds (nearly 60,000 kilograms) of explosive charge beneath the German stronghold. It was perhaps the greatest man-made explosion then devised. Much of the work fell to the 1st Australian Tunnelling Company.

On 15 May, the 14th Battalion in Ribemont entrained for Bailleul and, on arrival next morning, marched the 12 kilometres to their farm billets at Doulieu, where they began an intensive training regime for the battle ahead. General Plumer himself visited the area and met the battalion commanding officers at 4th Brigade headquarters. The 14th—with its VC winner prominent—was selected for him to inspect, and he pronounced himself suitably impressed.

Only now did the officers and men learn that Messines was to be the objective of the next front-line action. Jacka led the other company commanders to one of the battlefield models set up at headquarters. He spent hours at the site and made his own detailed notes for later study.

He had still not come to terms with being passed over in favour of Otto Fuhrmann, but consoled himself that the appointment was only temporary. He still had a chance to become the permanent replacement for Peck, who had fast become one of Monash's most valued staffers.

However, just before they were due to go into action, the news broke. Fuhrmann was dropped to 2-I-C, but his replacement could hardly have been more insulting to Jacka and offensive to the men of the 14th. Major Eliazar Margolin of the 16th Battalion (which the 14th disdained) had been born in central Russia 42 years previously and in 1901 emigrated to Perth, where he became a merchant. He had never properly mastered the English language and the men were quick to mock him. Indeed, when they were resting beside the road as the 16th marched by to the accompaniment of their lively band, one wit from the 14th called out, 'Give us your band and we'll give you back your bloody Russian.'[4]

For the moment, Jacka kept his feelings to himself. There was a battle to be fought. In the ten days before the scheduled start, Monash had sent out raiding parties to keep the Germans off balance. He had circulated propaganda stories of German ill-treatment of Allied prisoners to fire the blood of his own troops. He then used his tried and true call to arms among the Australians: 'Fight for yourself, Australia and the British Empire.' But he knew the greatest incentive he could give them was the prospect of victory. And if, after the recent reverses under Gough, he could succeed at Messines, Monash knew the Anzacs would follow him anywhere.

At 3.10 a.m. on 7 June, almost 100,000 men were lined up along a 12-kilometre front, the 4th Brigade containing Jacka's company on the extreme left flank and behind the New Zealanders. The artillery began its barrage, but no sooner had the guns sounded across Flanders than the 23 mines in the massive charge exploded with a shock wave that reached London itself. Even before the sound died away the 3rd Division went over the top and charged a German defensive force that was already broken and bewildered.

Over the next 24 hours the 3rd Division, followed by the New Zealanders, moved into the German trenches and consolidated their positions. Lieutenant George Mitchell wrote, 'Most of the fire came from the flank of the attack making the Australian front probably the hottest part of the line. Almost hourly it seemed that new guns, heavy and of light velocity were joining the fray. The peculiar snarling note of their shells seemed to dominate the land.'[5]

Then on 9 June, the 14th moved into the front line, relieving the 50th Battalion and other units. Jacka's D Company and B Company under Captain Reg Jones were ordered to head the advance. By now the Germans had retreated but left behind machine-gunners and snipers to impede the Allied thrust. Mitchell said, 'With darkness came our relief. Captain Jacka V.C., coldly efficient, came up with a bunch of men and took over from us.'[6]

The next day Jacka and Jones left their men in the trenches and personally reconnoitred the area ahead. Jacka spotted several machine-gun positions and decided to deal with them after nightfall.

As he returned he was walking along the top of the trench inspecting his men, oblivious to the sporadic gunfire coming from the German positions. A relative newcomer to the battalion, a big, strapping private named Bill Dawe, was crouching in the trench with his corporal, Bill Boyce, as Jacka passed.

Boyce asked him to get down into the trench. 'It's much safer down here, sir.'

'Don't worry,' Jacka replied, 'if they're going to get you, they'll get you wherever you are.'

Just then a burst of machine-gun bullets swished over the top of the trench. Dawe reached up and grabbed Jacka by the legs and pulled him in. As he hit the bottom, Dawe said, 'We can't afford to lose you, sir.'

For a moment Jacka bridled, then he nodded and set off down the trench. 'You shouldn't have manhandled the skipper like that,' said the corporal. Dawe responded, 'I'd give my life for that man as easily as I'd give you a cigarette.'[7]

That night the patrols went out but returned without eliminating the German rearguard. So at 11 p.m., with Jacka and Jones again in the lead, the two companies set out across the pitted, sloppy, wintry landscape as artillery and flares from both sides lit the scene. Under small-arms fire, they progressed from one vague feature to another, shooting at shadows and at times engaging knots of German defenders.

By morning the shelling had ceased and the two companies seemed to have the battlefield to themselves. Orders from brigade headquarters urged caution and consolidation. However, that was not Jacka's way. So once again he and Jones left their commands in the line and pushed forward in broad daylight reconnoitring the territory ahead. Jacka brought his men up and established forward posts at least half a kilometre ahead of the so-called 'green line' that had been the previous Allied objective. Then he contacted the British units on his left, bringing them forward to correspond to his own advance.

In case of counterattack, he established defensive posts on two farms—Deconinck and Delporto—then ranged outposts ahead of them, all the time coordinating with Jones, who had gone forward about 500 metres to reconnoitre a farmhouse then returned with his men, occupied it, cleared the area of snipers, and took over three abandoned German field guns. He, too, set up outposts ahead of his defensive line.

They held their positions for the next 24 hours before they were relieved. Wanliss said, 'The unit's work had been not only clean, crisp and efficient, but of a distinctly high order. The Corps Commander sent a congratulatory message.'[8]

The battalion CO, Major Margolin, in his best English expression, immediately recommended Jacka for yet another decoration.

He had a patrol out into hostile area, successfully drove back several snipers who were harassing our lines, seized a Machine Gun and occupied Deconinck Farm and returned to his main line. This he improved and after arranging co-operation with the British forces on left he established a strong line of outposts and occupied 600 yards in front of 'green line'. He send back most lucid and comprehensive information and throughout displayed his usual coolness and judgement.

Margolin's commendation for Reg Jones was in almost identical terms. However, when the honours were posted, Jones was awarded a Military Cross. Jacka received nothing. Clearly, coming on top of being passed over for the battalion command, it was a fierce blow. A little over a month ago, working in close harmony with John Peck, Jacka could see the way ahead as a professional soldier, making his way up the ladder of command and in a game that appreciated his special talents on the battlefield. Now, it seemed, he'd been knocked down from behind by an unseen opponent and there was no referee to intervene on his behalf, no natural justice in prospect, no one to whom he could appeal.

20

REBELLION

The battalion remained in the line and in reserve over the weeks ahead. Behind the lines the men were often on fatigue, working in shifts to clear away empty shells, and during off-duty hours many made their way to Bailleul, where the French wine was cheap and the rum freely available.

One afternoon, one of Jacka's men returned half-tanked and full of fight. He threw a few punches at some imagined slight and men began to gather. 'Jacka was one of the few who kept away,' Rule wrote. 'Although he was a staunch Rechabite, he was never hard on those who warmed their bellies with rum. What was more, he loved a joke and providing that men were good soldiers in the line, he turned a blind eye to their failings when out of it.'[1]

On this occasion, however, matters were getting out of hand. Jacka made his way through the crowd. 'What's all this about?'

The pugnacious pugilist identified himself. 'Well, Nugget,' Jacka responded, 'you can have what you like. Either come up before me in the morning, or else take me on now for a few rounds.'

Rule said, 'Nugget was in a dilemma. He did not want to fight Jacka—not that he was afraid, but it wasn't quite the thing—when a titter from the crowd settled it.'

'Come on now, make a ring,' said Jacka and in no time they were at it. Rule reported the brief proceedings. 'Whack, whack, whack. The crowd kept murmuring, "Oh, no."' Nugget soon lost interest in a fistic career. Jacka pointed to the billets. 'Off you go and have a sleep. You'll get all the fighting you want in the near future.'

Rule noted, 'Of course, it is not every officer that could do this sort of thing—perhaps there was not another that could fight with one of his men and preserve his dignity. But Jacka was . . . well, just Jacka.'

On one of his forays into no-man's-land, Jacka was hit in the leg by a sniper and he was shipped out briefly to London for treatment. There he was called upon to give evidence to the Dardanelles Commission inquiring into the Gallipoli disaster. Asked his opinion on the landing, he responded with his usual vigour. 'If at any time the arrangements made did not prove sufficient', he said, 'it was always remedied by volunteers from infantry battalions.' He couldn't resist a shot at the leadership then or now. 'In those days, of course, we didn't have the same ideas we have now, and everyone used his own initiative and detailed a certain number of men to assist. The probability is that the higher command did not know what was taking place.'[2]

Shortly after his return, the battalion's officers had a visit from Brigadier General Brand, who arrived on horseback. They had assembled at the front of a château and were chatting informally when he dismounted and tossed his reins to an orderly.

Lieutenant Edgar Rule recorded a scene so remarkable that it was etched forever on his memory. 'By way of a lead up to his subject, he commenced by giving us an outline of the military situation as it stood at that time,' Rule wrote. 'He said that the French armies were exhausted and were in no position to stand up to a prolonged attack by the enemy. To assist the French, and also to keep the Hun on the move, Sir Douglas Haig had decided to commence a series of operations that would be the means of driving the Germans from the Belgian coast.'[3]

Then Brand grasped the nettle. 'Now gentlemen,' he said, 'the point I am coming to is this. It has been decided by the High Command that the 4th Division shall be given a task in the coming battle.'

Rule said, 'This simply took everyone's breath away. It was the most unjust thing that had happened to us. After all the promises of a rest, it was heart-breaking to think that we were given so little consideration as to be flung in beside the other four fresh Aussie divisions, and be expected to do with war-torn and tired men what they did fresh from four months rest.'

However, Rule was not expecting what came next.

'What!?' It was Jacka.

Rule said, 'While the brigadier had been talking I could hear Jacka's voice muttering to those who stood around him.'

Brand responded. 'I've no doubt you heard what I said, Jacka. As I was saying before I was interrupted, our division is thought very highly of by the army commander, and there is not the least doubt that you will ever cover yourself with credit.'

But Jacka was not to be silenced so easily. 'Do you mean to tell me that this battalion is to be flung into the line right away, in spite of all the promises made to the men?'

Brand glared back. 'Hullo, Jacka—what's the trouble with you? Have you got the wind up?'

It was an absurd suggestion and Jacka passed it off. 'No', he said dryly, 'I'm only thinking of the men. I've been over in England swinging the lead this past week or so, and personally I don't care a damn. But I want to know why the promises made to the men have been broken. I reckon it's a damned disgrace.'

Rule said, 'It was easy to see that he was expressing the sentiments of the rest. After it was over, the old Brig. rode away looking very black. Jacka was growling, "These people make me sick. They go running after 'the heads' volunteering for everything—'My men will do this, my men will do that!' They take fine care that they're not in it themselves!"'

Resentment simmered. If Jacka had chosen to hose it down it is clear that his fellow officers would have followed his lead. But it seems he was in no mood to make life easy for Brand and his superiors.

The confrontation reached its climax in September, when once again the battalion's commanding officer was replaced. The departure of Margolin, the 'Mad Russian', was a cause for rejoicing, but the simultaneous announcement of his replacement—Lieutenant Colonel Walter John Smith, formerly of the 37th—stopped the celebration in its tracks. Once again, Jacka's claims were overlooked. And worse, when Fuhrmann, the 2-I-C, was transferred to the 5th Division at the same time, another outsider was appointed. Wanliss commented, 'He was succeeded by Major D. Thompson whose advent naturally blocked the promotion of 14th officers of long standing whose efforts had largely made the battalion what it was.'[4]

Jacka had obvious claims for the post, but so too did Captain Harold Wanliss, who had been adjutant for seven months and was warmly regarded by all who knew him.

Just at this time—4 September—Brand made another visit as the battalion was engaged in a new training regime ordered by Lieutenant Colonel Smith. Rule said,

> Our Lewis guns had not yet come along and this kept back our training in the elementary stages. One morning [Brand] made a bad mistake. He came along to A and B Companies and finding them at this elementary work he was very upset and spoke much too heatedly. He told the companies that they were no good, and that their officers were a lot of dopes and that the battalion was dopey too.
>
> Now the officer who commanded A Company was Captain Harold Wanliss, DSO, an officer without fear and beyond reproach, energetic and careful, idolised by his men, their *beau-ideal* of what an Australian should be in character and ability. The men took their own tongue-thrashing meekly, but when the lash descended on Wanliss their indignation knew no bounds. When we all came in for lunch the news went around, and a meeting of officers was arranged for that evening.[5]

After dinner, the officer corps of 14th Battalion assembled in their mess. The CO had been called to brigade headquarters, but Thompson, the new 2-I-C, was present. The meeting was rancorous but relatively short. There was no talk of mutiny; it was their unit pride, not their courage that was under the gun. But if Brand had it in for them, then they would respond in kind. 'Accordingly,' said Rule, 'we all went to our billets and wrote out our resignations, asking for transfer to some fighting unit outside the brigade.' Then they reassembled and handed them in to Thompson for delivery to the brigadier.

It was an extraordinary act of rebellion. In his battalion history, Wanliss attempts to minimise it and calls it simply 'an unfortunate incident'. Brand's 'slur' on the battalion, he says, 'was an attack on the unit's pride'. It was 'unwarranted' and caused resentment throughout the whole battalion, so 'the officers of the unit, acting promptly and with practical unanimity, made a very determined protest'.[6] Rule was less diplomatic, and in his telling it is clear that Jacka was the stormy petrel who spoke for his colleagues, if not the formal leader of the rebellion.[7]

The next afternoon, Brand ordered a meeting of all officers of the battalion in the mess hut and began by outlining the battle formations of future operations. 'But of course we realised this was only to make an opportunity for speaking to us,' Rule said. Indeed, he was barely into his speech before he broke off to say, 'Well now, about that silly thing you fellows have done—I've flung all those resignations into the waste-paper basket.'

The meeting broke up shortly afterwards, but the argument continued. Rule said, 'Outside the room Jacka and the Brig had a regular set-to. Jacka in his blunt, straightforward way telling him what he thought was the cause of all the trouble. It wound up by the Brig threatening to put him under arrest.'

When they reassembled inside, Rule said, Brand tried to smooth the matter over. He referred to Jacka on an issue of tactics. 'I think these movements could easily be performed by the battalion, don't you, Jacka?'

But Jacka wouldn't budge. 'Why do you ask me?' he responded. 'If I open my mouth you threaten to put me under arrest. I'll keep my mouth shut for the present.'

It was as close to diplomacy as Jacka would come. And even then, Rule believed, the only thing that held him back was the next 'stunt' in prospect. 'It is my opinion that the mere idea of another officer leading D Company to the attack while he himself cooled his heels awaiting a court martial made Jacka control his speech at that moment,' Rule said. 'That night we all wrote out our resignations again, and sent them in.'

Brand backed down. The next morning, he sought out A and B companies and told them he had been hasty; their officers were all that could be desired. Then he called a parade and said the battalion 'contained some of the finest officers in the brigade' and he was proud to serve with them.

It was enough; honour was satisfied; and Jacka would keep command of his men in the forthcoming battle of Polygon Wood. In many ways, it would be his finest hour.

21

COMMAND AT LAST

Polygon Wood in the autumn of 2005 is a place of stark beauty and soft, misty silence. The wood itself—named for its geometrical shape—is a rich, dark green and, at the base of the pine trees, waterlogged trenches are a wrenching reminder of a terrible conflict almost a century past. As the morning mist peels away, a butte or small plateau becomes visible in a cleared area and at its summit a phallic memorial rises defiantly from the green mound. Stone steps lead up its side. From the crest, in poignant array, hundreds of tall gravestones may be seen in the flat field adjoining. They are positioned in line of battle like the soldiers of a Roman army, frozen in the moment before their advance.

In September 1917, 'Wood' was an ironic misnomer. Not a single tree remained. Artillery from both sides had torn the forest to shreds. The open field, previously used as a rifle range, was churned to a cold, glutinous muck. The butte was heavily defended by the Germans. It was the first objective of the advancing Allied forces led by the 14th Battalion. Soon they would be 'Jacka's Mob' in deed as well as name.

By now, there had been yet another shake-up in the high command. The conscientious Australian division commander, Major General William Holmes, had been killed by a stray shell when he ventured close to the line. He was replaced by General Ewen Sinclair-MacLagan, a Scottish professional soldier who had adopted Australia and was training officers at Duntroon when war broke out in 1914. He landed at Gallipoli on Anzac Day and later commanded the 3rd Brigade at Pozières. Most recently he had been director of military training for the entire Anzac force. He answered to Plumer, who had now replaced the egregious Gough as head of the 5th and 2nd armies.

After his success at Messines, Monash was riding high and his counsel was sought in the lead-up to Polygon Wood. By now there was a sense among the troops that the tide of battle was on the turn. Monash was already putting together his formula for a massively coordinated attack that would bring such vital breakthroughs the following year. The one essential ingredient, he believed, was an aggressive and powerfully motivated infantry, and in this he and Jacka were in perfect accord.

The battle orders reached the 14th Battalion on 24 September:

The 4th Brigade, in conjunction with the 14th Brigade on the right, and the 13th Brigade on the left, will assume offensive operations in two stages. 1st stage (red line), 2nd stage (blue line). 16th Battalion will secure the red line. 15th and 14th Battalions on a frontage of about 500 yards will secure the blue line. 13th Battalion will be in reserve in position now occupied. The barrage will be put down 150 yards in front of our forming up line at zero.

It will begin to advance at zero plus three minutes at the rate of 100 yards in four minutes for 200 yards; thereafter and up to the red line, the rate will be 100 yards in six minutes. Just prior to movement from red line it will increase in intensity and troops will move up close under it.

Jacka was in command of D Company, together with Wanliss (A), Hayes (B) and Mitchell (C). At 12.15 a.m. they made their way forward towards the jumping-off point with D Company in the lead. Jacka later wrote, 'The going was very heavy in the advance as the terrain was a mass of shell holes filled with water.'[1]

Almost immediately, there was a change in procedure that would have a profound effect on the action. Jacka wrote, 'The original arrangement was that Battalion Headquarters [comprising Smith and Thompson] was to move forward behind [the battalion]. For some reason they made a change and moved around to a very safe dugout behind the 15th Battalion, and remained there. Either no notice was sent to the front line of the new situation of H.Qrs or if it was sent, the runners became casualties and no effort was apparently made to ascertain if the messages reached their destination.'

The result was that company runners were searching everywhere for battalion headquarters. So, in the absence of Smith and Thompson, company commanders were forced to send their messages all the way to brigade headquarters. Jacka said, 'Battalion headquarters was not heard of at the front line till the end of the 2nd day of battle.'

The implication is clear: dereliction of duty—if not a more serious charge—against the battalion commander. However, Jacka was not alone in making it. Battalion chaplain, Captain Frances

Rolland, wrote, 'The CO and the Adjutant were certainly very conspicuous by their absence.'² Rule noted, 'Cut off from its nerve centre, the 14th advanced into action at a tremendous disadvantage. Slashed about with shell and machine gun fire, the men looked in vain to the rear for assistance and support.'³

However, it is hard to escape the view that deep down Jacka welcomed a situation that, in effect, gave him charge of the battalion in circumstances where he excelled. Indeed, Rule says, 'Instinctively knowing that his day had come, Jacka grasped the opportunity with both hands. His friends had known that he longed for the day when he would lead D Company into the attack, but it is probable that he never dreamt of seeing the whole battalion at his heels. With a fixed purpose he set out to lift the men of the battalion up to his own standard.'

When they reached their jumping-off point it was shortly before zero hour, 5.50 a.m. Wanliss wrote, 'Immediately before zero all conversation ceased and then, with a stupendous roar, our barrage fell upon No Man's Land. [The battalion] had had previous experience of barrages but this transcended anything it had ever fought under—a gigantic thunderstorm of bursting steel hurled out of the lips of thousands of guns.'⁴

That morning, too, was misty, and above the haze Allied planes flew east to reconnoitre and to engage German aircraft similarly employed. Jacka rose from his shell hole and waved the men forward through the slippery mud and deepwater craters towards their first objective about 300 metres ahead. His way was relatively clear, but he quickly saw that to his left German pillboxes were taking their toll of the 16th Battalion. Some officers and men were turning back. Immediately, he called men from his unit to him and led them towards the concrete bunkers. He intercepted the retreating soldiers, and when they saw it was Jacka, they turned back. In short order the pillboxes were taken, the Germans killed or sent back as prisoners. Monash's biographer later wrote, 'The attack ran into trouble' as much from the Germans as from shells of their own artillery, and looked like failing until cool Albert Jacka steadied them.'[5]

Again the 14th forged ahead and reached its first objective, the blue line, at 8 a.m. However, the line coincided with a road that might well serve as a range finder for enemy artillery, so Jacka called a quick meeting of company commanders and proposed they move ahead another 50 metres. There were risks—their own barrage might come uncomfortably close—but he reckoned it was one worth taking. Wanliss, Mitchell and Hayes signalled their agreement. Jacka gave the order.

Tragedy struck when Harold Wanliss, in returning to his company, took the full blast of a machine gun and was killed outright. However, Jacka's decision had been a good one. When the German barrage opened up later in preparation for a counterattack, it passed harmlessly overhead and pulverised the blue line.

Now Jacka needed signal rockets to call down his own guns. But he had entrusted them to his batman who was nowhere to be found. In fact, he had been killed in the advance, but Jacka knew that if he gave the task of finding him to another he might have difficulty. So he personally made his way back some 400 metres. He was sniped at for much of the journey, one bullet passing through his tunic, another grazing his hand. But he returned with the flares, waited until the Germans had formed up 300 metres away, then at 3 p.m. called in his own guns.

They smashed into the German ranks. Newton Wanliss wrote, 'Our artillery mowed them down in hundreds. Only one man among them succeeded in getting as close as about 70 yards from our line. The German stretcher bearers were busy the whole afternoon. Probably four or five hundred were killed on the battalion front in that afternoon alone.'[6]

A second German counterattack was mounted at 6 p.m., preceded by a barrage that played havoc with the 15th Battalion. The men of the 15th feared this heralded an all-out frontal attack on their position and there were indications that the barrage had sapped their morale. Jacka sent a message down the line by word of mouth: 'If the Hun attacks the 15th we shall hop out and meet the blighters. Advise the 15th.' Rule noted, 'The enemy's appetite for fight had by then faded. Onlookers were therefore denied the spectacle of a hand-to-hand fight in No Man's Land between the 14th Battalion and some of the picked storm troopers of the German Army.'[7]

Similarly at 10 p.m., the Germans failed to follow up an artillery barrage that became a duel between gunners. The 14th held their position, a major advance through heavily fortified German territory that had previously defied all attempts to break into. Then they held it in battle through a third day, before finally at 8 p.m. on 28 September, they were relieved by the 45th Battalion.

Throughout, Jacka had called the shots and deployed his forces with tactical guile and sureness of purpose. He was everywhere he was needed, and his determination and confidence lifted the whole unit. His only significant communication with a superior officer had been on the first day when the Germans were in disarray. Then, he reached Brand, and sought permission to take the battalion forward still further. Brand refused and later Jacka wrote, 'It required another battle on the 4th October to capture what was ours for the taking that day.'[8]

Rule wrote, 'At Polygon Wood Jacka's handling of the fighting men astonished even his greatest admirers; it was a demonstration by a master for the benefit of his pupils.'[9]

Newton Wanliss, who had lost a beloved son in the battle, was even more generous:

> His personal achievements in previous battles had been the admiration of his countrymen, but at Polygon Wood when the opportunity came, he displayed in addition a power of leadership, a grasp of tactics, and a military intuition that many had not given him credit for.
>
> It is impossible to over-estimate the value of his services during those three days in the line. He carried the left wing of the Battalion forward with a magnificent dash to the second objective and there took practical control of the unit and was thereafter the guiding spirit of the storm of battle. His reckless valour, his excellent judgement, his skilful tactics, his prompt anticipation of the enemy's movements, and the force and vigour of his battle strokes gained the admiration of all ranks, and inspired everyone with the greatest confidence.
>
> Throughout the whole engagement he was a ubiquitous and fearless figure, the very incarnation of a great fighting soldier and a born leader of men. No more fearless or gallant soldier took part in the Great War.[10]

As they were returning, Brand sent a runner forward with a note saying, 'Congratulations, Jacka, I have recommended you for the DSO.'[11] And when they reached the rear, Brand sought out Jacka to show him the personal recommendation he had written. Smith also caught up with events and made a similar recommendation, calling him 'the soul of the defence'.[12] However, while the Polygon Wood triumph attracted many decorations, no officer from the 14th—Jacka's Mob—was included.

Many have speculated on the reason. The explanations range from the 'rebellion' in which Jacka was seen as a ringleader; to the notorious 'tank report'; to the battle-shy actions of Smith and Thompson that were intrinsic to Jacka assuming command. Smith was Brand's choice for battalion commander. If the real story were to come out, it would reflect badly up the chain of command.

Whatever the true cause—and most likely it was a combination of all three—it confirmed Jacka in the view that there was no place for him in the upper ranks of the professional army. All he could do, henceforth, was knock out as many of the enemy as possible to get the thing over and done with. There was still a job to be done, but then, by God, he could walk away from the military backbiters and bureaucrats without a backward glance.

22

THE SORROW OF LOSS

In August 1917, Lieutenant Bill Jacka had been detached from the 14th for a stint with a training battalion in England. When he rejoined the unit in December he brought news from home, which his elder brother—not quite 25, but looking years older—supplemented with his own letters from the family. But in Albert's case, there were also occasional letters from strangers—well-wishers in Victoria and even other parts of Australia.

He tried to answer them but in time had to put them aside. There were other priorities, particularly the heart-wrenching letters he had to write to bereaved mothers and wives of his men who had 'gone out'. Chaplain Rolland attested to the time and effort he put into this work. 'He always tried to write in a very personal manner,' he said. 'He would give them something special to remember and I could see that it took a heavy toll on him. But I believe that it consoled people to receive a letter from Bert Jacka himself.'[1]

Some letters survive as treasured family memorabilia, none more so than that of Captain Frederick B. Stanton of Caulfield, Victoria, who was killed on 11 April 1917. Jacka wrote to the dead man's brother, Lieutenant James Stanton DCM, at the 7th Battalion four days later. 'It causes me great pain to write and tell you of the death of your dear brother, Fred,' he wrote.

> I know that, being a soldier, you understand the chances we all take, and I am sure, although it may add to your great grief, you would like to hear exactly, when and how, Fred met his death.
>
> It was in the early morning of the 11th April, in our attack on the Hindenburg Line, in which Fred and his company took part. They had gained the first objective, and were pushing on to the second. A German machine gun was firing from the wire in front of the second line, and Fred went forward with five men to knock it out. He was successful in his mission, but paid dearly for his great gallantry. He was shot almost through the heart, the bullet entering his left breast and passing through him. Death was instantaneous. Fred's conduct throughout the fight was most gallant and all ranks are loud in their praise of his noble work. We can ill afford to lose such a brilliant officer as your brother.
>
> Would you please accept my heartfelt sympathy and also the heartfelt sympathy of the 14th Battalion. Yours sincerely, Bert Jacka V.C. Capt. 14th Battalion.[2]

Bill Jacka also recounted stories of the effect the famous name had on people he met. He was intensely proud of his brother and was not the slightest jealous of his celebrity. Jacka himself simply listened and shook his head. By now he had been a VC for more than two years and knew the responsibilities it brought. Rule said, 'His bravery is known far and wide—it was a by-word far beyond the AIF—but his good fellowship is not. His praise was never lavishly bestowed, but his men treasured it more than medals.'[3]

The battalion remained in the line and in reserve throughout the operations known generally as Passchendaele, but to the military historian as the Third Battle of Ypres. Journalist Phillip Gibbs wrote,

Every man of ours who fought on the way to Passchendaele agreed that those battles in Flanders were the most awful, the most bloody, and the most hellish. The condition of the ground, out from Ypres and beyond the Menin Gate, was partly the cause of the misery and the filth. Heavy rains fell, and made one great bog in which every shell crater was a deep pool. There were thousands of shell craters. Our guns had made them, and German gunfire, slashing our troops, made thousands more, linking them together so that they were like lakes in some places, filled with slimy water and dead bodies.

Our infantry had to advance heavily laden with their kit, and with arms and hand-grenades and entrenching tools—like pack animals—along slimy duckboards on which it was hard to keep a footing, especially at night when the battalions were moved under cover of darkness.[4]

Despite the heavy rain, Haig ordered further attacks towards the Passchendaele Ridge and now the advancing forces had to endure German mustard gas attacks. The men in the trenches hated the gas with a passion.

It had been introduced by the French as early as August 1914 in the form of tear-gas grenades. However, the Germans made a thorough study of gas warfare and responded in October with shells containing a strong chemical irritant that caused violent sneezing. Poison gas—chlorine—followed in short order with terrible effects on the respiratory system; and the British reacted with their own mixture in 1916. As the conflict escalated both sides developed mustard gas (or Yperite), an almost odourless chemical that not only interfered with breathing but brought about terrible ulcers on the skin and, more importantly, the internal organs.

The men of the 14th were issued with gas masks soon after their arrival in France and by the end of 1917 their use became second nature when the yellow-green chlorine fumes approached. However, the new mustard gas was an invisible enemy.

On 6 November, the village of Passchendaele was finally taken by the Canadian infantry. The offensive cost the British Expeditionary Force about 310,000 casualties. Haig was severely criticised for continuing with the attacks long after the operation had lost any real strategic value. At last the horror of death on such a massive scale was beginning to get through to the politicians. But Haig remained at his post.

In December, the Germans counterattacked south at Cambrai and punctured the British line. The Australian 4th Brigade, including the 14th Battalion, was ordered to entrain for the battlefield, after which began a hard slog over slippery, frozen roads to Moislains. But when they reached the village they learned that the Germans had been repulsed.

Wanliss reported:

On 20 December another march over frozen roads brought the 14th to Templeaux-la-Fosse where a stay of three weeks was made.

Here Christmas was spent—the last during the war. The locality was bleak, desolate and snow-covered but, nevertheless, enjoyment reigned supreme for one day.

The morning of the 25th was ushered in by Christmas carols, whilst the brigade pierrots provided an excellent entertainment, *Cinderella Up-to-date*. The thoughts of all turned that day to the land they loved and which many were destined never to see again. The Christmas dinner, in addition to the ordinary rations, was supplemented by gifts from the Australian Comforts Fund. The last week of the year was uneventful and was spent in the same locality.[5]

After a short rest, Jacka and his men returned to their northern sector and were immediately thrown into the front line near La Clytte. The German trenches were on the other side of a wide, boggy no-man's-land and there were similarities to the stalemate that had developed on Gallipoli. Sniping, patrolling and short, fierce raids were the order of the day. But there was no sense of shared honour as there had been with the Turks at Anzac. The Hun was the enemy and no quarter was asked or given.

Jacka set up a line of outposts ahead of his company, charged with the task of warning the front line of an impending attack, delaying the enemy advance and, if necessary, fighting to the death. It was a lonely and nerve-racking task and, while most commanders remained in the rear (as was expected), Jacka made his way out each night to check on his men and keep up morale.

Once in the outpost, he often led a small patrol or went solo on a 'hunt' to unsettle the enemy. The activities of this mysterious avenger played havoc with the German outposts. On 31 January, the

Germans rushed an Australian post and captured two NCOs, Corporal Ernie Frost and Lance Corporal Charles Jeffries.

Frost later said the Germans told him they were anxious to capture the man who spent his nights patrolling no-man's-land single-handed. Frost told them, 'You'd be better off if you didn't. That's Captain Jacka; try to take him and it would be damned dangerous.'[6]

23

DANGER MAN

Jacka took the capture of his men personally. The same instinct that drove him as a boy to defend and protect his younger siblings translated into a need to safeguard his men in the field and to punish their enemies. For the next several weeks, life for the Germans opposite D Company was indeed 'damned dangerous'. No records exist of the retribution he exacted, but he went out every night until honour was satisfied.

A spate of German gas attacks on the front line and at battalion headquarters almost debilitated the 14th in early February. Because of his work beyond the line in the outposts, Jacka was spared, but seventeen officers, including Lieutenant Colonel Smith, and more than 250 men, had to be evacuated.

Smith recovered quickly, but Brand took the opportunity to relieve him of his command and he was eventually posted back to Australia. By now Jacka had probably abandoned all expectations of promotion, but it cannot have been easy to accept yet another outsider, Major Charles Melbourne Johnston, who had been on Brand's staff at brigade headquarters, as battalion CO. Brother Bill said later, 'Time and again he demonstrated he was superior to a lot of chaps who held high positions in the Army. I think it's right to say he upset some of the generals severely when he criticised their tactics. I think the generals had him in the gun.'[1]

Jacka's own reaction has not been recorded, but by now, it seems, he was conducting his private war. D Company was his instrument. The men were more than happy to follow his lead.

He had been called away briefly on a mission that turned out to be stillborn. High Command decided they wanted to increase pressure on the Turks by helping to organise the Armenian minority who were being slaughtered in shocking numbers by the Turkish militia, and driving them out to Syria and Iraq. High Command suggested Jacka and 'Mad Harry' Murray form part of a small team to travel to the border area and get things moving.

In an interview with Colonel Byron from Dunsterforce, Jacka said he was up for it—as did Murray—but before anything came of it Birdwood vetoed both names and they returned to their units. Birdwood gave no reasons, but the prospect of a million angry Armenians led by Jacka and Murray would give pause to any military strategist, not least the conservative 'Birdy'.[2]

Finally, on 1 March, the 4th Brigade was relieved of its duty on the Ypres salient and withdrawn to a 'deep reserve' position known as Neuve Eglise for rest and recreation. Jacka took the opportunity to return to London on a brief furlough. For a week he relaxed and let the tension of months of battle drain away.

On his return, there had been yet another change of command. Major Johnston had moved on and been replaced by Major Henry

Crowther, a former master from Brighton Grammar School, one of Melbourne's better private schools. Crowther had served with the 21st Battalion from May 1915 to August 1916, when he won the DSO at Pozières. He was a man of learning, courage and good humour, and had the kind of confidence that Jacka respected. Almost immediately, they were on the best of terms. For Jacka, it was almost like having John Peck back at the helm.

However, while the situation within his military 'family' was again positive and congenial, the wider picture was suddenly as threatening as it had ever been. In October 1917, the Bolsheviks had taken control of Russia and ended that country's participation in the 'capitalist' war. And once the Germans were satisfied the threat had passed, they moved their entire Russian Front infantry—more than a million men—to the west. Ludendorff now had numerical superiority and gathered his forces for a decisive strike.

Among the British generals the backbiting and politicking continued unabated. The one positive development was that the Australian divisions were now being consolidated under an Australian commander. In May 1918, Monash would be knighted and promoted to major general. Meantime, no one was prepared for the sudden lunge from Ludendorff on 21 March 1918.

The Germans again chose Cambrai as the point of attack, but this time on a front of almost 100 kilometres against the British 3rd and 5th armies. The defenders were pounded and crushed by the German steamroller and at one stage Monash himself, who had rushed to the front, was in danger of capture from the advancing forces. The British territorial gains of two years were lost in a week.

The call went out for the 4th Brigade to once again make the journey south, but this time, they could be sure, there would be no last-minute reprieve from front-line combat. Jacka had been tapped by Crowther to attend the Second Army School of Instruction—a necessary prerequisite for advancement to higher command. But this would have to be postponed. On 25 March, after an early breakfast at 3.30 a.m. and a march through the spring countryside, the 14th Battalion climbed aboard a line of buses heading for battle. That evening they reached Bavincourt. Colonel Crowther, after dinner at the home of the local priest, and with Jacka at his side, made a rousing speech.

The 14th had a proud history, he said, and the coming battle would add another chapter of gallantry and unflinching determination. They would stand their ground. They would honour the men who had made the supreme sacrifice in a noble cause, all the way back to the Gallipoli landing. The fighting 14th had a great reputation, none better in the entire AIF. Their actions in the coming days would add lustre and glory to a great fighting unit.

The officers and NCOs responded, Jacka chief among them. The obvious affinity between the two men was a powerful factor in raising morale. So, too, next morning, was the attitude of the French villagers who crowded around the Australians. 'Vivent les Australiens! Vous les tiendrez!' (You will hold them!) To which the veterans of nearly two years in France responded, 'Fini retreat, Madame (or Monsieur); Fini retreat, beaucoup Australiens ici.'[3]

Back on the road, they struggled against the tide of retreating British soldiers. Their message could hardly have been more different from the French: 'Gerry will have your bloody guts for garters.'

Jacka was unimpressed. He had been let down by the Brits before. Once again, it was up to the Australians to pick up the pieces.

On 26 March, the 4th Brigade launched an offensive with the 14th Battalion in reserve and in twelve hours hard fighting they took the town of Hébuterne. At daybreak, the German artillery opened up and plastered the town. The Allies' response was weak; the big guns were still on their way forward. However, the Germans held back until they could gauge the Australian infantry strength.

Jacka spent the day patrolling forward of the line, making his own assessment of enemy strength. He discovered a yawning gap in the Allied line—only a handful of British troops remaining between the left of the brigade and the British 62nd Division to the north. If the Germans struck there they would break through and expose the brigade to a devastating flank attack.

Crowther responded and Jacka led his D Company out to plug the gap while the rest of the battalion occupied a ridge that allowed them to fire down on any advancing force. Wanliss wrote, '[It] was one of the neatest operations ever carried out by the 14th. Notwithstanding the very poor visibility and the fact that the ground crossed was hampered by old and very heavy wire entanglements, the most efficient liaison existed between the various platoons.'[4]

The manoeuvre was completed just before midnight, when orders arrived for a further advance to occupy some old German trenches from 1916 to the east, and to extend the brigade left to that point before daylight. This, too, was successfully accomplished.

It was now 28 March and the brigade had been in combat continuously for 36 hours. Hébuterne was now solidly in Allied hands and the six-day German advance had been halted, at least temporarily.

For the next four days the battalion remained in contact with the enemy, but the immediate pressure was off, and on 6 April Jacka was detached to attend the School of Instruction. When he completed the course, he would be passed up the line in May for further courses at the 4th Division Wing.

Meantime, the 14th rotated back and forth in reserve and frontline duty with sister battalions until the end of April, when the entire brigade withdrew to the rest area in the south at Allonville, not far from Amiens, on Anzac Day, 1918. This time, there were no celebrations. They were back where they had begun two years before. The war stretched endlessly ahead.

24

JACKA'S LUCK RUNS OUT

Jacka returned from his courses on 10 May. Lieutenant Edgar Rule, who by now had been decorated with both a Military Cross and a Military Medal, had been away on secondment and had rejoined the 14th. They were just in time for the struggle to hold Villers-Bretonneaux, the key position on the approach to Amiens.

The place had been heavily shelled by the Germans for the past six days; they were gradually blowing it to pieces. Men of the 14th were detailed as working parties, and when the shelling let up they wandered through the abandoned buildings searching for booty. Most prized of all by the 'bronzed Anzacs' were the frilly silk underclothes the French ladies had left behind in their haste. To men who had been tortured by lice—commonly known as 'chats'—for months on end, the silky smooth bloomers were sheer bliss. Edgar Rule said, 'Ladies nighties were quite the fashion and one of the boys lined up next morning for his breakfast arrayed in a beauty.'[1]

The battalion camped in a valley about half a kilometre from Villers, and on 14 May they moved up to the line on the right flank of the brigade and next to a Moroccan division. At about 3 p.m., the Allied artillery opened fire on a German garrison and virtually wiped it out. In the front line, Jacka and his D Company ate their dinner at 9 p.m. and stayed on watch throughout the night. In the morning, they cooked up their breakfast—mostly bacon and fried cheese with hard biscuits—in the trenches.

Rule's C Company was just behind Jacka's men. 'Suddenly,' he said, 'just as we were settling down for a bit of a nap after breakfast, the Hun starts in to shell us with gas. He placed about fifty 5.9 shells close to the front line, and pretty soon the smell of onions [the only hint of the almost odourless mustard gas] came to us so thickly that on went our masks.

'Then the Hun started to snipe,' he said. 'One shot hit the famous Bill Dawe.' This was the big, strapping soldier who had pulled Jacka into the trench at Messines. Dawe was mortally wounded, but unknown to him, the man he said he'd give his life for was also in terrible condition. Jacka's luck had finally run out.

He took the full force of an exploding gas shell and, together with two other officers and 30 of his men, was overwhelmed by the noxious chemical. In Jacka's case, the agony was exacerbated by his many wounds, external and internal, that were opened up and instantly infected. It was, as Edgar Rule said, 'Jacka's last fight' on the battlefield.

Almost immediately he was engaged in another, more desperate struggle, simply to stay alive. That night Rule wrote to his aunt in Australia. Everyone in the battalion 'family' was deeply affected, he said. By then Jacka had been rushed to the regimental aid post, then to the 47th Casualty Clearing Station and finally to the 8th General

Hospital at Rouen. He could travel no further for six agonising days.

'Never again were we to see his soldierly figure strolling through the trenches,' Rule wrote.

> The main prop in the battalion had been cut away. There was not a man in the unit but knew he basked in the reflected glory of Jacka's exploits.
>
> All of us had grown accustomed to hearing, as we marched along the roads of France, 'Hello, here's Jacka's mob.' But to those of us who were privileged to claim his friendship—and to call him 'Bert'—he was a constant urge to greater efforts, and there were few of us who escaped his displeasure at some time or another. His candid tongue left welts in men's memories, but war was a man's game and strong stimulants were needed.
>
> His fighting spirit and independent nature constantly brought him into conflict with those in higher authority. For some reason unknown to me, men who did not know him in action were sometimes under the impression that he fought without brains, like a mad bull in a crockery shop. Nothing could be further from the truth. Fate seemed to lead him to where desperate situations required desperate remedies, and stories of his audacity will be handed on to generations of Australians.[2]

On 20 May, they were able to load him gently onto the British hospital ship *Panama* for the journey back to the 3rd London Hospital. There he underwent two major operations and remained under treatment for almost a month before he was allowed to appear before his medical board.

Their decision was final. His fighting days were over. He was fit only for light duties, preferably sedentary. For the time being he accepted the decision. His body was desperately in need of rest. They placed him on the Regimental Supernumary List and posted him to Depot No. 1 at Sutton Veny in Wiltshire, perhaps the most beautiful part of England.

The surrounding villages, in the upper Wylye Valley area near Salisbury Plain, provided an ideal location for a training unit early in the war. Ten camps were built around Sutton Veny village, and the troops would live in trenches for a week at a time with food being brought out to them. Village women took in soldiers' laundry, and snack shops and tea huts were built nearby.

There were two village pubs—The Wool Pack and The Bell—and the Australian YMCA was located in Sutton Veny House, a mansion of more than 50 rooms with spacious lawns and grounds. The camp boasted two cinemas. A third had been burned by the troops—to the singing of 'Keep the Home Fires Burning'—when the projector broke down and the proprietors refused to refund the tickets.

One nearby camp was used for prisoners of war, and in 1916 the hospital camp opened for eleven officers and 1261 soldiers. The same year, No. 1 Australian Command Depot moved to Sutton Veny, where it remained until 1919. The Australian authorities would develop an agricultural training depot in the area to prepare soldiers for a return to civilian life. But for the moment it was an ideal place for Jacka to rest and recuperate.

The young English poet Siegfried Sassoon captured Sutton Veny's mood when he wrote of it in the 1915 work, 'On Scratchbury Camp'.

Along the grave green downs, this idle afternoon,
Shadows of loitering silver clouds, becalmed in blue,
Bring, like unfoldment of a flower, the best of June.

Shadows outspread in spacious movement, always you
Have dappled the downs and valleys at this time of year,
While larks, ascending shrill, praised freedom as they flew.
Now, through that song, a fighter squadron's drone I hear
From Scratchbury Camp, whose turfed and cowslip'd rampart seems
More hill than history, ageless and oblivion—blurred.

I walk the fosse, once manned by bronze and flint head spear;
On war's imperious wing the shafted sun ray gleams:
One with the warm sweet air of summer stoops the bird.
Cloud shadows, drifting slow like heedless daylight dreams,
Dwell and dissolve; uncircumstanced they pause and pass.
I watch them go. My horse, contented, crops the grass.

However, after three months of enforced 'holiday', Jacka appealed
to his medical board. His place, he said, was with his unit. They
were unmoved.

By then Monash had put together his mighty plan for the Battle
of Hamel and, with the 14th Battalion prominent, executed a great
victory. The Australian commander had combined every element in
the military armoury—aircraft, tanks, artillery and infantry—with
an engineer's attention to detail.

By incorporating the tanks into the infantry's operations
Monash had followed Jacka's recommendations in every respect.

The result was a tremendously effective fighting unit. The tanks, he wrote later, had undergone 'a remarkable evolution during the two years which followed their first introduction on the battlefield in the Somme campaign of 1916'.[3]

He continued:

The tank crews had improved in like proportion, both in skill, enterprise and adaptability . . . The tanks were organised into brigades, each of three battalions, each of three companies, each of twelve tanks. Nothing can be more unstinted than the acknowledgement which the Australian Corps makes of its obligation to the Tank Corps for its powerful assistance throughout the whole of the great offensive.

Commencing with the Battle of Hamel, a large contingent of tanks participated in every 'set piece' engagement which the corps undertook.

But the most telling factor, he believed, was the courage and the dash that the Australian troops brought to their task. The French premier, Georges Clemenceau, visited the scene of triumph and told the troops:

We knew you would fight a real fight, but we did not know from the very beginning you would astonish the whole continent with your valour.

I have come here just for the very purpose of seeing the Australians. I am going back tomorrow to see my countrymen and tell them, 'I have seen the Australians. I have looked in their eyes.'

I know that these men have fought great battles beside us in the cause of freedom, and will fight alongside us again until the cause of freedom is safe for us and for our children.[4]

Jacka could only read about it in the papers.

By now, the Americans had joined the fight. The German air raids over England had ceased. Then, late in August, Monash followed up his Hamel victory with a massive, coordinated advance on the Hindenburg Line that Ludendorff called 'the black day of the German Army'. It shattered the Germans' belief in ultimate victory. It was now clear that the war would have to be ended by negotiation.

In September, the Americans launched their attack in the Argonne. After a brief advance they faltered, but in the north Monash surged ahead. For months the AIF had been riding high and Monash took the opportunity to publicise the great deeds of Jacka, Murray and others whose heroics added lustre to the cause. His reasoning was quite cold-blooded—he knew that the stories would be picked up by relatives in Australia and sent back to the fighting men who would be inspired to fight even harder.

Even Monash, with his great capacity to anticipate events, would have been surprised by the effect the publicity would have on the heroes—particularly Albert Jacka VC.

25

RECUPERATING

Whether Monash's ploy was successful or not, it did have an immediate effect on the convalescing Jacka at Sutton Veny. Gradually, his letters from well-wishers whom he had never met began to increase. He was even famous in Britain, where Madame Tussaud's displayed his wax effigy in action. And at the same time, both he and his brother Bill fell in love.

One of the unsought letters had been from a Mrs John Jacka of Taffswell, Wales, who wondered if they might be related and invited him to visit. Albert's strong sense of family was piqued, and when he was able to get around, he made the journey to the small mining town near Cardiff. John Jacka managed a goldmine there and, despite their inability to discover a common ancestor, the family gave him a warm welcome. On Albert Jacka's return for a second visit he took Bill, who was also convalescing.

Bill and the eldest daughter, Joan, hit it off immediately.

Albert's scars had healed and, while his nose was still bent slightly to one side, he was ruggedly handsome and polite to women to the point of courtliness. Still a teetotaller, at 26 he may well have been the oldest Australian virgin soldier in the country—a condition we may believe was remedied at this time. The identity of the young woman is unknown. Her existence was revealed in an extraordinary interchange of correspondence between Jacka and AIF headquarters in London when, in August, they ordered Jacka to return home to Australia together with other VC winners in the conflict.

Prime Minister Hughes was still intent on introducing conscription, despite his rebuff in the second referendum on the issue in 1917. He knew that among the diggers in Europe the tide had turned. Now the men wanted reinforcements to finish the job. They had been through hell, many of them for almost four years, and now believed every able-bodied man should do his bit.

Hughes had a majority in both houses to alter the Defence Act that would allow conscripts to serve overseas and did not need a plebiscite to provide the mandate for change. However, he did need the kind of moral authority that would come from the support of heroes like Jacka and his fellow VC winners. So on 31 August Jacka received orders in Sutton Veny to prepare himself to return 'as early as may be convenient'.

This raised real problems for the man from Wedderburn. His father Nathaniel, the rock-ribbed Labor stalwart, retained his intense opposition to conscription. But Jacka, like most of his comrades on the battlefield, had come to believe that all able-bodied men should do their bit, particularly when it seemed that with a steady supply of reinforcements the retreating Germans might be put to rout. In their letters the two had fallen out over the issue.

But though Albert was prepared to advance against the might of the entire German Army, he was deeply reluctant to confront his father. Moreover, he was constitutionally unsuited to be a public advocate and wanted no part of it. So when the call came, he politely declined. In fact, he said, he needed to recuperate for six months but, when properly recovered, his place was with his men in the 14th Battalion. The army was shocked.

Birdwood himself, as general officer commanding the AIF, responded through his Adjutant that 'whilst very much appreciating the thoughtfulness of Captain Jacka and his self-sacrificing spirit, [the General] is of the opinion that it would be best that the decision already arrived at be adhered to'.

He went on, 'In arriving at this conclusion, [the General] is guided by the fact that Captain Jacka himself must realise that he is much in need of a rest when he admits that it would even be beneficial for him to remain in England for six months. In view also of the fact that the Minister has definitely expressed his wish that all V.C. winners be returned to Australia, [the General] trusts that Captain Jacka will now accept the decision without further demur . . .'[1]

Birdwood's trust was misplaced. Jacka did demur. In fact, so forcefully had he put his case to Colonel Tom Griffiths, the CO of No. 1 Depot, Sutton Veny, that Griffiths wrote back to Birdwood on 15 September: 'Before issuing these instructions to Jacka, may I place before you the following as explained by him to me:

Jacka is very strongly opposed to returning to Australia just at the present moment for the undermentioned reasons:

    1. He is engaged to a lady in England and has arranged to get married within the next two or three months.

215

2. He is at the present time somewhat estranged from his father who is a strong anti-conscriptionist in Australia, Jacka being of course a conscriptionist; and he feels that if he goes out to Australia to help in the conscription campaign it will considerably widen the breach between them—a thing which he is particularly anxious to avoid.

I feel that if Jacka is informed of your decision that he is to return to Australia that he will at once apply for permission to take his discharge in England. Jacka has always stated that he is fit to carry on and according to his statement to me a week or two ago, in his opinion he is quite fit (and anxious) to resume duty with his unit in the field.

His statement about remaining in England for six months was given at the time because he thought it was your desire that he should not for the present rejoin his unit and I gather from other sources that there has been a certain amount of unpleasantness between him and his brigadier [Brand].

I am afraid if we persist in returning Jacka to Australia merely because he is a V.C. man, we should come in for a great deal of criticism both here and in Australia . . .[2]

Clearly, the prospect of Jacka going public was sufficient for Birdwood to execute a neat about-turn. On 21 September, Jacka received a letter from Birdwood's adjutant: 'The General has asked me to drop you a note to let you know that your remaining in England has been approved.'[3]

A week later the French overwhelmed the Bulgarians, Germany's allies, at far-off Salonica and their leaders withdrew from the war, asking for an armistice. In Germany, food and fuel shortages spun out of control. The people were roused. It became clear that Germany was set to lose the war.

However, in mid-October Ludendorff was all for fighting on. The great Allied attack on the Western Front was running down. But in Berlin the civilian ministers had had enough and appealed directly to the American president, Woodrow Wilson, to assist in negotiating an armistice.

On 30 October, Turkey signed an armistice of surrender with Britain: the Ottoman Empire died. Austria–Hungary followed almost immediately. The Habsburg Empire collapsed. Then with revolution spreading to Berlin, Kaiser Wilhelm was forced to abdicate on 9 November 1918. 'I herewith renounce for all time claims to the throne of Prussia and to the German Imperial throne connected therewith,' he proclaimed. 'I release all officials of the German Empire and of Prussia, from the oath of fidelity which they tendered to me as their Emperor, King and Commander-in-Chief.'

On 11 November, the Armistice was signed with Germany. In a trice, all the Central Powers' thrones had toppled, in the wake of Nicholas II's downfall. The four years of terrible slaughter had meant very little by way of territorial gain. But they had worked a marvel in transforming the landscape of power. The men who connived in imperial splendour to sate their vaulting ambition were no more. The foppish tsar, the preposterous kaiser, the ludicrous emperor, the scatter-brained sultan, all were now a foolish anachronism, as distant as the Crusades. Only the dull, pedestrian, chain-smoking George remained, secure in Buckingham Palace, his deadly emphysema congesting by the day. And even he accepted that the age of

Franz Ferdinand, whose petty quarrels had triggered it all, was gone forever.

It was little enough. But it was something.

Among the 'grave green downs' of Sutton Veny, Bert Jacka was also facing a new landscape in the life ahead. The end had come so quickly that he, and others like him, were unprepared for it.

War had made up so much of their life's experience, it had almost come to define them. And the VC did the rest.

The eager lad who had bounced up the gangway of the *Ulysses* in Port Melbourne those many months ago was a shining innocent. The man who wandered the glades and twisting lanes of rural Wiltshire had changed profoundly. He had killed in the service of his country, in the protection of his 'family', and in revenge for the killing of his mates. But he had killed. He had taken life. Many lives. And not just from a distance through the sights of a rifle or machine gun (though he had done that too) but close up, hand to hand, bayonet to bayonet.

It takes time to absorb and assimilate that experience, to integrate it into a self-perception that allows a man to move forward. Jacka had the time—and the place—to make that adjustment. If, like so many of his comrades at arms, he struggled again with the aftermath of war's horrors, there are no records of his seeking treatment from the few medical specialists with knowledge of post-traumatic stress syndrome. Nor do we know whether he sought peace and consolation in the beautiful medieval church that dominates the village skyline, though, given his close fellowship with the battalion chaplains, it would not have been out of character to do so.

While we do not know the identity of his fiancée, the likelihood is that it was one of the nurses or young women of the county who volunteered their services to convalescent homes like Sutton Veny to help the soldiers recuperate. While nothing came of their engagement, there can be little doubt that the relationship was an important element in Jacka's recovering his equilibrium and peace of mind.

However, we do know that he turned to the one activity that was sure to act as a tonic for a young Australian of his temperament: sport. In early 1919, he took over as the depot's sports officer, and soon he was in his element. In short order, he organised a series of regattas and athletic competitions. He helped train some aspiring young boxers and developed a regular tournament for the hopefuls.

Around that time, his brother Bill called to visit with happy news. He had proposed to Joan Jacka in Wales and she'd accepted. Now he wanted Bert to be best man. He agreed immediately and the wedding was duly held in the small Taffswell Wesleyan Church on 11 June 1919. It had been a whirlwind wartime romance, but it would endure for the rest of the couple's lives.

On their honeymoon, Joan and Bill visited Albert at Sutton Veny and talked about the prospects facing them. By now Bill too was a captain and both men had saved most of their army pay, which was waiting for them in accounts in Australia. Bill had called himself a 'labourer' on his enlistment papers in 1916. Now, with all the courses he had completed and the on-the-job instruction he had received, he would not be going back to that. He had shown a facility for writing reports and would be looking around for something in that line.

Bert Jacka still hadn't decided what his future would be. But he wouldn't be returning to his old job either. Some of his mates from the battalion had been to see him. They had discussed a few possibilities, but you couldn't make definite plans from so far away. And who knew what Australia would be like when they finally returned? The brothers agreed: it was a different world. Somehow, they'd just have to find a way to fit in.

For the older man, chatting in the cool afternoon shade of Sutton Veny, Australia meant the open spaces and long straight roads of northern Victoria, the solitude of the bush and the quiet fellowship of family life. He also carried a picture of a bustling Melbourne with its cable trams and horse-drawn buses, the busy shopping streets and the turgid Yarra River; and, further south around Geelong where his mother's clan had settled with its sheep paddocks and dairy farms, a cheery welcome from all the relatives.

In truth, the country that awaited him was beyond his imaginings. Soon it would overwhelm him—the bravest man in Australia—with one part fear and three parts wonder.

26

RETURNING A HERO

Jacka boarded the *Euripedes* for the return journey to Australia on 7 September 1919. Like some other single men, he had volunteered to stand aside and let the family men move up the demobilisation queue. Once on board he immediately applied to be the ship's adjutant and the brass jumped at the opportunity. Throughout the voyage—between bouts of seasickness—he organised sporting contests, debates and other indoor activities and responded as well as he was able to the many questions on the lips of his anxious comrades, some of whom had been away from home for almost five years.

He also talked long and hard to two fellow officers in his 14th Battalion 'family', Lieutenants Reg Roxburgh and Ernie Edmonds. Roxburgh was 28 when he joined up in 1916 and came from a wealthy Melbourne family with a business headquartered at 'The Olderfleet', a prestigious building in Collins Street. His father, Thomas, was the senior partner in a shipping and wheat brokerage business. He was the founder of the Melbourne Corn Exchange, which had its earliest meetings in his Olderfleet office.

The second son in a family of seven children, Reg was living in salubrious South Yarra and operating as a 'stock dealer' when he enlisted and, physically at least, had been left relatively unscarred by the war. In the Battle of Amiens in August 1918, he was recommended for an award for 'conspicuous bravery' when he took over the company after Captain Harris, his company commander, was severely wounded. Battalion commander Lieutenant Colonel Crowther said he was 'conspicuous throughout [the battle], urging on his men and by his utter disregard for his personal safety earned the admiration of all'.[1]

Ernest John Leslie Edmonds had been a 23-year-old commercial traveller living with his mother in St Kilda when he enlisted in 1915 and shipped out on the *Port Lincoln* on 16 August. He too had distinguished himself in battle, and at Gueudecourt on the night of 6 February 1917, volunteered to dig a communication trench with 100 men to a newly captured position partially exposed to the enemy. The then battalion commander, Lieutenant Colonel Peck, wrote, 'By his coolness and skilful handling of the situation under shell and machine gun fire, he practically completed the trench after 10 hours work with only one casualty.'

While neither Roxburgh nor Edmonds received a decoration, each man had clearly won Jacka's respect on the battlefield. Moreover Roxburgh was an accomplished boxer, which would have appealed to Jacka. Now the three young men discussed how they might pool their resources to make a new life for themselves as partners in business. Roxburgh had access to the finance needed to start a business; Edmonds had the gift of salesmanship. Jacka had neither. He had the ability to organise men on the battlefield, but whether that would translate into business was a moot point.

The VC gave him a certain cachet, but Jacka was unwilling to trade on it. On the contrary, he had come to see the award as an obligation rather than an asset. He had been Jacka VC for more than four years by now. It had become second nature for him to measure his actions against the high standards it demanded.

He had a standing offer of £500 from the prominent, if somewhat shady, businessman and political fixer, John Wren, whose connection with Melbourne's Roman Catholic Archbishop Mannix had become notorious during the great conscription debates. Indeed, Wren presented something of a conundrum for the Jacka family.

Like Wren, Jacka's father Nathaniel was fiercely opposed to conscription but, as with most Methodists of his time, he could not abide the Catholic Church and abhorred Wren's gambling activities as proprietor of the infamous Collingwood 'tote'. By contrast, Albert's attitude to conscription had changed along with that of his comrades in the front line. And he had mixed with Catholic and Protestant alike in the rough and tumble of the battlefield and the *estaminets*. He would not be comfortable in taking a 'payment' from Wren for winning his VC. But that did not preclude him accepting it as a business investment if that was required for him to pull his weight in the prospective partnership.

However, all such concerns vanished when the *Euripedes* docked in Port Melbourne. News of Jacka's imminent arrival had been telegraphed from the ship's first Australian port of call in Fremantle. The civic authorities had decided to hold a small, dignified reception for him at the Melbourne Town Hall in Swanston Street. But thousands of Victorians had an entirely different idea.

They had farewelled him among all the other untried and untested young warriors in the march from Broadmeadows through the city streets. Now the shy country boy had returned a conquering hero who had not only won the first Australian Victoria Cross of the war but risen through the ranks and covered himself and his country with glory each step of the way. The Allies had won the war, and here at last was an opportunity to revel in the victory and pay tribute to the figure who epitomised the very essence of the Australian fighting man.

The Argus and *The Age* on the morning of 19 October alerted their readers to the return of their champion, along with a ship full of some of the last officers and men of the AIF to be repatriated. (*The Argus* carried a scrambled story that, since the war's end, Jacka had been on the Mediterranean island of Malta.) The news of Jacka's arrival triggered an outpouring of emotional release that amounted at times to near-hysteria.

The afternoon newspaper, *The Herald*, devoted the entire seven columns of its front page above the fold to the events of that day. The story ran beneath three-column headlines that read:

WELCOME OF WELCOMES FOR JACKA, V.C.
Melbourne Pays Spontaneous Tribute to Australia's
Most Popular Hero
Roman Triumph Through Thronged City Streets

The report began with a stirring opening paragraph: 'When Albert Jacka won the Victoria Cross at Courtney's Post in 1915, he became the symbol of the spirit of Anzac. Through the long campaigns that followed, he carried on the splendid tradition. Today Melbourne remembered these things and the welcome it extended to him was a notable and spontaneous tribute.'

It continued:

Great leaders have been received with honour on several occasions recently, but the people's response today was an unorganised and sincere expression of appreciation. Ringing cheers, the blare of military bands, excited women's voices and the warming mass of khaki and civilian clad manhood surging around and over his motor car like the waves of a human sea—these must be the impressions of his return which remain in the mind of Captain Jacka. He left Australia an unknown Digger; he returned a popular hero with the ribbons of the Victoria Cross, the Military Cross and Bar on his chest, and the cheers of a nation expressing its thanks ringing in his ears.

Under the cross-heading, 'Jacka Will Do Us', the big reporting team followed the action:

When the *Euripedes* berthed, Captain Jacka was among the first to leave, travelling at the head of a long procession. In his motor car were a number of other diggers, and practically all of them wore decorations.

On the way through Port Melbourne, schoolchildren, housewives and workers lined the streets and cheered as the man whose personal valour had won him a place in their hearts swept past. Many houses showed bunting and here and there amateur sign writers had been displaying their talents. 'Jacka Will Do Us' was the announcement on one cottage and if the letters were a little irregular, the spirit left nothing to be desired.

In the city the welcome grew even warmer. Men left offices and girls deserted shops to catch a glimpse of the compact, khaki figure who was hiding bashfully among his fellows. As the car passed, Melburnians suspended business for a few moments to indulge in a happy festival of hero worship.

Here another reporter takes up the triumphal progress of the procession.

Through a narrow lane of cheering people the motor car passed. Smiles were on every face; greetings were on every lip; and every hand signalled, 'Put it there'.

There was a flush on the features of Jacka and the welcome must have ranked as one of the most trying times he has experienced. Many successes have not robbed the soldier of his modesty and as the procession was on the lines of a Roman triumph, it was a trying ordeal for a typical digger.

Here the description gave way to a purple passage of editorialising, rare in the days of anonymous reportage in daily newspapers: 'That is what Jacka is,' wrote the unnamed journalist. 'His bearing, speech, appearance and courage are true to the Australian type, and that is one of the reasons why his fellows and the public attended in such numbers. Other VC winners have come home without great display, but in the general mind of the people Jacka is the symbol that stands for them all.'

Then it was back to the procession which, by this time, was bearing down on the Town Hall in the city centre.

In Bourke Street, the girls of the big drapery warehouses shrilled their feelings; the street was gay with flags and abloom with pretty girls.

A girl sprang up on to the steps [running board] of the car and finding her arms around the neck of the nearest soldier gave him a hearty-kiss. 'That's from Sister Susie,' she said and blushing at the cheers of the crowd she retreated hastily. A crowd of girls received her with delighted giggles but there was a hitch in their plan which, in their excitement, they had not noticed. Their deputy had not kissed Captain Jacka but a delighted and bashful digger in his car. Everybody was satisfied however—particularly Jacka's understudy.

The crowd entirely blocked Swanston Street and, according to *The Herald*, 'in front of the Town Hall the reception became so hearty that it grew too strenuous. Returned men of the 14th Battalion, in uniform and civilian clothes, had lined the narrow gangway beneath the portico and on a decorated platform, Alderman Cabena, the Lord Mayor, and leading citizens were in readiness to bestow the city's welcome.'

While waiting for the arrival of the procession 'the greatest good fellowship prevailed . . . Majors chatted with privates and all distinctions of rank were forgotten in the joy of the day. Patriotic workers distributed beautiful sprays of roses and spring flowers and there was a ripple of excitement as the char-à-banc, with the band playing "Over There", approached.'

But when they arrived, pandemonium broke loose.

Driven by Dr R. E. Weigall, president of the Royal Automobile Club, the car crept beneath the portico—and vanished. That was the impression that was given, for a human wave engulfed it. The Lord Mayor looked down, not upon Captain Jacka, but the shoulders of the returned men who greeted him. They swarmed over the car and pelted him with roses and flowers; they cheered and shouted welcome; and on every side men and women craned their necks or stood on tip-toe to see the man of the hour.

By now the crowd stretched all the way across the intersection of Collins and Swanston Streets 'as though drawn by a magnet'. Then, to the horror of Dr Weigall they converged on his car.

Surging, jostling and shouting, taking all the buffeting in the best of spirits, they sought a glance of the soldier, an opportunity to pat him on the back, shake his hand or in some other way express their feelings. The humble people who merely wanted to look upon him and the ambitious souls who sought to lay their hands upon him, met with an equal lack of success owing to those clustered on the car and who held on as though their lives depended upon it.

Amidst the cheering, someone shouted, 'Stand him up—let's have a look at him', and Jacka rose to his feet. 'A great shout went up when he was recognised and he subsided promptly to the disappointment of the well-wishers.'

However, what the reporters found 'most surprising' was 'the energy and strength' shown by the women. 'One and all were anxious to get close to the man who had fought with their sons, and they struggled pluckily in the crush.'

Dr Weigall was becoming understandably distressed. 'At one

stage the people standing upon every portion of the car numbered more than forty,' *The Herald* reported. 'The hood was broken beneath the weight and the springs were forced so flat that the tyres were jammed against the mudguards, and the wheels would not move. Behind, the long string of cars were hooting for a way to be made and Dr Weigall grew desperate.'

All plans for a quiet civic reception were abandoned. In fact, with the police 'powerless to cope', Dr Weigall 'fought the crowd off with his hands'. Thrusting people off the running boards, he struggled through the thickest part of the assembly, finally breaking through and heading for St Kilda Road to the Finalisation Depot where Jacka would formally end his service.

By now Jacka had been joined in the vehicle by none other than Brigadier General Brand, recently appointed the State Commandant, who was not averse to sharing the limelight with the man he had treated so shabbily for so much of the war. When they reached the depot, *The Herald* had another reporter waiting. By now, he wrote, Jacka was in a state of 'nervous tension'.

'Excited women shrieked in his ears and flags fluttered in his face as he moved along the walk to the depot entrance. The modest hero liked none of it. If he could have hidden, he would gladly have done so. Once inside, he heaved a sigh of relief and was heard to remark to the officer who greeted him, "Thank heaven that's over".'

He declined a cup of tea and refused to pose for the newspaper's photographer. And when the reporter tried a question he replied, 'I'm not going to say anything.'

Brand stepped in. 'He was one of the Fourth Brigade,' he said. 'They were doers, not talkers.'

However, this spurred the rebel in Jacka and he decided he did have one or two things to say. First, he had not been in Malta as reported. 'I was never near the place,' he said. Then, more significantly, he answered a reporter's question about conscription. The journalist said it had been reported that he opposed it. Not true, Jacka said. 'I was in favour of conscription.'

The debate was no longer relevant in the public arena. However, to the private Jacka it was a declaration of independence from his father. With it, he stepped out decisively from the paternal shadow. At the same time, whether deliberately or not, he sent a message to John Wren that politically he was his own man.

He then rejoined the *Euripedes* for the last leg of the trip to Sydney. As adjutant, he had a responsibility to complete the journey. But there can be little doubt that he also welcomed the opportunity to leave the near-hysteria behind him for the calmer waters of Port Phillip Bay.

Dr Weigall was left to contemplate his ruined vehicle. 'Cars which are built to carry five cannot be expected to carry forty,' he told *The Herald*. 'The women were as bad as the men. If such unruly demonstrations are repeated and the public shows no respect for the cars, then motorists will have to decline to undertake the transport of such popular characters.'

27

THE REAL HOMECOMING

While he escaped a public ordeal in Sydney by staying aboard the *Euripedes*, Jacka took genuine pleasure in the welcome home to Wedderburn among family and old friends on 29 October. In the interim he had returned to Melbourne where he stayed quietly at the Middle Park Hotel in St Kilda. He had driven out to Clifton Hill and enjoyed the soothing balm of his mother's family, who flocked around him.

Now, when he arrived home to the strains of the famous Wedderburn Brass Band, there was a banner proclaiming, 'Justly proud of her hero—welcome home', and Nathaniel was waiting on the station with his big, rough hand outstretched. It was a deeply emotional moment and the two men acknowledged it with the strength of their clasp. At last, the war, with all its terrible divisions, was over.

Then Albert and the 70 other returned men from the district assembled and marched up the main street, preceded by an honour guard led by Lieutenant Ephraim McHugh DCM to the Mechanics'

Institute where all the local members of Parliament awaited. The politicians vied with each other to express their pride in polysyllabic splendour, while the soldiers quietly shook their heads, remembered the horrors they had endured and the comrades they left behind.

Indeed, their small town and district had sacrificed no fewer than 53 young men to the war to end wars—seven families had lost two sons and the Ross family a devastating three.

That night at the Shire Council, beneath another banner proclaiming, 'A night never to be forgotten', 200 guests sat down to a dinner prepared by the Wedderburn Women's Welcome Home Committee. The seven decorated soldiers, led by Jacka, were presented with replicas of their medals on solid gold mountings from the Bendigo mines. They depicted a soldier on a shield surrounded by a boomerang and wattle boughs supported by a kangaroo and an emu. Again the Wedderburn Brass Band was called to service. And reports in the town's Historical Society declare that it was indeed an unforgettable night.

Jacka remained with the family, reporting on the wedding of brother Bill, who was still in Wales, and catching up with the news of the district. The place was full of Jackas. His eldest brother, Sam, owned and ran the butcher's shop. The kids from school had a rhyme they would chant as they passed the shop:

Sam Jacka is a naughty boy
He kills the baa-lambs every day.

His eldest sister, Fanny, had married Isaiah Olive, who had also served in France and been seriously wounded. Before the war, they lived on a sheep property at nearby Yuengroon. However, Isaiah was no longer able to work the farm himself and had moved the family into town.

Sister Elsie had married Alf Saunders and they too had a farm in the district. His youngest sister, Bessie, was still at home with the parents. And brother Sidney was home on leave from service in the Middle East before being demobilised in Melbourne, where he would establish himself as a bootmaker in suburban Prahran.

Like most returned men, Jacka was reluctant to talk of the war, particularly to those who had not been there. But it is clear from family conversations that he quickly resumed his close ties with his parents and revelled in the warmth of family life.

However, the bush no longer exerted an appeal for him and in January 1920 he returned to Melbourne where he was granted demobilisation. When he left the army his height was measured, as it had been when he joined up. According to the records he was now 5ft 8½ inches (174 centimetres), a full 2 inches (5 centimetres) taller than when he enlisted. And this was not the only change in his appearance. He was heavier and his brown hair had begun to recede. His facial scars had healed, but there was a new gravity to his bearing and a confidence in his steady gaze that reflected the extraordinary experiences of the past four years.

There is a persistent family legend that he was offered the post of Victorian police commissioner by Premier Harry Lawson's Nationalist Party. No official documentation can be found to support the claim, which includes the assertion that when Jacka turned it down, another distinguished soldier, General Thomas Blamey, accepted. However, Blamey did not take up the post until 1925 and, in any case, Jacka was quickly embroiled with his mates

Roxburgh and Edmonds in getting their new business venture off the ground.

It was at this time that Jacka met John Wren, who provided the promised £500. Jacka supplemented this with £200 from his own savings and, in March 1920, Roxburgh, Jacka & Co. Pty. Ltd., Importers and Exporters opened for business at The Olderfleet Building, 475 Collins Street.

It is significant that Roxburgh's name precedes that of the famous war hero; and equally significant that though he was a major investor, Wren's name does not appear at all. Roxburgh provided the respectable financial imprimatur and Jacka the popular appeal. Wren preferred to work behind the scenes, and this would certainly have suited the Roxburghs, who would have much preferred not to be publicly associated with such a controversial figure. Roxburgh would withdraw from the business entirely in 1923 despite its healthy bottom line. However, according to Roxburgh family members the main reason was Reg's descent into alcoholism as a result of his wartime experiences.[2]

Today Wren's reputation is inextricably bound up with the character of 'John West' in Frank Hardy's novel *Power Without Glory*, which was also made into a television series. West/Wren is portrayed as a gangster and an arch political manipulator with no redeeming features. In 1920, however, he attracted more controversy than contumely.

Born in 1871, the son of Irish immigrants in Collingwood, an inner, working-class suburb, he was determined to make his way in the world. In 1893 he established an illegal totalisator (betting shop) in a Collingwood hotel. This made him a rich man and also gave him political influence in the inner suburbs. He expanded his interests into pony and horse racing, gambling, cinemas, goldmining and professional cycling. In 1903 his horse 'Murmur' won the Caulfield Cup.

Wren became best known as a boxing promoter, and through this success was able to establish the Stadiums Limited organisation, which acquired venues in most major Australian capitals, including the famed Sydney Stadium, Melbourne Festival Hall and Brisbane Festival Hall. Unlike many Australian Irish-Catholics, he supported Australian involvement in World War I, but he opposed conscription and grew increasingly anti-British after the Easter Uprising in Dublin in 1916.

Under Archbishop Mannix's influence he was fiercely anti-Communist, and after the war he used his wealth to support politicians who opposed Communism and defended Catholic interests, but he also expected them to protect his business interests, both legal and illegal. Jacka was careful to keep him at arm's length. When Wren organised a 'parade' of VC winners shortly after his return, Jacka declined to participate. By the 1920s, however, Wren no longer needed to be involved in illegal betting, and most of his money came from legal, if not entirely respectable, businesses such as racing and boxing promotion. It was during this period that he began his lifelong love of Collingwood Football Club as president and patron.

Some of the charges of corruption levelled against Wren in Hardy's novel had a foundation in fact, but most were exaggerated, and some of the political conspiracies attributed to him were completely fictional. Hardy was tried for criminal libel in 1951 because of the depiction of 'West's' wife having an affair, but he was acquitted on the grounds that the work was fiction.

The other major player in the business, Ernie Edmonds, didn't rate a mention in the company's name, but he proved to be a major asset with his flair for salesmanship. And when the business was reorganised after Roxburgh's departure, it became Jacka, Edmonds & Co. Pty. Ltd., Merchants and Importers at 50 William Street. Here they specialised in the household electrical goods that were just becoming accessible to the growing middle class in the boom times of the 1920s. Among their more popular products were electric irons, cookers, kettles and radiators, as well as the more common gas bath heaters, stoves and coppers. They also featured an imported line of porcelain baths, sinks and nickel-plated bathroom fittings.

Wren remained a silent partner, and both his brother, Arthur, and his close associate, Dick Lean, became directors. But Jacka's relationship with Wren was strictly business. At this time Jacka joined the Masons and would remain an active member for the rest of his life. In the 1920s, the Masonic lodges were regarded as firmly anti-Catholic. But of greater appeal to Jacka was their mission statement that proclaimed a Brotherhood of Man under the Fatherhood of God, together with the bonds of male friendship and good works they encouraged.

The Masons represented another 'family' like the 14th Battalion, which had provided the emotional underpinning to his war years. However, his Masonic commitment was undoubtedly another barrier to a private relationship with Wren.

Jacka kept in touch with his mates of the 14th through regular reunions and quickly involved himself in the development of the Returned Soldiers' League. The RSL too would provide him with a congenial male-oriented social network.

The RSL had been formed in Melbourne in 1916 after a meeting of various state-based associations of returned soldiers. The resulting federal executive of the RSL would be primarily responsible for lobbying the federal government on behalf of their members. By 1920 the organisation had a membership of more than 150,000 nationwide.

Participation would inevitably fade as the returned men adjusted to civilian life, and new preoccupations of family and business took over their lives during the 1920s. But for Jacka, whose service had played such a part in defining the man, the role of the RSL in the proper memorialising of those who served, and providing help to those who needed financial, medical, housing or employment assistance, was both a duty and an emotional obligation. His St Kilda branch would become known as 'the Hero's Club' because of his leadership.

Jacka was becoming more comfortable with his public persona. In February 1923, he contacted *The Age* and urged his fellow returned men to pay tribute to Monash at a special dinner at the Melbourne Town Hall. The initiative was remarkable in that it revealed just how far Jacka had travelled from the man who had so feared and distrusted the press on his triumphal return. But it also revealed a new-found political savvy and a determination to accept a public role in righting a perceived injustice.

Monash, who had returned from the war on Boxing Day 1919, had been consistently snubbed by Prime Minister Hughes, who had manoeuvred to keep Monash in Britain until after the 1919 elections. The man who pictured himself as the 'Little Digger' feared that Monash would run against him. He had subsequently ignored Monash's claims for a governorship, or even a much-expected promotion to full general.

Undeterred, Monash had accepted the Victorian government's offer to create the massive State Electricity Commission and build the new town of Yallourn on the brown coal deposit that fired it. Monash had led the relatively small march, with Jacka in the front rank, on Anzac Day in the intervening years, but now, Jacka believed, the time had come for the soldiers themselves to pay tribute to their most distinguished leader. 'As a soldier', he told *The Age*, 'he's like one of ourselves, and doesn't like swank. I think he'd like an address from us better than anything else.'

His remarks set the ball rolling. The RSL organised a packed banquet at the Town Hall, where a 'digger spokesman', whose name is lost to history, gave him the ultimate accolade: he was 'dinkum'.

Monash responded with a powerful speech that ended with a standing ovation. Jacka's initiative had caught the mood of the returned men, who believed that, like Monash, they and their great achievements on the battlefield were being forgotten or ignored. And once again it strengthened the link between Australia's two most celebrated soldiers.

When *The Herald* asked Jacka on Anzac Day 1924 to recall the bravest deed he knew of in the war, he responded at length:

Among so many brave deeds that became almost commonplace during the war, it is difficult to choose the bravest. To do so would be an injustice to many others. All I can do is describe one gallant thing which made a great impression on my mind at the time, as an illustration of cool and calculating daring.

Shortly after the landing, when the 14th Battalion was in a position at the summit of the ridge that overlooked the beach, charged with defending the crest against the Turks, who occupied the next parallel range about 500 yards farther inland, this incident happened.

As the Turks came in open order across the little plain at the foot of the hills, we potted them with machine guns. Those who got across attained safety in the 'dead' ground under our own hill, and there got ready to storm our position.

At Courtney's Post on the summit, Lieutenant Rutland, of the 14th, was in charge of a Vickers gun which he was himself firing. As the Turks advanced in short rushes he fired continually until just at a critical time the gun jammed. No one could have blamed Rutland had he thrown the useless thing down. The Turks were shelling his position from the next ridge, and he was defenceless against the advance.

Rutland did not give up. He sat down coolly in his trench and pulled the gun to pieces. He found the defect, and put the thing together just in time to use it against the approaching Turks. He mowed them down and their officer, a German, led the remnant on. To such close quarters did they get that the German made a blow at Rutland with his sword, not quite reaching him. The advance was stopped, but at the cost of gallant Rutland's life. He fell, riddled with a dozen close-range Turkish bullets. Ballarat has reason to be proud of such a son.

Jacka's health had improved. After demobilisation he was granted a partial disability pension, but by October 1921 he was judged to be fully recovered and the pension was cancelled. By then he was on top of the world. Business was prospering and he was comfortable with his position as a public figure.

In his private life, his parents were healthy and content at Wedderburn. His brothers and sisters were married—except for Bessie, the baby, but she had come to Melbourne where he could keep an eye on her and was working in a bank. Bill was back in the country with Joan after spending a year in the UK and had taken a job on the railways at Wedderburn. And most important, Jacka himself had at last found a woman to love: Veronica Frances Carey— Vera to friends and enemies alike. Unhappily, in the Jacka family the latter would soon outnumber the former, by a country mile.

28

WEDDED MISS

Vera literally threw herself into Jacka's arms. One morning in May 1920 Jacka was in the lift on the ground floor at The Olderfleet preparing to ascend, when the short, sprightly 21-year-old burst in and embraced him in a manner reminiscent of 'Sister Susie' during the triumphal procession a few months before.

'I can well imagine her doing it,' said their daughter, Elizabeth Moss.[1] 'She was an extremely attractive young woman.'

Whether spontaneous or calculated, the gesture paid off, at least in the short term. Jacka hired her as a typist to work for the firm and eight months later she and Albert were married.

However, in the interim she had to run the gauntlet of the Jacka clan, a painful exercise. In the first place, she was a Catholic and thus anathema to the Wesleyan Jackas of Wedderburn. It was one thing for Bert to go into business with a papist, quite another for him to marry one.

In 21st-century Australia, it is difficult to appreciate the depth of feeling between Catholics and Protestants at the time. It arose in part from the Irish issue, but its roots extended back 400 years into British history. Australia's earliest European settlers continued the schism with Irish Catholics overly represented among the convicts, and the landed gentry overwhelmingly from Church of England or Reformist stock.

Many of the bushrangers had Irish backgrounds, not least the Kelly Gang that flourished in the late 1870s. They filled the role of rebel in the Australian narrative, and the forces of law, order and privilege used all their power of authority and propaganda to demonise them.

The mateship of the bush proved a fragile weapon against religious prejudice and even the binding force of the Great War had been cut through by the vicious debates on conscription. The Protestant–Catholic division began early in life, with the rise of Catholic schools, particularly in the first decades of the 20th century. Then came the social strictures applied by both sides—from the 'wowserism' of the Reformists to the marital demands of the Catholics. Albert and Vera were caught fairly in the middle and the wonder is that they married at all.

When he brought her to Wedderburn to meet his parents, Nathaniel and Elizabeth warned the rest of the family to stay away.[2] Accordingly, only family legends exist to throw light on the event, but there can be no doubt that Vera made an indelible impression. She was vivacious, colourful and, according to daughter Elizabeth, 'my mother was socially adept—very sure of herself in social situations . . . her background was nearer middle class than lower'.

This was a double-edged sword. Her social graces might well have put another couple at their ease, but Nathaniel was determinedly 'working class' and not easily seduced by the fripperies of etiquette. Moreover, Vera liked a drink and this did not sit easily with most of the family. Albert's Rechabite membership was still current and his brother Bill was no less resistant to the siren call of alcohol. 'If he ever went to the pub with the boys', said Bill's daughter, Josephine, 'he would have lemonade mixed with cloves so it looked like beer. I think Uncle Bert did the same.'[3]

There is no record of Jacka's meeting with his prospective in-laws, but it is hard to believe that the famous war hero would encounter any resistance from the Carey family. Vera's father, John, gave his occupation as 'gentleman'[4] and they lived in the modestly middle-class suburb of Prahran. Her mother Catherine's maiden name was Ford, a British surname not usually associated with Irish Catholics, so it is possible that she had converted at her marriage.

But whatever the private ructions within the clans, Albert and Vera were married at St Mary's Catholic Church in St Kilda on 17 January 1921 with Vera's sister Mary as chief bridesmaid. Not all members of the Jacka clan attended and, according to Jacka's daughter, Elizabeth Moss, Vera's brother Jim may well have been called to service as best man.

'I don't believe we went at all,' said Josephine Eastoe, Bill Jacka's only surviving daughter. 'We had a farm at Berwick at the time—it was one of those times we were out of contact.' In the excitement of the moment, Vera's mother misspelled her surname 'Cary' on the marriage certificate.

Jacka may well have promised that the children of the marriage would be brought up within the Catholic faith since at the time that was a condition of a wedding 'in front of the altar'. But as it happened, the promise was not immediately relevant since they were unable to have children.

It would be natural to assume that Jacka's war wounds were to blame for this, but according to Elizabeth—whom they adopted as a baby in 1927—this was not so. 'My mother was not able to have children,' she said. 'Not with my father nor with her second husband.'

In later years, Elizabeth traced her natural parents, who were named Smith. 'I was only five pounds at birth,' she said, 'so my natural mother nursed me for a few months before handing me to the Jackas. I understand that my natural father was known to Bert Jacka—probably a wartime meeting.'

However, the inability to have children was not the only impediment to a happy Jacka marriage. Whether or not his parents were reconciled to the match, other family members 'couldn't stand a bar' of Vera. This animosity was reflected in the attitude of their children. Almost 80 years later, Josephine still vividly recalls her emotional response to her favourite uncle's wife. 'When I met her, I thought, "What an unattractive woman." She had an Eton Crop—her hair brushed straight back and cut straight all round. I thought, "I wonder what Uncle Albert sees in her?"' Others assert, confidently but incorrectly, that she was 'an alcoholic'.

Family ructions aside, the business continued to grow and in 1926 the partners moved to bigger premises in Elizabeth Street. Jacka and Ernie Edmonds worked well together. Edmonds said, 'In all our time, we never once had a disagreement.'

As the years passed, Jacka would be called on increasingly for comment on military, repatriation and memorial issues. Unlike other figures who were fading from the public consciousness, Jacka was actually becoming better known.

By then Vera and Bert had bought a substantial home at Murchison Street, St Kilda, and on the surface Bert seemed to be making every post a winner. Indeed, he took to walking to the front of the shop and talking with customers eager to share a conversation with the VC winner.

Another member of the 14th Battalion, Sergeant Bill Groves, a teacher from Sebastopol in Victoria, met him at this time and would later write that 'everyone with half an eye' could see the 'wonderful success with which he adapted' to his role as a business leader.

> Here was a new man—of fine personal appearance and confident address, able to move the hearts and minds of the most cultivated . . . by his forcefulness and depth. [He was] as much at home and as cool in this previously foreign atmosphere as he had always been when the stuff was falling. [This was] a superhuman trans-formation—an attainment possible only in those who are born to be great and who in some extraordinary way appear to remain unconscious of it.[5]

But despite appearances, serious problems were developing. Vera had long since given up work and with no children to look after was becoming bored with suburban life. In the evenings Jacka was often involved in meetings of the Masons or the RSL and the inevitable reunions of the 14th Battalion and the 4th Brigade. And when he did come home to bed this brought its own trials.

Ever since the war, he'd had difficulty sleeping. One of the after-effects of the German mustard gas was a hacking cough that persisted into the night. And then there were the dreams. Like so many of his comrades, Jacka suffered shocking flashbacks to the horrors of war. He would later tell his doctors that the dreams brought a terrible restlessness that often kept him awake for most of the night.[6]

Undoubtedly, this impeded the couple's sex life, and cracks appeared in the marital facade. In all likelihood it was at this time that Vera began to spend time in the city, lunching and later enjoying a drink at the fashionable Hotel Australia.

In 1926 Jacka was 33, comfortably well off, fashionably dressed and ruggedly good looking. He was coming out of his social shell and was increasingly aware of his attractiveness to women. The jazz age of the 1920s was in full swing; hem lines were rising; vaudeville was booming; 'flappers' were flaunting their charms in a new, permissive atmosphere; Melbourne was kicking up its heels in a way that hadn't happened since the Gold Rush of the 1850s. As relations with Vera deteriorated it is possible that Albert might have sought consolation elsewhere.

However, the evidence is not very substantial. 'He was not pure,' Elizabeth said.[7] 'My mother never spoke ill of him to me—just mildly amusing anecdotes.' But Vera was not amused when she handed Elizabeth a leather-bound, flip-up notebook for her homework. 'Here, you can use this,' she said brusquely. 'It was your father's. I've torn out the women's addresses.'

Elizabeth wrote years later, 'I still have that notebook with the jagged edges left from angrily (?) torn pages.'

Clearly, the adoption of Elizabeth ('Betty') herself in 1927 was an attempt to rebuild the relationship. The child would not only fill Vera's empty hours, she would provide Albert with an outlet for his powerful family instincts. And for a time, it seems, the situation improved. He was a kind and affectionate father. Elizabeth's earliest memories are of waving him goodbye each morning as he left for work in the car. There was most likely a period of calm and renewed commitment in the relationship. The family travelled up to Wedderburn for Christmas and family occasions and, though Vera was never really accepted by most of the Jackas, she did have a friendly relationship with Jacka's eldest brother Sam and his wife, Elizabeth.

But if there was a new and welcome calm in the Jacka household, outside the confines of St Kilda, and indeed the young nation itself, forces were gathering for an economic storm that would exact a terrible price. It would fling Albert Jacka into a new battlefield, one where the rules of engagement were never stated, where the enemy was all but invisible, but where the casualties in rank and file would be starkly scattered in limitless number across the bleakest of landscapes.

29

THE OTHER WAR

The signs were everywhere apparent. By 1928, Australia's economy was intricately linked with that of Britain. Despite the introduction of a protectionist trade policy in the first decade of the 1900s, Australia was still dependent on the importation of manufactures, such as Jacka and Edmonds' electrical goods, together with investment capital, from the Mother Country.

These imports were paid for by the export of primary products, principally wool, wheat and coal, back to the UK. However, the British economy had never really recovered from the Great War, which had depleted its savings and raised inflation. This meant Britain could not afford to keep pace with its import of commodities, so Australia's own balance of payments suffered.

At the same time Australia was taking hundreds of thousands of assisted British migrants, adding to the demand for public spending. But when Australian governments wanted to invest in new infrastructure, such as the Murrumbidgee Irrigation Area, the state railways or the Sydney Harbour Bridge, they had to borrow overseas, either on the bond markets of the City of London or on Wall Street.

Unemployment fluctuated between 6 and 10 per cent and by late 1928 it threatened to go higher. Australia had pegged its currency to the pound sterling, and in 1926 Britain had returned to the Gold Standard at pre-war parity. The effect was to increase the value of the Australian pound and make the country's commodities less competitive in the international marketplace.

At first, Jacka, Edmonds & Co. were relatively unaffected. The influx of new settlers triggered a housing boom, and the latest electrical appliances were much in demand. However, that was about to change. Because of falling commodity prices, employers in the affected industries—notably coalmining—were unable to meet pay demands from their workers and a series of crippling strikes ensued. The Bruce–Page government in the new Parliament House in Canberra reacted by seeking to shut down the Arbitration and Conciliation Commission, thereby deregulating wages; and at a Hunter Valley coalmine, police moved in and shot dead a striking teenage miner.

The economy threatened to descend into chaos. In the election of 1929 the Labor Opposition under James Scullin won in a landslide, with Prime Minister Stanley Bruce himself losing his seat, the first and only time a prime minister has done so. Scullin had promised to 'save' Australia and its high living standards from what he saw as the conservatives' program to destroy Australian working conditions. But two days after he was sworn in came the Wall Street crash. In the ruinous Depression that followed, Scullin could not even save himself—he lost office in 1931—much less the country.

Among the returned men, who could see all they fought for suddenly in jeopardy, a group of hotheads began agitating and organising under various banners, most notably the New Guard. This would produce the memorable spectacle of Francis de Groot finessing the official opening of the Sydney Harbour Bridge in 1932 by slashing the ribbon before Premier Lang could do the honours. But in the late 1920s the New Guard was active in Melbourne and provincial areas and called for Monash to lead a military putsch.

Monash quickly disabused the ringleaders of their hopes and ambitions, declaring that he did not fight for democracy only to abandon it when the civil authorities needed all the support they could get. Jacka publicly stood with him and entered the public arena himself. He was elected to local government at almost the same time as the Labor Party was handed the poisoned chalice of power in federal Parliament and was sworn in as a St Kilda city councillor on 23 September 1929.

It was a natural progression from his work in the local RSL and the Masons, but there was something almost beyond coincidence that found him signing up for the new struggle. As a councillor he was in the front lines, dealing with the daily battering of his extended 'family' in St Kilda. And just as he had thrown himself into the thick of the battle at Anzac, Pozières, Bullecourt and Polygon Wood, so he now set out to confront the economic shellfire that was devastating his constituents.

His first act was to propose a move to meet with other nearby councils 'to consider means of providing employment for the relief of those families affected by the present economic slump'. The vote went his way and he was chosen as St Kilda's delegate to the meeting.

The councils decided to coordinate their efforts, and Jacka was given the task 'to investigate ways of relieving unemployment', which was rising exponentially as businesses in the area closed their doors.

But he quickly realised that there was very little local government could do to beat back the invader. At best councils could keep their own charges down and provide a kind of 'first aid', just as a field ambulance unit patched up casualties on the Somme.

The federal government at the time lacked a centralised unemployment assistance program. In thousands of city households, the men 'went bush' in search of work; the state and local governments were left to deal with the cries for help from the families left behind.

Scullin and his treasurer, 'Red Ted' Theodore, sought to make funds available for 'relief' work but were largely frustrated by a hostile Senate, still controlled by the conservatives. Then in mid-1930, the British banks who were demanding loan repayments from Australia sent an envoy, Sir Otto Niemeyer, to lecture Australian governments on the virtues of austerity and 'belt-tightening'.

It was exactly the wrong prescription for the time. The young British economist John Maynard Keynes understood and urged that such old-fashioned nostrums would only worsen the situation. Governments needed to kick-start the economic engine, to use their spending power to get the economy over the top. But the men in charge were locked into yesterday's mould in much the same way that Haig and Gough had trumpeted the virtues of the cavalry charge while sending thousands of young soldiers to futile death.

Unfortunately, Australia remained in thrall to the British establishment, and a conference of state and federal governments in Melbourne that year agreed to slash government spending, cancel public works, cut public service salaries and decrease welfare benefits. Once more, 'the heads' were savaging the rank and file with a combination of arrogance and incompetence.

Moreover, Scullin accepted advice to raise tariff barriers to 'luxury' imports. In a single stroke, the electrical goods of Jacka, Edmonds & Co. were rendered inaccessible even to those who continued in work. One crisis meeting followed another in the company boardroom. John Wren, the hard-headed businessman, made his position clear: there was no point at all in throwing good money after bad; the company would have to close its doors.

Neither Edmonds nor Jacka could argue against the reality of the bottom line. The company owed creditors £21,289; its liabilities exceeded its assets by £19,942. The two major unsecured creditors were the National Bank (£11,544) and John Wren himself (£6051). Almost overnight, it seemed, the partners' dreams of financial security simply evaporated. In September 1930 they held a final closing-down sale and walked away. The creditors received 8.73 pence in the pound.

It was at this time that Wren offered to organise a seat in Parliament for Jacka, either at the state or federal level. Whether Wren had the political influence to accomplish such an outcome is debatable. According to Wren's biographer, James Griffin, it was highly doubtful.[1]

'How many seats did the great "fixer" have at his disposal?' Griffin asks.

With the Labor landslide of 1929 increasing the party's representation in hard times from eight to thirteen [in Victoria], who would have resigned at Wren's instigation for Jacka? Had Wren been accused of offering to contrive some Labor or Country Party back-bench [seat] for Jacka in the Victorian state parliament, the story could just be credible, but a federal prospect of this sort at that time must seem like fantasy, but it is not untypical of the tales vulgarly spun around Wren.

Griffin protests too much. Jacka had no reason to contrive the affair when he told Edgar Rule that he had been 'pressed' by Wren to 'take a seat in parliament'; nor did he say whether the parliament involved was federal or state. Instead he told Rule, 'No Eddie, they are not my style; and if I did accept, they'd say, "Look at Jacka—a failure in business climbs into a safe job as an M.P."' Wren's actions could just as easily be seen as an attempt to help a valued business colleague or even to assist a national icon through a rough patch.

Either way, Jacka declined. And for twelve months he too was unemployed. This allowed him to devote himself wholeheartedly to the work of the council. He was back in the front lines but was racked with frustration as there seemed no way to come to grips with the enemy.

He organised functions at the Town Hall in aid of sick and disabled soldiers. He voted funds to the Ladies' Benevolent Society to distribute food parcels to the unemployed. He led a delegation to the state government to protest the government's incompetence in managing unemployment relief. He headed a sub-committee to oversee the building of a retaining wall on the St Kilda foreshore with funds wrested from the state government's Unemployment Relief Fund. Then on 1 September 1930 he was unanimously elected mayor of St Kilda.

It was a proud occasion. The position came with an honorarium of £500 a year that would help tide his family over. This was some consolation to Vera. She enjoyed dressing up and accompanying Jacka on the formal events as lady mayoress. But it also meant that he spent every waking hour in the front lines of council business.

He was soon known as the 'Lemonade Mayor', for his teetotal commitment remained firmly in place. But he was able to break free of his Methodist upbringing sufficiently to organise a series of entertainments at the Town Hall to raise funds 'to relieve distress'.[2] He created a 'Jobs Bureau' designed to ensure St Kilda residents would have first preference for council work projects.

The entertainments were a great success, and Vera was in her element. But as he devoted himself single-mindedly to his St Kilda 'family', many of the old marital resentments resurfaced. Jacka was never home. And when he did return late at night he was exhausted, physically and emotionally.

It is possible that the 'women's addresses' that so piqued Vera were entered in Jacka's leather-bound notebook at this time. But in this case it is highly unlikely that he overstepped the matrimonial bounds. They were 'family', and they were in terrible distress. It would have been a denial of his basic character to have taken advantage of their vulnerability.

Not all council business was concerned with the Depression. For example, Jacka led a successful delegation to the police commissioner, General Blamey, to increase police supervision of St Kilda beach. Other bread-and-butter issues clogged the council agenda: with the arrival of a new post office in the area, newsagents lost the right to sell postage stamps. Money was also needed to relieve the debt of the Soldiers' Memorial Hall.

Jacka abandoned the usual end-of-year 'smoko' for council

employees and transferred the money into the Unemployment
Relief Fund. He reserved an area in the huge Town Hall basement
for the meagre possessions of those who had been evicted from their
homes. And whenever possible he talked with the men and women
who were suffering in a peacetime war over which no one seemed to
have any control. The sense of frustration and powerlessness to a
man of action like Jacka must have been very hard to bear.

30

BACK IN THE FRONT LINES

There was no prospect of relief. Indeed, 1931 offered not just more of the same but a deepening of the Depression. Delegations of the unemployed called on Jacka as mayor seeking ever more assistance from the council. At the same time, ratepayers sought a reduction in their contributions to council while the state government—and influential leader writers in *The Age*—demanded that councils balance their books. It presented a fiendish dilemma to a man who, quite without his willing it, felt an overbearing sense of responsibility for the less fortunate members of the St Kilda 'family'.

The £500 mayoral allowance was well above the basic wage and should have been more than enough to keep himself and his small family in reasonable comfort. However, he was a notoriously 'soft touch' to old comrades in arms down on their luck, and when a doorknock brought forth scores of old shoes for the destitute, he insisted on paying for them to be repaired from his own pocket before they were distributed.[1]

The strain was putting his health under pressure. He decided that he had to limit his mayoral tenure to a single year, but this meant he had to find a job in an overcrowded marketplace. At the time, he was in correspondence with Newton Wanliss, who had completed his history of the 14th Battalion and was starting work on a Jacka biography.[2] Jacka was willing to cooperate and, at Wanliss's urging, was writing his memories of Polygon Wood.

But inevitably, the return to that wasteland of horror brought forth the dreams and the flashbacks. He would wake in a lather of sweat and sometimes hours would pass—to the accompaniment of that persistent, irritating cough—before he was able to return to sleep.

In an aside, he wrote to Wanliss, 'Thank God my term of office as Mayor ends at the end of August and I hope that I will be getting another start to life then. I have every hope of getting started with Shell Oil Co. and that is the reason I have not yet asked you to write to General Monash.'[3]

Clearly, if all else failed, he would draw on the long association with Monash who would, no doubt, do all in his power to assist. But for the moment he did at least have some prospects, unlike so many of the poor devils he had to work with each day.

The coming of winter meant that the need for blankets and warm clothing for St Kilda's poor and destitute became ever more acute. He developed yet another initiative—a special SOS week—and joined other council workers and volunteers knocking on doors with a personal appeal for help.

He began to organise a fundraising 'carnival' for the end of the year which would include a series of picture shows and stage acts.

Organising it was enormously time-consuming and demanded qualities of diplomacy that had not been part of his natural make-up. But when his fellow councillors devoted most of his final meeting as mayor, on 31 August, to a unanimous tribute to his contribution over the past twelve months, it must have provided some sense of satisfaction.

At the very least, he would have left the meeting secure in the knowledge that he had done his bit. Moreover, he would remain a councillor; he would do what he could for as long as he could. To walk away from the fight—however ill-equipped he was for the struggle—was simply not an option.

However, at home his marriage had collapsed. Vera had resumed her visits to the Hotel Australia in Collins Street, and on the rare occasions they had time to talk together the conversation quickly descended into mutual recrimination. In June 1931, Vera took four-year-old Betty and moved to 38 Malvern Road, Glen Iris; then in August she made a second move to Kingsley Hall in Cathedral Road, East Melbourne. She found a job as hostess of the Venetian Room—where afternoon teas were served—in the Hotel Australia, and quickly took up with a wealthy businessman, Frank Duncan of Clifton Hill.

Jacka was shaken to the core. He put the Murchison Street house on the market and moved to rented accommodation at 60 Chaucer Street, St Kilda. The house sold quickly, but after the debts were paid there was little or nothing left to share between them. As his health deteriorated with the onset of bronchitis, he reapplied for a war service pension for Vera and the child, and it was quickly granted. He found a job as a commercial traveller for Anglo-Dominion Soap, a subsidiary of William Angliss Co., and according to brother Bill he 'did well' at the job.

However, the agony of mind over his marriage failure and the endless demands of his role as councillor were taking a terrible toll. He proposed a new scheme to help relieve unemployment in the area: the sustenance handouts should be replaced by large-scale work programs using funds from federal and state governments. This would get the local economy moving again. 'There would be an immediate demand for manufactured goods which would stimulate industry and further relieve the position,' he said.

The state government expected to raise £1.4 million by taxation and to receive £1.6 million from the Commonwealth. 'If, of this amount, 1 million pounds were set aside to give 40,000 men 10 weeks work at, say, two pounds ten shillings a week, there would be an incredible [increase in the] demand for goods.'[4]

This was the essence of the Keynesian view of 'pump-priming' the economy at a time of downturn, and the council gave Jacka its full backing. But it was almost impossible to move the massive government bureaucracy required to turn theory into action.

His successor as mayor, Councillor Herbert Moroney, was absent from council meetings for the next two months, and Jacka returned to the chair. Indeed, he was deputising for the mayor on 8 October when his old commander, Sir John Monash, succumbed to a series of heart attacks. And on 19 October, at the next council meeting, he proposed the motion of condolence.

He had marched with Monash on every post-war Anzac Day, from the few thousand returned men of the early days to the magnificent turnout of 1927 when 30,000 paraded before the Duke of

York and established the occasion as a vital and continuing element of the Australian experience.

He had supported Monash in his resistance to the extremists who wanted him to lead a military takeover when the economy faltered. By joining the democratic process himself, he set an unmistakable example to those who would abandon the system they had fought to preserve. And now the 'old man' was gone, worn out at 66, years before his time.

It was yet another blow, and as Christmas approached Jacka faced the prospect that for the first time in a decade he would make the journey to Wedderburn alone. The nay-sayers of the family, who 'always knew' he had made a terrible blunder in marrying Vera, would have their predictions realised. It was not a happy prospect, but like everything else in life, it had to be faced and overcome.

Meantime, he attended the Monash funeral with its formal panoply and the military march-past outside the steps of Parliament House. In the streets, Melburnians came out to pay a last tribute as the procession made its way to Brighton Cemetery. Jacka was among the mourners at the graveside where, after the Jewish ceremony, a trumpeter played the 'Last Post'. A seventeen-gun salute followed.

The two men were of totally different background and temperament—Monash the cultivated intellectual, Jacka the straightforward, self-made country man—but they had been joined in a great endeavour and their mutual respect was unbounded. It had been Monash who recommended to Hamilton that Jacka be awarded the VC. And it had been Monash who understood and appreciated just how much the fighting qualities of Jacka and his ilk could be used against the enemy, both for psychological advantage as well as their astonishing feats on the battlefield. Together, they epitomised the best of Australia's fighting force.

But, once the funeral was over, Jacka returned to the struggle at hand. During the day he made his rounds to the retail outlets—from corner shops to the big department stores. And at night he fulfilled his obligations to the Masons, the RSL and, most of all, the victims of the Great Depression.

The strain began to tell. A fellow VC winner, W. C. 'Bill' Joynt, saw him in the city at the time and was shocked by his appearance. 'I could not believe it was the same man I'd seen only a couple of months ago. He had aged terribly,' he said. 'He had gone completely grey.'[5]

At the council meeting of 14 December, Jacka rose with a proposal that a council project to repair the Elwood Park Kiosk be reserved for the local unemployed. The motion passed. Then in a surprise move, Councillor Moroney presented Jacka with an Illuminated Address containing the text of the fulsome and unanimous resolution passed on the occasion of his final meeting as mayor. It was beautifully and colourfully—even flamboyantly—illustrated. Jacka accepted it with an uncharacteristic tremor in his voice.

His planned fundraising carnival was scheduled for only four days hence and there were a hundred last-minute details to be finalised. After the meeting he went towards his office with a list of people to telephone. He never reached it. He collapsed; an ambulance took him to an emergency centre and thence to Caulfield Military Hospital. His last battle was upon him.

31

GOING OUT

For several months, Jacka had been aware that his health was deteriorating. In May when he applied for a part pension, Dr Crowe at the Repatriation Commission detected a 'loss of tone' of the heart and some infection of the lungs. He diagnosed 'Pulmonary fibrosis [scarring of the lung] and Bronchitis'. The patient, he said, suffered regular attacks of bronchitis, which were 'direct sequels of gassing on service'. He granted Jacka a 20 per cent disability pension with the recommendation that it be reviewed in twelve months. The money went directly to Vera.

When he collapsed in December, Drs Silverberg and Rosenfield discovered an infected kidney with 'heavy albumin and much blood in the urine'.[1] There was a thickening of the arteries and the heart was seriously enlarged. 'Gallop rhythm is present.'

Dr Rosenfield declared, 'I regard him as suffering from a severe degree of Nephritis [kidney disease] with cardio-vascular degeneration. Rest in bed and vigorous treatment is essential.'

However, no matter what treatment the doctors applied, they could not reverse the downward spiral. Before Christmas he had been well enough to respond to visitors. His niece Josephine remembers he gave her a penny. 'He was such a lovely man,' she said. 'I wish now that I had kept it. But of course at the time I probably spent it on lollies or something.'

Vera brought little Betty to see her father. 'My only visual memory of him is in hospital,' she said. 'I remember thinking that Daddy's bed was very high.'

St Kilda Councillor Unsworth urged council intervention to have Jacka moved from Ward 5 of the Caulfield Hospital to a single ward at the Alfred Hospital. 'Ward five is noisy and Jacka is held up as an exhibit by other patients and visitors,' he said.[2]

However, nothing came of the move and on 7 January he was placed on the Dangerously Ill list. Three days later came his 39th birthday. He was only vaguely aware of it. As his kidneys shut down, Jacka became blind and only close relatives were permitted to visit. The newspapers heard of his struggle and, according to *The Herald*, his last message was to his father: 'I'm still fighting, Dad.'

Brave words, if true. However, by now the myth-making demons were at work and the evidence for their authenticity is thin at best. Indeed, Vera had begun the pretence that they had been living together at 60 Chaucer Street until his collapse. Elizabeth is unequivocal: they had parted 'when I was three and a half or four—well before his final illness.'

But there is no gainsaying the astonishing interest suddenly directed to the dying man who had now become critically ill. Telegrams and cards poured in to the hospital from every part of Australia and overseas, particularly Britain. The family gathered, but the occasion was fraught with unspoken resentment towards Vera.

Still he lingered, unaware of the emotional currents swirling around him. State and federal governments were put on notice and quietly arrangements were being made for a state funeral. The newspapers established a 'death watch', with hospital authorities primed to pass the word when the inevitable occurred.

It came in the early hours of Sunday 17 January, and even for those who had been aware of the struggle of the past week the bald announcement arrived as a terrible shock. Jacka was a symbol of the fighter who survived shot and shell while others fell around him, the personification of the Anzac spirit that defied the gods of mortality. And now, suddenly, he was gone. It was impossible, and yet it had happened.

Behind the scenes, the Army and Navy Club stepped in to help Vera with the funeral arrangements. Jacka had been president of the club and remained a prominent member. They engaged the funeral directors, W.G. Apps P/L, and the head of the firm, Arthur Apps himself, took charge. They moved the body from the hospital to 60 Chaucer Street for the family to pay their private respects on the Sunday. The following day they took it to the Apps' Chapel in St Kilda.

Then on Tuesday 19 January at 9 a.m., they loaded the best kauri polished coffin, silver mounted with an engraved nameplate and the Masonic emblem, into the hearse for the journey to Anzac House. There, draped in a Union Jack, it would lie in state for four hours while at least 6000 mourners filed passed.

Four sentries—all members of the 14th Battalion—were mounted over the coffin on which were his sword, decorations and slouch hat, as the crowds paid their respects. At 2 p.m. a short service was held, before the eight pall-bearers—all VC winners—carried it out into the sunshine and the waiting gun-carriage. One of the pall-bearers, Bill Joynt, said, 'Melbourne had come to a halt. As we marched alongside the casket I was conscious of what a great Australian we were honouring that day.'[3]

The turnout by the people of Melbourne was almost unbeliev-able. By 2.30 p.m. the temperature had climbed to a scorching 108.9 F (42.7 C), the highest for a quarter of a century, yet the procession's progress through the city was almost brought to a standstill by the dense crowds.

The Herald reported 'a city whose roar had faded to a murmur' where 'solid phalanxes of people stood bareheaded in the blistering sun'.

His little niece, Josephine, said, 'It was so hot I almost fainted. They took me inside a building and made me lie down on the cold floor.'

The Herald said the city streets were

> so choked by a wedge of people that mounted police had to push them back to make a lane for the assembly of Diggers. Every window in shop and office was populous with clerks, shop girls and typists.
>
> The crowd flooded over the Swanston Street intersection and packed the parapets of the Town Hall and other adjacent build-ings. For an hour the sun beat down mercilessly on the files of people who pressed forward to the tram tracks. It did not deter them from paying a last tribute of respect to a great soldier.

A contingent of former soldiers of the 4th Brigade—at least 200 strong—fell in behind the catafalque with the RSL band playing the 'Dead March in Saul'.

They marched in fours, medals flashing in the pitiless sun. Some of them, lame and worn-looking, walked with difficulty over the tram tracks. But personal discomfort was forgotten in a general desire to honour 'poor old Bert'.

There were Diggers in faultless suits who swung canes jauntily as they strode along. There were others who were collarless and whose boots were falling to bits, those who had been overwhelmed in the war after the War. There were frail men, prematurely aged, with greying hair and eyes that had lost their old-time brightness.

It was a remarkable gathering that Fate had dealt with in different ways in the years since they had fought with Bert Jacka, or thrilled to the recital of his exploits. Gusts of heat hit their faces from the surcharged pavements, yet nobody 'fell out'.

The gun-carriage, drawn by eight horses, passed over Princes Bridge to the strains of Chopin's *Funeral March*. In the procession of cars led by the family came Brigadier General Brand.

'The scene along St Kilda Road was remarkable,' *The Herald* reported. 'As the head of the procession passed the Shrine of Remembrance [initiated by Monash and supported by Jacka] the procession was still passing over Princes Bridge.'

After receiving a salute at the Shrine, the procession was joined by more than 300 of St Kilda's unemployed men on whose behalf Jacka had fought so long. This, perhaps, was the most poignant reminder of his willingness to enter the lists on behalf of his comrades. And by the time they reached the St Kilda Cemetery the crowds were overwhelming.

The Age reported, 'Deep personal respect was the predominating characteristic amongst the many thousands of citizens of all creeds and classes who mourned the passing of Captain Albert Jacka VC.'

The service was conducted by former Chaplain F. W. Rolland, now headmaster of Geelong College. Sergeant Angus MacDonald of the 14th told the assembly that Jacka 'had proved himself the greatest fighting soldier of the A.I.F.'.[4]

'He had a marvellous ability to inspire others,' he said, 'and time and again he went back into the firing line with a cheering smile and a grand optimism.'

The headstone proclaimed him:

A Gallant Soldier
An Honoured Citizen

Steel facsimiles of his hat and sword were riveted to the top of the gravestone.

The mourners lingered, some unwilling to say a final farewell until the sun went down.

Daughter Elizabeth said, 'I was with Aunty Liz [the wife of Sam Jacka, Albert's oldest brother] and Ivy [her young daughter] at my father's funeral. That memory has never left me.' Sam and Liz Jacka were the only members of the family who would maintain any contact with Vera and Betty.

Part of the reason may well derive from the interview Vera gave the following day to *The Herald*. While some of the sentiments can be attributed to journalistic excess and proprietor Keith Murdoch's posturing, Vera made no attempt to correct the record or to decline the extraordinary response it engendered.

The story began with an emotional tribute that set the tone for what was to follow: 'Worn out by financial worries, reduced to desperate need, and torn with anxiety about the welfare of a courageous wife who had struggled on through the economic fight with him, Captain Albert Jacka V.C., Australia's foremost frontline soldier, died in indigent circumstances.'

It then concentrated on Vera's 'plight':

Today Mrs Jacka, weary and jaded from days and night[s] of watching at the bedside of her husband, sits in their rented home at St Kilda surrounded by masses of telegrams of condolence from all parts of Australia but with the bleak future ahead of having to subsist on a pension of two pounds two shillings and sixpence a week . . .

His widow is convinced that many months of worry and his desperate struggle to make ends meet reduced his chances of fighting the illness which was the legacy of his war injuries.

Then came the 'solution':

Yesterday, 30,000 people lined the route of the funeral procession to do honour to the memory of Australia's greatest frontline soldier. The Directors of The Herald and Weekly Times Ltd feel that among those thousands there are many who have the means, and would welcome an opportunity, to pay an even more tangible tribute to the memory of Australia's first V.C.

They can do this by helping to provide a home for Mrs Jacka.

The Herald therefore has decided to start a fund with a contribution of 25 pounds for the provision of a cottage for her.

It is felt that the whole of the people of Victoria will be glad of an opportunity to help such a fund.

Individual readers are invited to contribute and any money received will be entrusted to a small committee which will arrange for a suitable cottage to be either built or bought. Any surplus beyond requirements would probably be invested for the benefit of Captain Jacka's child.

Then followed 'revelations' about the 'battering' which Jacka received 'in the economic war which followed the war of steel'. It traced his financial collapse in excruciating detail before returning to Vera's ordeal.

A few days before his death, he said to Mrs Jacka, 'This is a rough spin, but we have been through many rough spins together. I'm afraid, Mummy, you'll have to struggle on alone, I feel I'm done.'

Mrs Jacka did her best to cheer him and mentioned to him that although they had a long, rough spin, it had been good in parts. 'Yes, Mummy,' he replied, 'It was good in parts.'

Jacka often in the last days expressed to his wife his appreciation of the way she had struggled on gamely with him.

It ended in pure bathos: 'A pathetic feature of his illness, however, was that for some time before his death, his sight had failed, and he was unable to see his wife's face or even her hand as he held it before his eyes.' Surprisingly, it failed to mention that Jacka had died eleven years to the day from his wedding on 17 January 1921.

While the newspaper story may be read today as mawkish, ingenuous and more than a little self-serving, it had an extraordinary effect upon the readership, and indeed other Victorian bodies. It triggered an outpouring of public sentiment almost unheard of at the time.

The newspaper was overwhelmed with hundreds of donations from the public. Simultaneously, the RSL and St Kilda Council began appeals to their own associated groups, the council's chief clerk writing to every other city, town and shire council in Victoria. And in the next several weeks hundreds of pounds poured into the consolidated fund.

As the appeal reached several thousand pounds, a leading Melbourne architect, Harry Johnson, offered to design the 'cottage' without charge. His offer was politely declined. Instead, by March, Vera was able to write to the St Kilda Council treasurer, A. J. Chamberlin, 'I am going to town for a few days next week to purchase a home and I do dread the lonely task of unpacking and settling down. I have been going out a good deal and have avoided being alone as much as possible but, of course, there are bad hours in plenty. I hear on all sides all sorts of tales as to my movements. Even little Betty is brought in. But on the advice of my solicitors I am just going to ignore it as much as possible.'

According to Betty, Vera did buy the house with the funds, but mother and daughter never lived in it. According to council records, there was more than £800 left over. Half the surplus was invested with the income to be paid to Vera until Betty was 21, at which time the capital would be liquidated and paid to Vera. The other £400 would go to Betty when she was 25.

Meantime, Vera received a pension of £4.4 shillings a fortnight. That was cancelled when she married Frank Duncan at St Patrick's

Church six months later. Duncan already had a family from a previous marriage. The *Truth* newspaper of 26 September noted, 'Only very intimate friends of the couple were present at the wedding and immediately after the happy pair left for Sydney where they are spending their honeymoon.'

Bill Jacka continued his extraordinary parallel of his famous brother's career by becoming mayor of another Melbourne city council, Footscray, in the early 1940s. He had left the railways and taken a job as a reporter on the *Footscray Mail*. He also became a Mason.

He too suffered from his war wounds. According to daughter Josephine, he had one 'perished' lung and the other was 'scorched'. He had stomach trouble until an operation when he was 50 replaced some intestine with 'pig gut'.[1]

'This made a big difference,' she said. 'He could eat anything after that. When he retired from the *Mail* they went to Frankston and bought a farm.'

After her Uncle Albert's death, Josephine said, 'We didn't see much of Vera or Betty.'

Betty wrote, 'I had a happy life as the youngest member of a large family. My husband and I lived overseas for a few years because we liked to travel. We came home to have our family. We've had a pleasant and uneventful life together. The far past of my life hasn't entered my head for many a long year. I prefer to keep it that way.'

In the late 1930s, Nathaniel and Elizabeth's house in Wedderburn burnt down and they moved to Melbourne. When Elizabeth died in 1940 Nathaniel resolved to spend six weeks at a time with each of his children.

Albert's other brother who served in the war, Sidney, who had spurned the opportunity to join his brothers in the 14th Battalion, retained his Prahran boot-repair shop until he had a heart attack in the 1950s. Thereafter he worked as 'keeper' at the St Kilda Town Hall.

Vera died in Melbourne in her late sixties.

By then the ranks were thinning, but every year scores of men and women—old comrades from the Great War and admirers from Jacka's days of civic service, as well as the extended family—made the pilgrimage to Jacka's graveside.

It continues to this day.

EPILOGUE

I n December 2005, I attended the C. E. W. Bean Foundation
dinner at the Australian War Memorial to hear an address from
the Turkish prime minister, Recep Tayyip Erdoğan. The speech was
lost to me because just prior to his introduction I had a short conversation with the man sitting next to me, a junior member of the
Australian Army's History Unit. When he learned I was writing a
biography of Albert Jacka his response was immediate and devastating. Jacka, he declared, was a social misfit. Indeed, the implication
was even more serious—that he was some kind of uncouth, unlet-
tered, killing machine.

Though it came as a shock, it should not have done so. It was
consistent with the attitude of those members of the military
establishment who had been discomfited by Jacka's willingness to
challenge their authority when they were sending his mates to a
needless death.

It was the same attitude that, more than 70 years ago, had
impelled Edgar Rule to write his memoir. At the time, he said, Jacka

had been 'painted by men who did not know him as a sort of caveman, uncouth, ruthless, undisciplined by law of man or God'.[2]

I had just spent more than a year researching a figure whom I had come to know and admire. It had not been easy to penetrate to the essence of the man. But I believed that I had finally understood what motivated him to such extraordinary deeds on the battlefield. Indeed, it had not been until I discovered the selfless way he sacrificed himself in the final battle that claimed him—what *The Herald* called 'the war after the War'—that the essence of the man's character finally emerged.

As a boy, he had slipped naturally into the role of the defender and protector of his brothers and sisters. He took it because it seemed right. He was fast and strong for his age. He felt responsible. And he was good at it. As well, he not only defended them from strangers but, if necessary, from the stern patriarch, Nathaniel, with his set ideas and the chip on his shoulder born of resentment of 'the bosses' and which found expression in his devotion to Labor politics.

As he grew to solitary manhood he became stronger and faster. He was bright, intelligent, but under-educated. There was nowhere to go, no outlet for the drive within . . . until the war.

They were made for each other. The war gave him a cause and he responded with all he had to give. And then, no sooner had he launched himself against the foe in the great crusade, he won the Victoria Cross.

It is impossible to over-estimate the power of the VC, not just on fellow soldiers but on the recipient himself. The effect was to rekindle and reinforce that self-image of the protector and defender of the weaker members of the 'family'—which now meant the battalion that provided such strong emotional support at a time of the highest psychological intensity.

In 1923, Charles Bean wrote to Newton Wanliss: 'Unlike many other men who won the V.C., he was not spoiled by it . . . It left him afterwards as he was before.'[3] Bean's words were more accurate, I believe, than he fully understood. The man and the honour fused, and a remarkable character emerged. Jacka VC was a powerful force to be reckoned with.

His actions at Pozières, Bullecourt and Polygon Wood were truly extraordinary and would have led to very high decorations in anyone else. Bean himself said, 'Everyone who knows the facts, knows that Jacka earned the Victoria Cross three times'.[4] I presume he meant Gallipoli, Pozières and Bullecourt, though Polygon Wood saw him at his finest.

Jacka's instincts demanded that he take the lead and throw himself into the thick of the fighting. But according to fellow VC, Lieutenant Colonel Harry Murray:

Many people have the impression that Jacka went berserk in action. That is wrong. He was the direct opposite—cool, deliberate and calculating—always fighting to win, not merely by sheer bulldog tactics, but by out-generalling the opposition, and *saving the lives of those whom he commanded.*

At all times he was considerate to those junior to him, and was most tolerant to those who served under him and who had not his courage. Kind-hearted, quiet and unassuming, [he was] ever ready to recognise good work done by another, always rejoicing at honours awarded to comrades, keen to keep the name of the A.I.F. clean, and his units efficient.[5]

Murray recognised the quality that rankled with the high command. 'Fearless of all if he thought his opinion right', he wrote, 'Jacka's sense of justice was of the highest.'

Undoubtedly, he was seized by an overwhelming sense of injustice at the arrogance and incompetence among the leadership that threatened his men's lives. It was this outrage that so offended 'the heads' that they refused him promotion and downgraded his honours. Moreover, they counterattacked with a whispering campaign.

No one could impugn his bravery or his efficiency. Nor could they challenge his capacity to absorb the tactical and strategic lessons of the officer training schools and other courses where he invariably distinguished himself. So Jacka was 'a handful'. He was 'not sound'. He was, in short, 'not one of us'.

In truth, the military establishment, for all its fulsome praise, finds VC winners awkward to deal with at the best of times. These men have stepped beyond the chain of command; they can't be slotted into 'the system'. In this sense, Jacka was the VC winner *ne plus ultra*. Even Bean, the British-educated historian, was prey to this tendency when he wrote confidentially to Wanliss, 'I think if you regard Jacka as a good fellow of a rather crude type, you will probably arrive at the best estimate of him.'

Wanliss was not impressed. 'He has a higher order of brain than he is popularly credited with,' he responded. 'In my opinion he is a born soldier with true tactical intuition and had he received fair play he was capable of greater things than he was ever entrusted with. But he did not get fair play . . . There was underground work used. I won't say any more: I have said perhaps more than enough.'[6]

Walter Manie, a sergeant in the 14th, was president of the Battalion's Association when Jacka died. He knew the man well. 'Much has been said and written of Jacka's exploits which brought him decorations or renown,' he wrote,

> but little of the transformation which took place in him after the war. He settled down with that determination and grit he was famed for, to carve for himself no small niche in the community he had fought for so magnificently.
>
> Four years ago he appeared to be nearing his goal . . . then came one blow after another, and though Jacka fought with all his old-time courage, these enemies—of economic depression, ill-health and worry—were not to be denied.
>
> Although himself in dire need of assistance, he gave freely of his time and unceasing effort to alleviate the suffering of the unemployed of his municipality, and so drained his body of that vitality which may have made the difference between life and death.
>
> As an example to Australian youth, Bert Jacka's name should never die.[7]

In fact, his name is commemorated in a St Kilda boulevard, the Wedderburn memorial park and most recently a suburb of the National Capital. And as the thousands of young Australians gather every year at Anzac Cove, the spirit of Albert Jacka lives on.

From distant London, the Metropolitan Police send their some-what mysterious wreath. My frequent co-author, Peter Thompson, who lives there, made personal inquiries as to the sender of the wreath, but the police department were unable to track down the specific source within the service. 'However,' they wrote, 'we are pleased that this Australian hero has been remembered.'

He was, indeed, a very Australian hero.

Notes

Chapter 1

1. Lord Birdwood of Anzac and Totnes, *In My Time: Recollections and anecdotes*, p. 142.
2. The designation habitually applied by the diggers to the staff officers, usually British, who directed their activity. It was seldom used affectionately.
3. Newton Wanliss, official historian 14th Battalion, *Reveille*, 31 January 1932.
4. Official report of Lieutenant Wallace Crabbe to Army Command, 21 May 1915.
5. In his official report, Lieutenant Wallace Crabbe wrote 'b——s'; Charles Bean chose the euphemistic 'beggars' for his *Official History*. Jacka's language was much more salty; it could equally easily have been 'bastards'.
6. Letter from Charles Bean to Keith Murdoch, 1916.
7. Perry, *Monash*, pp. 206–7.
8. The name was immortalised in Edgar Rule's 1933 account, *Jacka's Mob*.

Chapter 2

1. The *McIvor Times*, July 1914, record his third place (off a six-minute handicap) in the 12-mile road race; on the next day he kicked two goals for Heathcote v Pyalong.
2. Brownridge and Ring, 'Laughter and Learning Difficulties', p. 6.
3. *Jacka VC* (documentary).

CHAPTER 3

1. Morrison is not as well remembered now, but had first come to prominence when he exposed the Kanaka 'blackbirding' in *The Age* in 1881, then the following year walked alone from the Gulf of Carpentaria to Melbourne, re-enacting the ill-fated Burke and Wills expedition. He then led an unsuccessful expedition to cross New Guinea from south to north, in which he received a serious wound from a spear. As special correspondent for *The Times* of London while in Peking from 1887 he wielded great influence and in Australia was spoken of as a potential prime minister. See Peter Thompson and Robert Macklin, *The Man Who Died Twice*, Allen & Unwin, 2004.

2. Mitchell, *Backs to the Wall*, p. 168.

3. Wanliss, *History of the Fourteenth*, p. 9.

CHAPTER 4

1. Tronson, *A Soldier's Book of Life*, quoted in Stanley, *Quinn's Post*, p. 9.

CHAPTER 5

1. Hamilton, *Gallipoli Diary*, p. 42.

2. Wanliss, *History of the Fourteenth*, p. 13.

3. Commentary on Dardanelles Commission, 1916.

4. Maxwell, Letter to War Cabinet, March 1915.

CHAPTER 6

1. *The Times*, 27 March 1915.

2. Perry, *Monash*, p. 170.

3. Perry, *Monash*, p. 172.

4. Wanliss, *History of the Fourteenth*, p. 16.

5. Wanliss, *History of the Fourteenth*, p. 17.

6. Ashmead-Bartlett, *Uncensored Dardanelles*, p. 37.

7. Ashmead-Bartlett, *Uncensored Dardanelles*, p. 38.

8. Ashmead-Bartlett, *Uncensored Dardanelles*, p. 39.

9. Perry, *Monash*, p. 172.

10. Wanliss, *History of the Fourteenth*, p. 17

CHAPTER 7

1. Jacka, Diary, 24 April 1915.

2. Askin, *Gallipoli*, p. 21.

3. Mitchell, *War Diaries*, 25 April 1915.

4. Mitchell, *War Diaries*, 25–26 April 1915.

5. Ashmead-Bartlett, *Uncensored Dardanelles*, p. 50.

6. Ashmead-Bartlett, *Uncensored Dardanelles*, p. 51.

7. Jacka, Diary, 26 April 1915.

8. Jacka, Diary, 27 April 1915.

9. Carlyon, *Gallipoli*, p. 83.

10. Wanliss, *History of the Fourteenth*, p. 20.

11. Wanliss, *History of the Fourteenth*, p. 21.

12. Stanley, *Quinn's Post*, p. 27.

13. Wanliss, *History of the Fourteenth*, p. 23.

CHAPTER 8

1. Jacka, Diary, 1 May 1915.

2. Ashmead-Bartlett, *Uncensored Dardanelles*, p. 54.

3. Jacka, Diary, 3 May 1915.

4. Ashmead-Bartlett, *Uncensored Dardanelles*, p. 94.

5. Ashmead-Bartlett, *Uncensored Dardanelles*, p. 101.

6. Ashmead-Bartlett, *Uncensored Dardanelles*, p. 103.

7. Wanliss, *History of the Fourteenth*, p. 41.

8. Mitchell, *War Diaries*, 20 May 1915.

9. Wanliss, *History of the Fourteenth*, p. 41.

10. Wanliss, *History of the Fourteenth*, p. 45.

11. Mitchell, *War Diaries*, 24 May 1915.

12. Ashmead-Bartlett, *Uncensored Dardanelles*, p. 107.

13. Ashmead-Bartlett, *Uncensored Dardanelles*, p. 113.

CHAPTER 9

1. Carlyon, *Gallipoli*, p. 154.

2. Jacka, Diary, 6 August 1915.

3. Perry, *Monash*, p. 221.

4. Wanliss, *History of the Fourteenth*, p. 53.

5. Perry, *Monash*, p. 222.

6. Wanliss, *History of the Fourteenth*, p. 59.

7. Wanliss, *History of the Fourteenth*, pp. 60–1.

8. Wanliss, *History of the Fourteenth*, p. 61.

9. Wanliss, *History of the Fourteenth*, p. 71.

CHAPTER 10

1. Ashmead-Bartlett, *Uncensored Dardanelles*, p. 218.

2. Ashmead-Bartlett, *Uncensored Dardanelles*, pp. 240–3.

3. Wanliss, *History of the Fourteenth*, p. 75.

4. Monro would never publicly acknowledge it, but he was the step-brother of Australia's most infamous bushranger, Frank Gardiner, who had shared the Jacka stamping grounds of western Victoria 40 years before Albert was born. Gardiner's mother, Jane Christie, married Henry Monro, a pioneer of the Campaspe district, northwest of Wedderburn, in 1841 but later died in child-birth. Charles was the youngest son of Monro's second marriage.

5. Author interview with the Jacka family, January 2006.

6. Wanliss, *History of the Fourteenth*, p. 79.

7. Perry, *Monash*, p. 231.

8. The original 1933 Angus & Robertson publication of *Jacka's Mob* in many cases used aliases to disguise the identity of men still alive at the time. In 1999, Carl Johnson and Andrew Barnes edited the manuscript and, with the assistance of Australian War Memorial records, identified almost all of the participants from the 14th Battalion. Rule says he took notes during the war with 'no other object but keeping fresh the writer's own memory'.

9. Rule, *Jacka's Mob*, p. 2.

10. Rule, *Jacka's Mob*, p. 5.

11. Perry, *Monash*, p. 232.

12. Rule, *Jacka's Mob*, p. 11.

13. Rule, *Jacka's Mob*, p. 11.

14. Wanliss, *History of the Fourteenth*, p. 79.

15. Mitchell, *War Diaries*, 21 December 1915.

CHAPTER 11

1. Wanliss, *History of the Fourteenth*, p. 92.

2. Rule, *Jacka's Mob*, p. 14.

3. Perry, *Monash*, p. 211.

4. Perry, *Monash*, pp. 247−9.

5. All quotations by Wanliss are from Wanliss, *History of the Fourteenth*.

6. Rule, *Jacka's Mob*, p. 15.

7. Wanliss, *History of the Fourteenth*, p. 95.

8. Rule, *Jacka's Mob*, p. 15.

9. Rule, *Jacka's Mob*, p. 15.

10. Rule, *Jacka's Mob*, p. 17.

11. Rule, *Jacka's Mob*, p. 17.

12. Rule, *Jacka's Mob*, p. 17.

13. Grant, *Jacka VC*, p. 57.

CHAPTER 12

1. Charles Bean's private letter to Newton Wanliss in 1923 implies that Jacka was in the habit of nursing such resentments.

2. Rule, *Jacka's Mob*, p. 23.

3. Rule, *Jacka's Mob*, p. 23.

4. Wanliss, *History of the Fourteenth*, p. 123.

5. Wanliss, *History of the Fourteenth*, p. 131.

6. Rule, *Jacka's Mob*, p. 24.

7. Bean, correspondence with Wanliss, March 1923, Australian War Memorial.

8. Rule, *Jacka's Mob*, p. 24.

9. Rule, *Jacka's Mob*, p. 25.

CHAPTER 13

1. Gammage, *The Broken Years*, p. 149.

2. Wanliss, *History of the Fourteenth*, p. 138.

3. Bean, *Official History*, vol. III, p. 699.

4. Bean, *Official History*, vol. III, p. 718.

5. Rule, *Jacka's Mob*, p. 30.

6. Rule, *Jacka's Mob*, p. 29.

7. Rule, *Jacka's Mob*, p. 29.

8. *Reveille*, 31 January 1932.

9. *Jacka* VC (documentary).

10. Wanliss, *History of the Fourteenth*, p. 140.

11. Bean, *Official History*, vol. III, p. 719.

12. *Reveille*, 31 January 1932.

13. Rule, *Jacka's Mob*, p. 48.

CHAPTER 14

1. Bill Jacka, Letter to Wedderburn Historical Society, 21 September 1969.

2. Australian War Memorial, 88/190. Personal records of Capt. A. Jacka VC, MC & Bar.

3. Rule, *Jacka's Mob*, p. 48.

4. Rule, *Jacka's Mob*, p. 49.

5. *Reveille*, 31 January 1932.

6. Rule, *Jacka's Mob*, p. 62.

7. Rule, *Jacka's Mob*, p. 55.

8. Rule, *Jacka's Mob*, p. 61.

CHAPTER 15

1. Rule, *Jacka's Mob*, p. 62.

2.   Rule, *Jacka's Mob*, p. 55.

3.   Wanliss, *History of the Fourteenth*, p. 169.

4.   Rule, *Jacka's Mob*, p. 67.

5.   Rule, *Jacka's Mob*, p. 66.

6.   Mitchell, *Backs to the Wall*, p. 68.

7.   Mitchell, *Backs to the Wall*, p. 69.

8.   Wanliss, *History of the Fourteenth*, p. 182.

9.   Rule, *Jacka's Mob*, p. 68.

CHAPTER 16

1.   Wanliss, *History of the Fourteenth*, p. 185.

2.   Wanliss, *History of the Fourteenth*, p. 187.

3.   Rule, *Jacka's Mob*, p. 75.

4.   Rule, *Jacka's Mob*, p. 75.

5.   Rule, *Jacka's Mob*, p. 75.

6.   Mitchell, *Backs to the Wall*, p. 89.

7.   Wanliss, *History of the Fourteenth*, p. 191.

CHAPTER 17

1.   Wanliss, *History of the Fourteenth*, p. 194.

2.   Mitchell, *Backs to the Wall*, p. 91.

3.   Wanliss, *History of the Fourteenth*, p. 195.

4.   Mitchell, *Backs to the Wall*, p. 91.

5.   Rule, *Jacka's Mob*, p. 77.

6.   Mitchell, *Backs to the Wall*, p. 97.

7.   Rule, *Jacka's Mob*, p. 79.

8.   Wanliss, *History of the Fourteenth*, p. 207.

9.   Wanliss, *History of the Fourteenth*, p. 207.

10. Rule, *Jacka's Mob*, p. 81.

11. Rule, *Jacka's Mob*, p. 81.

12. Murray, 'Some Reminiscences', 1950, quoted in Franki and Slatyer, *Mad Harry*.

CHAPTER 18

1. Wanliss, *History of the Fourteenth*, p. 213.
2. Rule, *Jacka's Mob*, p. 81.
3. *Reveille*, 31 January 1932.
4. Holmes, 4th Div General Staff War Diary. AWM 4.
5. *Reveille*, 31 January 1932.
6. *Reveille*, 1 December 1936.
7. Bean, *Official History*, Vol. IV, p. 351.
8. Rule, *Jacka's Mob*, p. 83.
9. Rule, *Jacka's Mob*, p. 83.

CHAPTER 19

1. Rule, *Jacka's Mob*, p. 83.
2. Wanliss, *History of the Fourteenth*, p. 216.
3. *Reveille*, 31 January 1932.
4. Rule, *Jacka's Mob*, p. 88.
5. Mitchell, *Backs to the Wall*, p. 144.
6. Mitchell, *Backs to the Wall*, p. 156.
7. Rule, *Jacka's Mob*, p. 95.
8. Wanliss, *History of the Fourteenth*, p. 222.

CHAPTER 20

1. Rule, *Jacka's Mob*, p. 87.
2. Dardanelles Commission Evidence, AWM 51.
3. Rule, *Jacka's Mob*, pp. 108–11.
4. Wanliss, *History of the Fourteenth*, p. 233.
5. Rule, *Jacka's Mob*, p. 109.
6. Wanliss, *History of the Fourteenth*, p. 235.
7. Rule, *Jacka's Mob*, p. 110.

CHAPTER 21

1. Letter to Charles Bean, 1923, in Bean, *Correspondence*.

2. Rolland to Wanliss, August 1931, quoted by Grant, *Jacka VC.*, p. 142.

3. Rule, *Jacka's Mob*, p. 112.

4. Wanliss, *History of the Fourteenth*, p. 240.

5. Perry, *Monash*, p. 295.

6. Wanliss, *History of the Fourteenth*, p. 243.

7. Rule, *Jacka's Mob*, p. 112.

8. Letter to Bean, 1923, in Bean, *Correspondence*.

9. Rule, *Jacka's Mob*, p. 112.

10. Wanliss, *History of the Fourteenth*, p. 245.

11. Rule, *Jacka's Mob*, p. 112.

12. Recommendations for Honours and Awards, AWM 28.

CHAPTER 22

1. Rolland to Wanliss, August 1931, quoted by Grant, *Jacka VC*, p. 142.

2. Papers of Capt. F. B. Stanton, Australian War Memorial, DRL155, 12/11/3116.

3. Rule, *Jacka's Mob*, p. 122.

4. Horne (ed.), *Source Records of the Great War*, vol IV.

5. Wanliss, *History of the Fourteenth*, p. 257.

6. Wanliss, *History of the Fourteenth*, p. 260.

CHAPTER 23

1. *Jacka VC* (documentary).

2. Franki and Slatyer, the authors of *Mad Harry*, confirm the approach but suggest the force would be organised around Tiflis (Tbilisi), the capital of Georgia.

3. Perry, *Monash*, p. 319.

4. Wanliss, *History of the Fourteenth*, p. 271.

CHAPTER 24

1. Rule, *Jacka's Mob*, p. 119.

2. Rule, *Jacka's Mob*, pp. 121–2.

3. Monash, *The Australian Victories in France*, pp. 266–9.

4. Monash, *The Australian Victories in France*, pp. 62–3.

CHAPTER 25

1. Jacka's Official War Record, Australian War Memorial. His mate Harry Murray would similarly decline. Like Jacka, he did not see himself as a political performer for Billy Hughes.

2. Jacka's Official War Record, Australian War Memorial.

3. Capt. Albert Jacka, VC, MC & Bar, personal record file, AWM.

CHAPTER 26

1. Jacka's Official War Record, Australian War Memorial.

2. Interview with Roxburgh Family Members, Feb–March 2006.

CHAPTER 28

1. Interview with author, January 2006.

2. Author interview with Jacka's niece, Josephine Eastoe, January 2006.

3. Interview with author, January 2006.

4. Albert and Vera's marriage certificate.

5. *Reveille*, 31 January 1932.

6. Medical report, A. Jacka, Form B103, Australian War Memorial.

7. Personal communication, January 2006.

CHAPTER 29

1. *Quadrant*, Jan–Feb 2002.

2. St Kilda Council minutes, 22 September 1930.

CHAPTER 30

1. Whether he sent them to brother Sidney in Prahran for reconditioning is unknown, but given his attachment to family, highly likely.

2. It was never completed.

3. MSS 143a, Australian War Memorial.

4. St Kilda Council minutes, September 1931.

5. *Jacka VC* (documentary).

CHAPTER 31

1. Jacka's Official War Record, Australian War Memorial.

2. St Kilda Council minutes, books 25, 26, August, September 1931.

3. *Jacka VC* (documentary).

4. *The Age*, 20 January 1932.

EPILOGUE

1. Interview with Josephine Eastoe, January 2006.

2. Rule, *Jacka's Mob*, Preface.

3. AWM 43, A414; correspondence between Wanliss and Bean, 1923.

4. *Reveille*, 31 January 1932.

5. *Reveille*, 31 January 1932; author's italics.

6. AWM 43, A414; correspondence between Wanliss and Bean, 1923.

7. *Reveille*, 31 January 1932.

BIBLIOGRAPHY

BOOKS

Ashmead-Bartlett, Ellis, *The Uncensored Dardanelles*, Hutchinson, London, 1916

—— *Despatches from the Dardanelles*, George Newnes, London, 1915

Askin, Mustafa, *Gallipoli: A turning point*, Keskin Color, Canakkale, 2004

Bean, C. E. W., *Official History of Australia in the War of 1914–18*, vols I–IV, 8th edition, Angus & Robertson, Sydney, 1942

—— (ed.), *The Anzac Book*, London, 1916

Birdwood, Lord, of Anzac and Totnes, *In My Time: Recollections and anecdotes*, Skeffington, London, 1946

Brenchley, Fred and Elizabeth, *Myth Maker*, John Wylie and Sons, Australia, 2005

Carlyon, Les, *Gallipoli*, Pan Macmillan, Sydney, 2001

Franki, George, and Slatyer, Clyde, *Mad Harry: Australia's most decorated soldier*, Simon & Schuster, Sydney, 2003

Gammage, Bill, *The Broken Years: Australian soldiers in the Great War*, Penguin, Ringwood, 1975

Gibbs, Phillip, *Realities of War*, Heinemann, London, 1920

Giles, John, *The Western Front Then and Now*, Battle of Britain Prints, London, 1992

Grant, Ian, *Jacka VC: Australia's finest fighting soldier*, Macmillan, Sydney, 1990

Bibliography

Hamilton, Ian, *Gallipoli Diary*, Doran Edition, New York, 1920

Holmes, A., Lorraine, J., Pay, B., and Ring, K., *Wedderburn Revisited*, Korong Historical Society, Wedderburn, 1997

Horne, Charles F. (ed.), *Source Records of the Great War*, vol. IV, Edwin Mellen, New York, 1923

Lee, John, *A Soldier's Life: General Sir Ian Hamilton 1853–1947*, Macmillan, London, 2000

Mitchell, G. D., *Backs to the Wall*, Angus & Robertson, Sydney, 1934

—— *War Diaries*, 1915–18, Australian War Memorial

Monash, John, *War Letters of General Monash*, Angus & Robertson, Sydney, 1935

—— *The Australian Victories in France in 1918*, Angus & Robertson, Sydney, 1937

Perry, Roland, *Monash: The outsider who won a war*, Random House, Sydney, 2004

Rule, Edgar John, *Jacka's Mob* (ed. C. Johnson and A. Barnes), Military, Melbourne, 1999 (original edition first published in 1933)

Stanley, Peter, *Quinn's Post: Anzac, Gallipoli*, Allen & Unwin, Sydney, 2005

Staunton, Anthony, *Victoria Cross: Australia's finest and the battles they fought*, Hardie Grant, Canberra, 2005

Taylor, A. J. P., *The First World War*, Penguin, London, 1963

Tuchman, Barbara W., *The Guns of August*, Macmillan, London, 1962

Wanliss, Newton, *The History of the Fourteenth Battalion, A.I.F.*, Arrow Printery, Melbourne, 1929

DOCUMENTARY
Cooper, R., and Beusst, N., *Jacka VC*, Monash University, 1974

MANUSCRIPT SOURCES
Bean, C. E. W., Correspondence, 1919–42, Australian War Memorial, 3 DRL 7953

Bean, C. E. W., Diaries and notes, Australian War Memorial, 3 DRL 7953

Commentary on Dardanelles Commission, 1916, AWM 51

Jacka, Bill, Letter to Wedderburn Historical Society, 21 September 1969

Jacka, Captain Albert, Personal Records file, National Archives, Canberra and Melbourne

Jacka, Captain A., Diary, 1 October 1914–18 December 1915, AWM 224 Mss. 143A

Jacka, Captain A., Correspondence, Personal Records 88/190

—— William Jacka; Sidney Jacka; Harold Wanliss; G.D Mitchell. Personal Records files, AWM.

Maxwell, Letter to War Cabinet, March 1915

St Kilda City Council records, 1929–31

Stanton, Captain F. B., Papers, 14th Btn A.I.F., AWM, 2DRL 155

Unit War Diaries, 14th Battalion, 48th Battalion, 4th Australian Division General Staff, 1914–18, AWM 4

Whitham, Colonel J. L., Arrangements for Funeral of the late Captain A. Jacka, V.C., M.C., Reserve of Officers, 18 January 1932

NEWSPAPERS AND JOURNALS

The Age, selections, 1919–32

The Argus, selections, 1919–23

Brownridge and Ring, 'Laughter and Learning Difficulties: Serious and not so serious tales of Wedderburn and its schools', Wedderburn Joint Schools Anniversary Committee, 1986

The Herald, selections, 1919–32

McIvor Times, selections, 1913

Quadrant, selections 2002–04

Reveille, 1928–36

Truth, 26 September 1932

Wedderburn Express, 1914–33

INDEX

293